770

CHILDREN AND DRAMA

CHILDREN

Also by Nellie McCaslin:
CREATIVE DRAMATICS IN THE CLASSROOM

and
DRAMA

EDITED BY
Nellie McCaslin

THE PROGRAM IN EDUCATIONAL THEATRE
THE SCHOOL OF EDUCATION
NEW YORK UNIVERSITY

DAVID McKAY COMPANY, INC. / NEW YORK

Foreword

KENNETH L. GRAHAM

Kenneth L. Graham, chairman of the Department of Theatre Arts at the University of Minnesota, is a past president of the American Theatre Association and the Children's Theatre Association. His involvement in both college and children's theatre has taken him to various campuses in the United States and abroad. He has conducted institutes for teachers in creative drama and has been a research consultant for the Arts and Humanities Branch of the U.S. Office of Education. Dr. Graham has received numerous awards and honors, including the American College Theatre Festival Award of Excellence in 1973. His wide experience makes him one of the most knowledgable leaders in the educational theatre field.

In *Children and Drama* Nellie McCaslin has collected the current thinking of fourteen of the leading practitioners in the field, giving each free rein to express his philosophy in his own distinctive style. The range, both in content and form, makes for provocative reading. And to widen the scope, British and Canadian writers as well as those from the United States have been included. The editor has called on such early innovators as Winifred Ward and Gerald Tyler; those well known for some time; as well as some newer on the scene, such as Moses Goldberg, Elizabeth Kelly, and Joanna Kraus. Virginia Tanner's personal reflections on creative dance and Aurand Harris's illuminating thoughts on playwriting for young audiences are welcome treatments of these respective specialities. The individual writing ranges from the scholarly to the sheer poetry of Agnes Haaga's "Reflections on a Spring Day."

Evident throughout the book is a clear theme: The creativity of the individual leader is what makes for exciting results in drama by and for young people. In these essays one may enjoy insights into new directions which reflect the individual viewpoints of each writer, but they have as a unifying concept the power of drama to unlock and to stimulate in young people meaningful aesthetic experiences.

When one compares this new book with collections written ten years ago, it is evident that the field has indeed moved forward. Of particular note is the Dartmouth College Conference (discussed by Geraldine Siks in "Drama in Education: A Changing Scene") where the significance of drama was manifest for the learning of language and communication skills. Yet current research indicates that educators are still reluctant to place drama centrally in teacher-training programs. Hopefully, this stimulating book will be a strong incentive toward the further accomplishment of that worthy goal.

Children and Drama is highly recommended for all practitioners in theatre—and especially for administrators involved in teacher training at the elementary and secondary levels.

A Retrospect

WINIFRED WARD

Winifred Ward's distinguished contributions to the field of child drama are well known. In articulating the principles and demonstrating the effectiveness of creative dramatics as opposed to formal theatre for children, she was instrumental in changing the direction of education in the dramatic arts in this country. She is the author of four texts, Creative Dramatics, Playmaking with Children, Stories to Dramatize, *and* Theatre for Children. *Her convictions regarding the improvisational approach developed during her early years as a public school teacher and culminated in the establishment of the now famous Evanston Program. Dr. Ward, professor emeritus of the School of Speech, Northwestern University, speaks appreciatively of the influence on her work of such educators as Dean Ralph Dennis, Hughes Mearns, and Harold Ehrensperger. Perhaps her most lasting accomplishment was founding the Children's Theatre Association, the national professional organization devoted to the promotion of drama for and with children. In this retrospect Winifred Ward has chosen to share some of her personal reminiscences rather than repeating her philosophy, which as she says, she has already written.*

Do you consider creative dramatics important enough in a child's education to be included in the curriculum of every public school along with music and art? Do you who believe in its value enough to practice it, write books about it, give workshops for teachers—feel satisfied with its present status?

Shortly after I had published my first book, *Creative Dramatics,* in 1930, I was shocked when I came upon this statement by a widely experienced educator: "Whenever a new idea in education is proposed, it is at least fifty years before it becomes common practice."

How do new subjects get into the public schools? Because a need is strongly felt. And in the case of creative dramatics, the need was felt by Mr. Skiles, superintendent of the Evanston, Illinois schools. He had come to Evanston in 1918, had visited all the grade schools, and had recognized that the middle grades were lacking in interest. He talked with a school board member, Ralph Dennis, who was also dean of the School of Speech at Northwestern University, asking him to recommend a teacher. Mr. Dennis came to my office, hoping I would be interested. Since I had begun to teach a course in drama for teachers, and this would open the door for my students to gain experience, I knew it was a wonderful opportunity. But I was not sure that I wanted to undertake it myself, so I hesitated, and he said, "Think it over and I'll talk with you in a day or two."

I was torn as to whether or not I should accept, especially as it was likely to become a larger responsibility than I wanted to add to my already full program. When Mr. Dennis came back, I decided I must tell him the reason why I hesitated. "I'm very much afraid," I said, "that this offer will develop into a full-time job and I would have to leave Northwestern, in which my roots go very deep." The dean stood up from where he was sitting by my desk, put his hand gently on my shoulder, and said, "It will *never* take you away from here." Then, as if embarrassed by his show of sentiment, he strode to the window and stood looking out at the lake.

Of course, I then agreed to undertake the position, even though I was not at all sure how I could find time to do all that I was sure it would involve. Soon afterward I met Mr. Skiles and we had a long talk in his office. I knew at once that he would be wonderful to work with.

During our first conversation he had discussed the lack of interest in the fifth- and sixth-grade courses of study; they needed the liveliness that drama would supply. It was not long before the idea spread and other grades were added. Both Mr. Skiles and I had been retired for some years, however, before all the grades had dramatics.

I have begun with a short history of the drama department in the Evanston elementary schools, which is almost unique in our country. Is it because the Evanston schools were rich? Not at all. The superintendent who established the department was known as a very careful man concerning finances. The answer is simple and clear: He believed in the importance of dramatics. That was sufficient.

In recent years, with high taxes and new superintendents unsympathetic to this art, the whole department has been threatened. So strong, however, have been the protests of parents and children that, as of now, Evanston still has a fairly large dramtic staff, ten teachers in all. And I thought we might have to settle for a home with the language arts!

Few people start at the top of their careers. I was not one of them, in spite of what my opening story might indicate. I had graduated from the two-year course at the School of Speech at Northwestern, and until I could find a teaching position, I had to be content with coaching high school students for oratorical contests and senior plays. The first real offer came in the middle of the year from the public schools in Adrian, Michigan, where I was to have the following assignments: coaching students for high school contests in public speaking, directing the senior play, teaching reading in the upper grades, coaching girls' basketball, dancing, and conducting calisthenics once a week with the primary grades.

The declamation contests were easy; my student won the state contest the first year. My reading classes were successful, especially when, occasionally, they could read stories in "parts." And the senior play "went over" best. My basketball girls rarely won an intercity game; however, they were always good friends.

I met with some surprises in my many duties with physical exercise in the lower grades. I found that if I could add a dramatic element, the children would have enjoyed physical training all morning. For instance, one exercise designed to give the first grade a change was as simple as this: As the children stood alongside their desks, I told them about a snowman standing in front with arms stretched out at his sides like sticks. One child at a time took this part. Then all the other children at their seats were to pick up some snow, pat it into balls, and on a signal throw it with all their might at one of the arms of the snowman. They always aimed accurately and the arm was knocked off, of course. Then, on a signal, the other arm met the same fate; next the snowman's head fell forward; and finally, the big climax—the last snowballs knocked the snowman down and he crumpled to the floor!

I had no idea how popular that game was going to be! Every child in the room had to have his chance to be the snowman; after a while we had several snowmen at once lined up along the front of the room. By that time all the children had had plenty of exercise and fun for the morning and were content to sit at their desks.

Creative dramatics! Why didn't I think of it then? The children and I could have had the joy of it several years sooner.

For the next two years after my experience in Adrian, I was finishing my master's degree at the University of Chicago and making ready to move to Evanston. Here I was to teach for the next thirty-two years, until my retirement.

I had come to teach at Northwestern at the end of World War I. No other invitation could have made me so happy as the one that came from Agness Law who, with Professor Hardy, had been heading the speech department during the absence of Dean Dennis, then filling a wartime post as vice-consul in Russia.

I am sure that my years of teaching in Michigan, coming to know and work with children of all ages, had much to do with my invitation; for my future at Northwestern was quite sure to involve the preparation of students who would be teachers of children.

Almost as soon as I came to live in Evanston, I began to hear the names of John Dewey and his followers. I had heard of him before, but it was different now. I was close to a center where many of his devoted followers lived and worked. As I read in a book published in 1964 by the Southern Illinois University Press called *John Dewey and the World View*, edited by Douglas Lawson and Arthur Lean,

> No other professor in American history has had so powerful, so lasting and so widespread an influence in the whole field of education as had this shy, simple, gangling son of Vermont.
>
> He had his own school in Chicago for seven-and a half years, but his real career was at Columbia University where he influenced educational practice in his role as teacher of professors of educational theory. They in turn profoundly affected the course of educational development through the many thousands of teachers and administrators they helped to prepare for service in the schools. A philosopher of growth, change and

experimentation, John Dewey may long remain one of the world's most frequently misunderstood and misinterpreted scholars.

One of the earliest schools I visited was the Francis Parker School in Chicago. I thoroughly liked what I saw. The attitude of both teachers and pupils was unlike any I had ever seen. There was no lifeless response to teachers' questions, no looking at the clock to see if it was almost time for the class to be over. There seemed to be a feeling of responsibility on the part of the young people. If this was the "new education," I approved most heartily.

In those first years I wanted to find out more about these schools and their philosophy. I read several of Dewey's books, including *The School and Society*, one of his most popular works. From Kilpatrick's works, I read *Foundations of Method*; I liked especially Rugg and Shumaker's *The Child-Centered School* with its interesting chapter on the Children's Theatre. But when I read Hughes Mearn's three books, *Creative Youth, Creative Power*, and *The Creative Adult*, I knew that, for me, these were the best!

All Mearns' books were acclaimed, but *Creative Power* carries on its jacket such kudos as, "Here's the great book of intellectual adventure and psychological experiment that burst upon the world of ideas like a bombshell and has been hailed as a step forward in education—praised by such people as Louis Untermeyer, Carl Sandburg, Angelo Patri, Dorothy Canfield Fisher, and a host of famous men and women of distinction and success—'A new force in the field of creative education,' says the *New York Herald Tribune*."

By this time I was enthusiastic about creating a new course which I would call *Creative Dramatics*. It was based on the philosophy of Hughes Mearns and the "new education." So began what turned out to be a far-reaching plan for spreading ideas whose time had come.

The three books written by Mr. Mearns became classics in their field. I was to use *Creative Power* as required reading in my course. My students were always so enthusiastic after reading it that their reports were glowing. One girl was so fascinated that she stayed up practically all night to finish the book. Any author, it seemed to me, would be happy to know that young people were thinking about his book, and so I occasionally sent Mr. Mearns one or two of the best of these written reactions.

To my surprise and delight he responded with notes so gracious and clever, expressing his appreciation for the comment, that I saved all of them. Here is one he wrote after receiving a report from Margie Owens, one of my students.

Dear Winifred Ward:

Your contagious spirit always sets me up and makes me feel worthy of good deeds ahead. And you knew that Margie Owens' honest and sincere critique of *Creative Power* would do the same. What delights me so much, and assures me, is that she has told very simply what I intended by the writing of that book but could not be certain that I had really done it until some intelligent person like herself came along and said, "It's here!" I wanted the inexperienced—inexperienced professionally, I mean—reader to feel stirred to interest in the possibilities of finding hidden powers, generally unnoticed gifts; and I wanted the professional teacher to get from the book practical help in finding them in herself and in her charges. Well, I must have done just that, or Margery Owens would not have announced it as true.

I have so many other things that I hoped readers would sense in the motive and the method I have used in this trilogy on creative education; and verification has come from so many discoverers that I am made most happy. Professors have scolded me for being colloquial, for telling stories of real children, for making my material out of human endeavor instead of translating it into cold abstractions, for deliberately avoiding, in short, the method of the learned for the sake of helping others to see and to perform in a region, the creative arts, where learning without feeling, precept without illustrative example, is useless if not fatal. Every common illustration I used out of my own experience was placed with a deliberate teaching purpose, never merely for entertainment, and I have proof that the plan has worked into the heart as well as into the mind of others.

Thanks for the assurance you have always given me and for this added one from Margie Owens.

Fifty years of teaching and the three volume report, seem to me to make a completed thing. I have nothing more to add, and I do want to finish some belated creative work of my own. It is taking the form of light verse, an avocation of a life time. Some of it is pure nonsense—the Carolyn Well's forthcoming Anthology will contain some of that. David McCord will be the editor. But nonsense with always a foundation in truth, as this one:

Live And Learn

By clever planning I contrived
To come before I had arrived,
But uselessly my time was spent—
I should have gone before I went.

Isn't it the truth for all of us!

For you and Margie I am enclosing another type of verse. Don't ask when the whole shall be published. Sometime, no doubt, but we'll have to find an insane publisher first.

Here is an excerpt from a later letter:

You are right about the effect of the recent attacks on "progressive education." I predicted long ago that that would happen after Dewey's death. None of them would have dared to speak up while he was alive. They are hashing over the same old stuff of fifty years ago, "putting the screws on 'em"—stuffing 'em with irrelevant "facts," and that old phantom, liberal arts, concerning which, the last named, I could never get anyone to give me a clear definition.

Well, cheerio! Good things do not die. Reactionaries do not take the trouble to investigate what they are attacking. This is my contribution to the subject:

The Perfect Reactionary

As I was sitting in my chair
I *knew* the bottom wasn't there,
Nor *legs* nor *back*, but I just sat,
Ignoring little things like that.

When Hughes Mearns died, newspapers all over the country, instead of noting his three remarkable books, printed his best-known nonsense rhyme:

As I was going up the stair,
I met a man who wasn't there.
He wasn't there again today
I wish, I wish, he'd stay away.

Volume 9 of the *Encyclopedia of Education* contains this statement:

The Soviet launching of Sputnik [an artificial satellite] in 1957 intensified both popular and professional doubt concerning the quality of American education. We had obviously fallen behind in the science curriculum. Where else were we inferior? Education suddenly took on international overtones, and because of the climate of opinion, it was suddenly possible to enact in the National Defense Education Act 1958 all the ideas which had been brewing for almost a century.

In addition to Sputnik what had brought about this strong reaction to Progressive Education? Why had so many of the best minds, influenced by the outstanding scholar of the century in the field of education—John Dewey—failed? The answer is clear: Too many teachers in the country attempted to use Dewey's methods with little or no understanding of them. An illustration of the kind of teaching carried on with little or no judgment is that of one such teacher who asked her pupils to choose what they would like to study for the coming year; and their choice turned out to be "Shells!"

Some years ago, I was introduced to the head of the School of Education of a large university whose two teachers of creative dramatics I had trained. Minutes after speaking of them with genuine admiration for the quality of their work, he voiced his scorn for Progressive Education. I smiled inwardly. I knew that his teachers had been using the very creative approach he had been condemning.

Years after the downgrading of Progressive Education, the effect of it was felt in many ways. A sudden move toward education in science sent young men into that study in such numbers that soon the country had educated more scientists than we needed. The arts were slighted for years. Washington had only one theatre of any note, and we never heard of government grants for projects at home or for foreigners wishing to study here. In recent years, worthy ventures in the arts, both for native American groups and for foreign visitors, are more and more common. Washington itself has become a cultural city with the completion of Kennedy Center and its program of performing arts.

When the schools in Evanston began offering electives to the students of seventh and eighth grades, I had saved time for two classes I would teach and had one or two very capable seniors who had taken the course and were ready to do student teaching. But the registration was so much larger than we expected that we had to increase the number of students in each section.

We found the children eager to participate, and the classes went well. During those first years I wanted to find out what the children felt they were getting from the course. Some said, "It gets a person over being afraid to speak out." But many of them just enjoyed dramatics. As with all electives, it gave them more time to spend on what they especially liked. In later years, instead of electives, every child has spent a certain amount of time in various fields.

To be convinced that creative dramatics should have a place in the public school curriculum you should observe it in action with a good teacher. You may not see anything spectacular in one visit, though a single visit will give you a very good idea of the respect in which it is held. At other times, something happens which is inspiring.

There was the second-grade class, for instance, which was playing out a barnyard story. One little boy, well liked by the class, but who never had anything to contribute, surprised the other children by volunteering to be the rooster.

In the midst of the playing, at precisely the right moment when the animals were in high dispute, Jimmy came forth with a tremendous "cock-a-doodle-do," so loud that the whole action stopped and the barnyard fowls forgot their playing and looked at Jimmy, amazed and delighted. They crowded around him, full of praise. After the class, Jimmy said almost unbelievingly to his teacher, "Gosh, Miss Taylor, wasn't I wonderful?" The teacher's comment to me was, "If Jimmy never does anything else, he has had one real triumph."

If we are accustomed to praise ourselves, we can't know how important it is to a slow child to have the joy of success now and then. But I have seen evidences enough of what success does to a child to wish that even the slowest boys and girls might have praise once in a while. But a wise teacher will be wary of praising an overconfident child.

Another child I remember from dramatic class I shall call Mary. Mary was a quiet, timid little girl who spoke so softly in class she could hardly be heard. In an assembly program she played one of the three witches in *Macbeth*. No trouble to hear her there! Her eighth-grade teacher exclaimed afterwards, "I couldn't believe it was Mary! In the classroom I can hardly hear her!"

I do not often know the future of children who have been in our public school dramatic classes, but Mary has kept in touch with me during all the years since. In a holiday note when she was in high school, she told me how much easier dramatics had made it for her to adjust there. Later she wrote me about college and how much more assurance she had now because of her dramatic work. Nowadays, married and with two children, she cannot come to see me, but she writes at Christmas about her Boy Scout group and her work in PTA where she is unafraid to speak.

On opening night at the Civic Opera in Chicago a few years ago, a young man came up to me and said, "You don't know me, but I was in your *Rumpelstiltskin* when I was a boy and that experience opened up a whole new world to me. If it were not for that, I wouldn't be here tonight shouting my lungs out for Joan Sutherland."

I trust there have been many Marys and Jims and Bills whose lives have been made more effective because of their participation in creative drama. But I am perhaps just as grateful for the implication of the boy who wrote, "I like dramatics because I'm right more times."

I have reserved for the last the most remarkable teacher of creative drama we ever had in Evanston: Ann Flagg.

Ann was black. I met her in Cleveland at Karamu House, a center for teaching arts and crafts. Ann was teaching creative dramatics and was all excited because I, "who had written a book on creative dramatics," was there to see her! She needn't have worried. She was exceptionally gifted and I could truthfully praise her work. Ann was especially concerned, I think, because she was hoping to win a scholarship to Northwestern the following year. I could enthusiastically write a letter of recommendation for her.

Ann was a college graduate and came to Northwestern the next year for her graduate work. While there she took a course in play writing from Professor Walter Scott and wrote a play titled *The Great Gittin' Up Mornin'* which told of a little black boy sent to school for the first time. Dr. Scott considered it good enough to enter in a Samuel French play contest where it won first prize; later that year, Ann was flown to California to oversee its production for television. With her delightful sense of humor, she told us later that during rehearsals she sat in a *chair with her name on the back!*

We kept her in Evanston doing part-time teaching until she had her master's degree; from then on, she taught a full schedule for several years. Nearly all her time was spent at Foster, a black school in Evanston. She found that most of the children there felt inferior, and she did magnificent work in building real pride in being black.

"What country did our race come from?" she asked one class.

They named every continent except Africa.

"Where else?" she prodded.

Finally a timid little girl said, almost in a whisper, "Africa?"

"Yes," she echoed in a strong voice, "Africa!"

In every way possible she emphasized dignity in their cultural background. Ann felt deep pride in her race and taught it to her students. She saw to it that the school library had the best books from which the children could learn about their people, and they sang songs which fostered this love and pride. Ann was interested in children as individuals. When a child was lacking in confidence, she gave him parts to play to bolster his courage. And he never let her down.

Though I had retired from teaching, Hazel Easton and I always went to Ann's plays which were built up in classwork. One such, which was remarkably effective but was never recorded or photographed, grew out of what the children had studied concerning their race. The children had learned about many black leaders of whom they could be proud. They had read poetry by Paul Lawrence Dunbar and James Weldon Johnson, among others; they knew the historical fact that the first man in the Revolutionary War to die for his country was black; they knew the accomplishments of George Washington Carver, a revered name to them.

This production, I recall, had both a singing and a speaking choir. The singing choir sat in the front rows of the auditorium; the speaking choir was grouped on the steps leading up to the stage, some of them sitting, some standing. On the stage itself, scenes were enacted depicting historical events such as the Underground Railroad and the dedicated work of Harriet Tubman. As a climax, the speaking choir on the steps called the names of people of note in their race of whom they could be proud: "Marian Anderson! Ralph Bunche! Martin Luther King!" Sometimes one strong voice would call a name, at other times two or several voices; but all of them ringing loud and clear and building with intensity of feeling—a spine-tingling effect. It was a thrilling performance. When it was over, the audience, visibly moved, gave a standing ovation. I remember it as one of my most moving experiences in the theatre.

It would be profoundly interesting to know how much those years of Ann's teaching influenced the children of Foster School. There were not many years—her health was never good, and at a teachers' meeting after school one afternoon she suddenly died. It was a sad loss and a very great one.

A memorial service was held in the school auditorium, and the room was packed with parents and teachers. The service was as unique as Ann. A children's choir sat on one side of the stage, and there was a lectern on the other side with one large jar of flowers in front of it. Each of Evanston's drama teachers paid a short tribute to Ann, many of them simply repeating lines Ann had spoken to her classes. Simultaneously pictures of Ann teaching her classes were thrown on a screen. And finally the principal of the school came to the podium with a letter he had directed to Ann. It called to mind anecdotes, some of them very humorous. Among them was a little ritual that he and Ann spoke when they met in the hall. Mr. Hill would say, "How's your behavior?" And Ann would respond,

"You've stopped talking and gone to meddling." Mr. Hill finished his letter simply, "See you later." It was the most moving aspect of a ceremony which ended with the choir coming down from the stage and walking out, singing the song that had given the title to her play—"The Great Gittin' Up Mornin'."

Introduction

NELLIE McCASLIN

Nellie McCaslin, editor of Children and Drama, *teaches in the Program in Educational Theatre at New York University. Dr.* McCaslin *is the author of the college text* Creative Dramatics in the Classroom, *four books of plays for children,* Children's Theatre in the United States: A History, *and numerous reviews and articles. Her B.A. and M.A. degrees were granted by Western Reserve University, her Ph.D. by New York University; she also studied with Maria Ouspenskaya. Dr.* McCaslin *has taught at National College of Education, Teachers College of Columbia University, and Mills College of Education, and has lectured and led workshops throughout this country and England. She is currently president of the Children's Theatre Association, a division of the American Theatre Association.*

This collection of essays may be best described as having originated in postconference rumination. Heading for home after days of meetings, I habitually found myself in the comparative isolation of airline or bus, attempting to sort out the various opinions I had heard expressed and contested. Challenged by questions raised in discussion and stimulated by workshops and demonstrations, my reflections in time took a practical turn. Others must share my dilemma of fragmented recollection. Why not try to collect and publish together the viewpoints and procedures of a number of leaders? The result is *Children and Drama.*

Much has been written and said in the past sixty years regarding the place, practice, values, definition, and role of drama in education. Many leaders have demonstrated the ways in which this area of the arts might be incorporated into the curriculum or used to enrich community offerings. A variety of programs has been introduced over the years, some of them still in existence, most of them altered, others discarded in favor of new ideas or changing interests and needs. Nevertheless, drama in one form or another is now recognized as a subject worthy of inclusion in the curricula of many schools and colleges. Realistic objectives have been stated, and content appropriate to differing age levels and circumstances has been suggested. Drama has long since moved from its place on the periphery of the curriculum to a more central, if still unstable, position. Education for the teachers of creative dramatics and children's theatre today is a carefully organized program, though there are few of us who would not like to see an expansion both qualitatively and quantitatively throughout the country. Finally, through the structure of the American Theatre Association, divisional organizations representing special areas of interest have been established. One of the largest of these divisions is the Children's Theatre Association.

The professional journals and conferences of this organization offer us opportunities to share our ideas as well as to explain and explore both traditional and innovative programs. We are constantly examining the relationship of theatre to education and education to theatre. Yet, in spite of our burgeoning channels of communication, we have not yet succeeded in reaching all our colleagues in these fields, few outside them. Indeed, we have not always reached one another. Many articles and books on child drama have been published in this country and in England, it is true, but no collection that has as its single purpose the presentation of current thinking and practice as expressed by some of the leading practitioners in the United States, England, and Canada. Thus the rationale for this book, which I hope will be welcomed by all who are concerned with children, education, and drama.

As editor, I began by polling a number of colleagues to see if they shared my enthusiasm for such a collection. The results were both encouraging and helpful. There was a unanimous willingness to share ideas and a desire to learn more about the thinking of others. The selection of the contributors was a more difficult task than I had anticipated, for there are today many outstanding teachers of educational theatre and child drama. An arbitrary number, necessary as it was, obviously eliminated many educators, whose reputations and work in the field would qualify them for inclusion in any book purporting to represent significant contribution to theory and practice. I regretted this need for selection, yet I fully understood the practical necessity.

The question may well be raised as to why no one from community or professional theatre has been included. I gave this point careful consideration at the outset, then reached the conclusion that, in spite of the excellent and imaginative work that is going on in a number of places under their auspices, the thrust of this book is drama in education and I must be parochial in my interpretation. To spread the focus to cover related areas could lead us far afield and perhaps defeat the original purpose. I am sure that some readers will take exception to this delimitation but it was the result of considered judgment—right or wrong—not disregard or unawareness of current practice.

I should like at this point to mention a new concept of theatre for youth that has emerged in the past decade. Created first to meet the needs of older children and adolescents, it tends to deal with contemporary subject matter and problems cast in nontraditional forms. Whether it should be considered as an alternative to traditional child drama or an extension, I am not yet prepared to say; but some exciting results have been obtained under the leadership of a new group of young director-leaders with strong social concerns. Their influence has already been felt.

In many instances, however, the three major areas of school, community theatre, and professional company are working together toward common goals. When this takes place it is most often the school or university that initiates or assumes responsibility for the program.

After much deliberation the following criteria were adopted in the selection of the contributors: a clearly defined point of view and a substantial record of achievement based on that point of view. All the authors are well known regionally, nationally, and in some cases, internationally. When asked if they could condense their statements into twenty manuscript pages, all agreed to attempt it, though admittedly this was not an easy assignment. I have been gratified both by the results and by the fact that the contributors represent so broad a spectrum. If this book is received with the enthusiasm I think it deserves, it is my hope that there will be subsequent volumes.

I have tried to avoid the pitfall of superficiality through the use of a single focus—children and drama—believing that one topic discussed in depth has greater value than a collection of topics dealing with various aspects or areas. Although the word "child" is used in the title, the implications for all age levels, including high school and college, are to be found in the writing of many contributors. The book is philosophical rather than practical by intent. It does not aim to tell the reader how to teach but examines the base from which each leader works. Inevitably, in many instances procedures must be described as an integral part of the presentation.

The variety I hoped to obtain is achieved through the differing attitudes and goals of the writers. Some give the highest priority to the educative process; others, to the aesthetic; and others to the social and personal growth of the participants. Yet I was aware in assembling the manuscripts that all of us share a portion of basic agreement as to the raison d'être of drama for and with children. In the final analysis, the individual teacher in his particular situation must determine his goals and thereby his emphasis. Regardless of personal bias and skills, each of us well might, given a different set of circumstances, realign his priorities.

There is no one right approach. Our methods must be our own, to be tested, modified, altered, or scrapped as we relate our objectives to the situation. Moreover, there is the constant reality of the changing times. To be flexible and open to new ideas and at the same time adhere to a philosophic conviction requires confidence in oneself, perception, and judgment. We have all witnessed the popular methods, the gimmicks, the shortcuts to showy results; but we have also seen the slow evolution of concepts and methods that have proved viable and thus earned acceptance.

My own point of view is well known through my writing. Nevertheless, I must acknowledge indebtedness both to those colleagues who have preceded me and to those currently engaged, whose work I have observed and respect. Their influence and my own experience have led me to the conviction that informal or creative dramatics is the only sound approach to drama for children under high school age. Committed as I am to this point of view, however, I am willing to admit that sharing with an audience is at times valid; but I should hope that these occasions are rare and to be considered as demonstrations, not performances.

As to material for improvisation, I believe strongly that both literary and life experiences should be included. To omit good prose and poetry is to deprive the young of a part of their cultural heritage; to avoid personal human experience, on the other hand, is to deny the essence of drama. Drama as process can and may include both; product belongs to a later stage of development, when the art of the theatre is the major concern. It is on these points that we find the greatest difference of opinion.

The experience of this past year has been richly rewarding for me and, I hope, for the authors with whom I have had the pleasure of working. I am particularly pleased to be able to present three essays by authors from England and Canada, outstanding leaders who have had a significant influence on many teachers and students in the United States. Gerald Tyler and Dorothy Heathcote have not only lectured widely in this country but have also been particularly hospitable to Americans studying theatre in education abroad. Mr. Tyler has been generous in arranging visits to British colleges and theatre centres, and some of Mrs. Heathcote's American students have followed her to England to observe her work at Newcastle upon Tyne. Margaret Faulkes from the University of Alberta also is well known in the States, for she is a member of the Children's Theatre Association and has participated in its convention programs.

Among the fringe benefits of editing this publication have been the renewal of old friendships and a lively correspondence with colleagues at a distance. I am keenly aware of the time that this task has taken from already heavy schedules, but the collective hours and efforts have produced a work that is long overdue. May I take this opportunity to thank all the authors for their cooperation and generosity? The result of their contributions creates a whole that is, I believe, far greater than the sum of its parts.

Contents

CHILDREN AND DRAMA

DRAMA IN EDUCATION—
A CHANGING SCENE

GERALDINE BRAIN SIKS

Geraldine Brain Siks is a national leader in the field of children's drama. Co-author with Ruth Lease of Creative Dramatics in Home, School and Community, *Mrs. Siks is author of* Children's Literature for Dramatization *and* Creative Dramatics: An Art for Children. Marco Polo, Prince Fairyfoot, The Sandalwood Box, *and* The Nuremberg Stove *are among her published plays. With her sister Hazel Dunnington she edited* Children's Theatre and Creative Dramatics, *a monograph requested by the American Educational Theatre Association. Mrs. Siks contributes frequently to professional journals. Currently and for many years a faculty member of the School of Drama at the University of Washington, Seattle, Mrs. Siks was recipient of a contract with the U.S. Office of Education to research Theatre Arts Materials for Use in Children's Drama in seventeen European countries.*

"The old order changeth, yielding place to new . . ." *Tennyson*

On a flight across the country on a sunny August day a few years ago, the plane flew low over the Mississippi River Valley. From this vantage point one could see how forceful currents of water had first cut the river channel, and how torrents of floodwaters, at later times, appeared to have changed the initial path of the river. I recall that I pondered on an analogy between the river and the historical flow of human events. More particularly, since I was flying to a

1

Children's Theatre Conference, I remember that my analogy related to the children's drama movement. I contemplated on the desire of persons concerned with drama in education to imagine a high enough point where they might view the pattern of historical events that have shaped the field. If it were possible to view events in proper perspective, I reasoned, it might, also, be possible to perceive in current happenings some major implications that would serve to advance the field.

The purpose of this essay is twofold. First, it examines, briefly, the flow of major educational events that have etched out the creative drama movement in our country. Second, it points out a new thrust for drama in education based on current educational trends that appear to be cutting new channels for the future.

HISTORICAL OVERVIEW

Creative drama in our country is linked inseparably with the person of Winifred Ward and with the history of education in the United States. A brief glance at these factors shows that it was Miss Ward and her influence that served to develop and advance creative drama at all educational levels during an approximate fifty-year span. This is evident in many ways, predominantly: the introduction in 1925 of a course in creative dramatics in the curriculum of the School of Speech at Northwestern University and, later, classes in creative dramatics for children in the Evanston public schools; the publication in 1930 of a text, *Creative Dramatics*, and the continuing publication of textbooks, articles, and a government bulletin from that time to the present; the founding of the Children's Theatre Conference in 1944, providing an opportunity for persons in the field to confer and exchange points of view; collaboration with Rita Criste to produce a teaching film, *Creative Drama: The First Steps*; and her influence on students, colleagues, administrators, and children concerning the philosophy, enjoyment, and values of creative dramatics.

Winifred Ward based her philosophy of creative dramatics and its practices on her perceptions of child development and on trends in education. These included primarily an emphasis on creative education, on "creative self-expression," "learning by doing," "child-centered school," "tolerant understanding of self and others," and "education for a democracy."

In 1957, in the second edition of *Playmaking with Children*, Miss Ward observed that during the advancement of creative drama four widely different attitudes had evolved concerning its use. First was the attitude of classroom teachers to use it as a *tool*, a tool to involve children in learning facts. A second attitude was that it was purely *recreation* with no concern for education. A third designated its use entirely as *therapy*. Fourth was the attitude that regarded creative drama as an *art* with such unquestioned value that it should be a part of every elementary school curriculum, on equal footing with music and the graphic and plastic arts. This assessment, made nearly twenty years ago, describes the four principal attitudes toward creative dramatics at the present time. For the most part, it is used in relationship to the first three attitudes. There is little if any evidence to support a trend toward the inclusion of creative dramatics as an art in basic education in primary and elementary school curricula throughout the country.

EDUCATIONAL DEVELOPMENTS

A major educational revolution in our country since 1960, at all educational levels, has effected change in the attitude toward the arts in education. From my perspective, I perceive four major educational and historical events that have contributed directly to this change.

U.S. Office of Education

Of first importance is the interest and initiative taken by the U.S. Office of Education in the educational aspects of the arts and humanities. USOE provides the services of its specialists to educational institutions concerned with fostering programs in the arts and humanities. In 1962, USOE established an Arts and Humanities branch to develop a program of research and related activities to advance education in the arts and humanities. This branch with consultants in the various arts spearheaded the development of programs designed to promote extension and improvement of education in the arts and humanities at all educational levels. Effective action, in the nature of national and international conferences, was aimed at strengthening theatre arts at professional and educational levels. Theatre arts' consultants, particularly Kathryn Bloom, Jack Morrison, and Irving Brown, have promoted research aimed at designing curricula to improve education in theatre arts in elementary and secondary schools and at higher education levels.

Federal Support

A second major event was the recognition at the federal level of the importance nationally of the arts and humanities in the lives of the American people in our society. This occurred with the passage of the National Foundation of the Arts and Humanities Act in 1965, which was signed into law by President Lyndon B. Johnson on September 25 of that year. Historically unprecedented, the law created a national foundation to "develop and promote a broadly conceived national policy of support for the humanities and the arts in the United States."[1] The foundation consists of a federal Council on the Arts and the Humanities and twin endowments, a National Endowment for the Arts and a National Endowment for the Humanities, each having its own advisory body. The purpose of the federal council is to coordinate the two endowments and relate their activities to other federal programs. The 89th Congress in session from 1965 to 1966 passed an unprecedented amount of educational legislation which was as applicable to the fields of the arts and humanities as to any other fields of study.

Through Titles I and III of the Elementary and Secondary Education Act of 1965, considerable research supported educational efforts in the fields of the arts. Some of the most innovative projects, aimed at improving and advancing arts education, were research programs designed by National Regional Educational Laboratories. An example of this kind of research was initiated in the summer of 1967, by the Central Atlantic Regional Educational Laboratory (CAREL) and conducted at Airlie House in Warrenton, Virginia. A research team of twenty-five artists and educators, working five days a week for a period of six weeks, formed a unique task force concerned with the arts in education for young children. I was privileged to be a member of this task force. The mission focused on ways to present the arts effectively to children in early childhood education. Research centered on identifying commonalities in the fundamental creative processes of the arts, seeking ways to impart to young children a sense of the substance and processes of the arts, finding ways to integrate basic arts' elements, and writing behavioral objectives for teaching the arts to young children. Although all project goals were not accomplished during the six-week period, research was continued by smaller teams and by individuals.

Aesthetic Education

Evolving out of the two events previously cited are two comprehensive programs in the arts—CEMREL's Aesthetic Education Program and the JDR III Fund for Arts in Education Program. CEMREL, Inc. (Central Midwest Regional Educational Laboratory), a private, nonprofit corporation, is a national educational laboratory in Saint Louis, Missouri, supported in part by funds from the U.S. Office of Education. CEMREL's major thrust in this program has been the development of a "massive, systematic and rational exploration" of education in the arts. CEMREL has designed a curricular system of modular resources or learning packages for children in the primary grades that focuses a child's enthusiasm for learning on "experiencing the beauty, the order and the form to be found in the arts and the environment."[2] Essentially this program aims at developing a child's aesthetic sensibility and human spirit and at helping a child develop and shape his perceptions, his patterns of thinking, his creativity, and his judgment. CEMREL's long-range plans for this program include the designing of learning packages for grade levels K-12, and the developing of a program in aesthetic education for teacher education.

The JDR III Fund for Arts in Education Program aims primarily at making the arts an integral part of the general education of every child. Since 1967, this program has been in process of research and development. It has focused on three pilot projects designed to complement existing arts programs and to stimulate more comprehensive programs. Development centers on the inclusion of the arts as part of the total curriculum rather than as separate and specialized subjects. "All the arts for every child" is their stated mission, and to achieve this in a way that enriches the general curriculum rather than reinforcing the segregation of the arts.

International Conference on the Teaching of English

A fourth event was the Anglo-American Conference on the Teaching of English held at Dartmouth College in the summer of 1966, a conference now referred to as the Dartmouth Conference. Forty-eight British and American educators and one representative from Canada convened under the auspices of the American Modern Language Association, the American National Council of Teachers of English, and the British National Association for the Teaching of English. The conference considered solutions to critical problems concerned with a need to improve the teaching of English at all educational levels. During the month-long seminar, the conference identified a need for various kinds of research. A major outcome, spearheaded by the British, was a realization of the importance of drama in the lives of children and youth to foster their learning of language and communication skills. Drama was viewed as an experience natural to a child's way of learning and a means of involving the child in a whole range of human interaction.

Following the conference, James Moffett researched at Harvard University and, in 1967, developed the thesis that drama and speech are central, not peripheral, to a language curriculum. They are its base and essence. His thesis placed drama as the matrix of all language activities, subsuming speech and engendering the varieties of writing and reading. It is Moffett's assumption that "dramatic interaction—doing things verbally in situations with other people—is the primary vehicle for developing thought and language."[3] In 1968 Moffett published *Teaching the Universe of Discourse* and *A Student-Centered Language Arts Curriculum, Grades K-13: A Handbook for Teachers*. These books, focusing on theory and application, were followed by extensive instructional materials titled *Interaction*, a whole new concept in English education. For example, activity cards focus on Acting-out, Imagining, Moving, Speaking, Listening, Characterizing, Improvising, Dramatizing, and Enacting Play Scripts.

A further result of the Dartmouth Conference was the international cooperation that has resulted in efforts to advance drama in education. Two significant actions include: (1) the adoption in many American colleges and universities of a text from England written by Brian Way, *Development Through Drama*; and (2) the influence of Dorothy Heathcote, one of England's outstanding drama educators, who has conducted summer workshops at Northwestern University and other American universities. She has developed and made available a series of teaching films illustrating her theory and practices. Mrs. Heathcote's films communicate her unique technique of teaching "in role" and demonstrate how she relates drama to other subject areas by involving children in in-depth discussions and experiences.

Collectively these historical and educational endeavors appear to be cutting a new channel for the inclusion of the arts in education, particularly for the inclusion of drama in education. Concerted efforts aim at positioning the arts in a central rather than peripheral position in education at all levels. Along with private and public forces at the state and local levels, federal efforts will now serve to produce permanent and significant results. The U.S. Office of Education views research and development as indispensable approaches to the improvement of educational aspects of the arts and humanities. Continuing research, testing, and dissemination of instructional materials by CEMREL and the JDR III Fund will advance aesthetic education at all educational levels. Moffett and followers of his theory will no doubt create more extensive instructional materials emphasizing drama as the core of the language arts process. International cooperation in this area appears to be heading in an effective continuing direction.

Consider these efforts and endeavors from the perspective of drama in education. On the one hand, it seems evident that creative dramatics will and should continue *to be used* as a tool for teaching facts, for therapy, for recreation, and for teaching language. On the other hand, it seems equally evident that drama will not be included as an art in education until it is reconceived as an art in education.

NEW DIRECTION FOR DRAMA IN EDUCATION

Thesis and Assumptions

I believe that if drama is taught primarily as an art in education at all educational levels, including teacher education, it will affect child development and learning, and simultaneously serve to advance drama as an art. This thesis is based on four assumptions:

1. The involvement of an individual (regardless of age) in the fundamental processes and content of the art of drama affects his thinking, feeling, and doing. This serves him in living.

2. If a teacher learns drama as an art and gains an organic understanding of its structure by actively *experiencing* its processes, applying its concepts, and enjoying the act of creation, drama will be more effective when the teacher uses its processes and concepts with children as a tool, as therapy, as recreation, and as the core of a language arts' program.

3. If a teacher learns drama organically, as described above, the teacher will know more effectively how to integrate a child's learning with the other arts and other subject areas.

4. If a child or youth responds with enjoyment in learning drama as an art and becomes involved in its creative and collaborative processes, that individual will continue his experience in the art as an adult, probably as a member of an audience or perhaps as a practicing artist in one of the related drama and theatre arts.

Proposed Direction

If drama is to be taught as *an art in education* for children and youth, I propose that drama be taught *as an art* in teacher education on the undergraduate and graduate levels in college and university programs and in inservice programs for teachers in public schools. I propose further that the art of drama be structured and taught from a process-concept approach.

What is meant by a process-concept structural approach in teaching drama as an art? Clearly this question calls for a comprehensive answer in the nature of a book or books which, I suspect, are now being researched or written. The approach is not new. It grew out of conferences and research stimulated by the U.S. Office of Education which examined fundamental processes involved in imparting to children a sense of the substance and nature of the creative processes of the art of drama. Persons interested in examining initial efforts in this direction are referred to two available sources. The first was prepared for California public schools and the other for drama in education in Washington State schools.

Drama/Theatre Framework for California Public Schools. This 127-page syllabus is a 1972 reproduction of a working draft. It was developed and prepared over a five-year period by the California Office of the State Superintendent of Public Instruction in cooperation with a Drama Framework Committee, special consultants, and a statewide Fine Arts and Humanities Framework Committee. Twenty individuals, including theatre artists, educators, and members of the California Educational Theatre Association, assisted the official Drama Framework Committee of eight members and three special consultants. Their document is available through the California Educational Theatre Association. As explained in the Preface, it is intended to function in several capacities: "as a statement of policy by the State Board of Education; as a guide to district superintendents, consultants, and school administrators; as a guide for curriculum planners; and as a guide for the classroom teacher until more comprehensive courses of study have been initiated."[4]

The "Framework" goal states: "Every child should be educated in kindergarten through grade twelve to develop his dramatic imagination, his problem-solving abilities, and his communicative potential, and to provide him access to his cultural heritage."[5] The Framework Method is clarified as follows: "Far from being simply another 'subject' in a crowded school day, the drama/theatre program proposed in this document is a fundamental, interdisciplinary approach to learning. To achieve the framework goal, the student must experience theatre by engaging in its processes and understand theatre by applying its concepts. Because theatre is in essence a process, an engaging act, its proper academic discipline is to study it and practice it in this context."[6]

The "Framework" represents a soundly researched and comprehensively conceived drama/theatre arts program. It provides a conceptual design for structuring curricula at all educational levels. It appears to represent an educational breakthrough for including drama/theatre arts in basic education. It will no doubt serve as a model for the advancement of drama/theatre arts for California schools and for schools throughout the nation.

Drama Education Guidelines for the State of Washington. Published in 1972, this 56-page document is available through the Office of the

State Superintendent of Public Instruction, Olympia, Washington. The publication was prepared by a five-member committee of the Washington Association of Theatre Artists (WATA) under the direction of personnel in the Washington State Superintendent of Public Instruction's Office. The WATA Guidelines Committee, meeting over a three-year period, determined a number of criteria applicable to drama education in Washington schools. These criteria serve as the base for several sets of guidelines for public school administrators and teachers. Taken together they provide a direction for a program of drama education for the first twelve school years. Unlike the California "Framework" the *Guidelines* address themselves to five areas of concern: (1) reasons for education in the theatre arts; (2) space and equipment requirements for teaching drama; (3) drama education in the elementary school; (4) drama for the junior and senior high schools; and (5) preparation for teachers of drama.

The elementary program described in the *Guidelines* "is regarded as a process which aims primarily to educate children in the broad field of the art of drama. Education today is recognized essentially as a process of changing behavior—behavior in the broad sense of thinking, feeling, and doing. Thus, drama education seeks to change the natural, imaginative spontaneous behavior of the child evident in his perceptions and representations of his experiences in role-taking and dramatic play, to more consciously controlled behavior required to do drama."[7] Although the *Guidelines* objectives are admittedly ambitious, they focus toward one clear end: "to exercise and develop a child's learning processes so he learns to do and receive the art of drama with enjoyment. Learning drama from this view should enable a child to function as a more imaginative, perceptive citizen responsive and responsible to his society, his environment, and himself."

Unlike the California "Framework," the Washington *Guidelines* do not provide strategies, resources, and activities for implementing the curriculum. However, a newly formed Washington State Drama Committee, working with personnel in the State Superintendent of Public Instruction's office, is currently at work revising the elementary school program. Their aim is to clarify the theory, and to design activities centered in basic drama concepts that will involve children in exploring and applying them as they engage in fundamental drama processes. Activities are being designed, also, from a content point of view, to provide an interdisciplinary approach to learning through drama.

CONCLUSIONS AND IMPLICATIONS

Viewing drama as an art in education from an imaginary vantage point on high is challenging. It cannot provide a clearly defined course for the art of drama in the future, but it can reveal new and forceful thrusts. It is much too early to judge what kind of channel will be cut, or whether two or three of the current surgings will reinforce one another as effective tributaries moving in a new direction. Nevertheless, three factors emerge clearly.

First, it is only in the schools—nursery, primary, elementary, junior and senior high schools, and colleges and universities—that the tide can be turned for the arts and the drama arts in basic education. Second, if change is to occur, it is essential that teacher education in a broadly conceived concept of the art of drama be advanced simultaneously with the advancement of the arts in basic education of children and youth. Because of the unique nature of drama, it can serve many effective purposes in education. However, this will occur only if teachers as learners first experience drama organically as an art. Drama, as an art, engages the whole human being—his senses, imagination, feelings, intuition, and intellect. Third, research is imperative for a continued movement toward new knowledge in the broad field of the arts in education and for drama in education. Research serves as a vanguard for the advancement of the field.

To effect change calls for the combined efforts of many persons working in a variety of educational endeavors. It calls for innovation. It asks for research task forces of theatre artists, psychologists, educators, and interested adults willing to give their time, effort, imagination, and expertise to seek ways to reach desired goals. It seeks individuals with the vision, spirit, and dedication possessed by Winifred Ward, one of our country's great women in the arts.

Must we wait for time to cut its natural course for the art of drama in education? Or will there be in our midst persons who perceive in the nature of human beings and in current happenings that:

There is a tide in the affairs of men,
Which, taken at the flood, leads on to fortune;
Omitted, all the voyage of their life
Is bound in shallows and in miseries.

WILLIAM SHAKESPEARE, *Julius Caesar*

NOTES

1. "The Arts and the Humanities: Educational Developments," *Progress of Public Education in the United States of America. 1966–1967* (Report of the Office of Education, U.S. Department of Health, Education, and Welfare to the Thirtieth International Conference on Public Education, Geneva, Switzerland, 6-15 July 1967), p. 27.
2. Stanley S. Madeja and Sharon Bocklage, "The Aesthetic Education Program CEMREL, Inc." (Report of the Aesthetic Education Center, AE-TA Convention, August 1971), p. 45.
3. James Moffett, *Drama: What is Happening* (Washington, D.C.: National Council of Teachers of English, 1967), p. vi.
4. Drama/Theatre Framework for California Public Schools (Reproduction by the CSCLB Theatre Arts Department of a draft prepared by the Office of Wilson Riles, Superintendent of Public Instruction, California State Department of Education, 1972), p. iv.
5. Ibid., p. 13.
6. Ibid., p. 14.
7. Geraldine B. Siks, "The Elementary Program," *Drama Education Guidelines* (Office of Superintendent of Public Instruction, State of Washington and Washington Association of Theatre Artists Committee, January 1972), p. 10.

CREATIVE DRAMA-
IMPROVISATION-THEATRE

MARGARET FAULKES

*Margaret Faulkes, associate professor of drama at the University of
Alberta, Canada, was educated in England, where she attended
the Royal Academy of Dramatic Art and London University Goldsmiths'
College. She has taught in the City of Leicester Education Department,
at Loughborough College, and in the Hinckley and West Ham secondary
schools, as well as acted in the West Country professional children's theatre.
She was co-founder and co-director with Brian Way of the well-known
Theatre Centre in London in 1954, where she remained until 1965, when she
became visiting lecturer at the University of Washington. She assumed
her present position in 1967; in addition, she has lectured and conducted
numerous drama workshops throughout Canada and the United States.*

Drama: *a set of events having the unity and progress of a play and
leading to catastrophe or consummation.* The Oxford dictionary's definition provides an apt choice of prognoses for twentieth-century
drama in education, brought sharply into focus through controversy
among protagonists in the field preventing unity and impeding
progress. Dichotomy and polarization in objectives and techniques
of educational drama have been aggravated during the past twenty-
five years by developments in educational philosophy and
psychology, by the influence of pioneers in 'creative' approaches to
drama in schools, and by the evolution of theatre itself with its
emphasis on experimentation. At first glance, the controversy seems
well founded, for drama teachers have widely differing objectives
embodying confusing and sometimes contradictory techniques.

Four major objectives for drama in education may be identified, each involving variations in teacher orientation:

1. *Exposure to (and sometimes training in) traditional theatre arts and crafts.* While this approach may be found at any grade level, it is most commonly associated with the secondary school where the drama specialist, fully trained (most often in traditional approaches to formal theatre), will philosophize that the experience of theatre as an art "for art's sake" nonetheless integrates educational and cultural principles.

2. *The development of personal resources, including creativity and social awareness, with some experience of theatre arts.* The drama teacher may have some orientation to and knowledge of theatre arts, but also has a commitment to education in the broadest sense. It is likely that training, if any, has included creative drama* and, if formal theatre is attempted, its techniques may be deemphasized in favor of process rather than product. Being less concerned with the preservation of theatre tradition, this teacher may well utilize improvisation as a core for the teaching of drama as an option.

3. *The teaching of other subjects, or for personal enrichment (sometimes defined as "having fun").* The general teacher or specialist in another subject recognizes that dramatic method involving improvisation is useful as an educational tool. In this classification we find elementary and secondary teachers of English, language arts, and social studies. Many teachers in this category are unfamiliar with the basic elements of any kind of drama, let alone the techniques involved in creative drama; consequently, the classroom becomes a setting for chaos in the name of creativity.

4. *The development of interpersonal relationships, "group trust," social and/or political awareness.* Comparatively recent, this utilization of drama on the one hand takes advantage of the trend toward "social conscience" by limiting theatre experience to documentary themes of political import; on the other, and more dangerous, side, drama techniques have been adapted by amateur psychologists and some drama teachers who have been diverted by the specter of drama as a panacea for all human problems, for sensitivity training, and for

*Creative Drama is here used as a generic term embracing *child drama, children's drama, educational drama, creative drama, creative dramatics, developmental drama,* etc. Later (p. 17) it will be used to denote a specific approach to drama.

"confrontations" in the classroom. Regrettably, teachers in this category seem unconcerned about the art of theatre although they label their activities "drama"; there is an unfortunate trend for administrative encouragement of these activities and, in one area of North America at least, government grants have been given to drama teachers and actors with some experience of participation children's theatre to do creative drama in mental hospitals. It should be noted that these teacher/actors had no training in psychology. Such identification of *creative drama* with therapy and its related fields of sensitivity training, etc., or with questionable propaganda, brings the whole field of drama into disrepute.

To a great extent, those of us who have pioneered in creative drama are to blame for the increased use of our techniques in other fields. Zealous in our well-meaning efforts to convince the traditional theatre arts teachers that a non-performance-oriented "creative" approach to dramatic art is not only desirable but essential for young children, we have so negated theatre itself that we have antagonized our colleagues and have provided strong arguments for equating creative drama with everything *but* theatre. Indeed, some leaders in the field have spent long hours trying to find alternative titles and descriptive terms in order to emphasize the dichotomy between "drama" and "theatre."

More damaging is the manifestation of confused thinking among the exponents of creative drama: some view it as an art form, suggesting that it is the child's style of theatre; others call it art, but discourage any connection with the art of theatre; some insist that it is a subject in its own right but is concerned with personal rather than drama development; still others argue that it is a basis for eventual drama experience; some deny its existence as a subject at all, designating it as an educational tool—a core for all subjects.

Further perplexity arises because the pioneers at first focused their attention on the young child, so that creative drama became associated with elementary education; but later developments applied the techniques to work with teen-agers, and it is not uncommon today to hear people talking about "the creative drama approach to theatre." With utter disregard for rationale, creative drama is described as a non-theatre-oriented activity and defined as improvisation which, historically, has always been a part of theatre art and, in this century, has become integral to actor-training—while avant garde, highly publicized, professional theatre groups have declared that improvisation is a viable theatre art form. Meanwhile, developments in theatre for young audiences (long associated with creative dramatics in teacher-training) have included the interpretation (or misinterpretation) of audience participation as creative drama; trouping companies have promoted improvisation in lieu of script, "poor theatre" in any shape and in any place, and actor-audience interraction with the proclaimed educational objectives of promoting creative drama as a classroom activity.

The layman, bombarded by such inconsistencies, selects whichever words or phrases make the most sense, and often ends up with the all-too-familiar prejudice against any kind of drama in education; and it is not surprising that the traditional theatre arts teacher suspects the creative drama teacher of being anti-"real theatre." At the same time, "traditionalists" who have been known to dismiss both creative drama and participation children's theatre as "pixie drama" are reluctant to acknowledge that contemporary playwrights, directors, designers, and actors have effected comparable—in some cases identical—innovations. Instead of applying such unconventional, adventurous explorations to theatre arts programs, the quasi-conservatory system in many high schools perpetuates an outdated mode of theatre which evidences an abysmal disregard for progress in either theatre *or* education, Similarly, some elementary school teachers, while fully endorsing creativity in a general educational sense, resort to conventional styles of production and performance in the name of drama expression for children. Such anomaly arises from ignorance or obstinacy.

One reason for the continuing dichotomy between the "traditionalists" and the "progressives" is that neither group envisions the total spectrum. If the whole field of drama in education is viewed in terms of the definition of drama itself—"a set of events having the unity and progress of a play"—then any course or program of drama must include a beginning, a middle, and an end. To begin at the beginning, where drama in education is concerned, seems to be an excercise in futility. The "traditionalists," focusing on formal theatre techniques, invariably begin at the end, equating process with product. The "progressives," emphasizing development of personal resources, seem with increasing regularity to end at the beginning, equating product with process. It is important, therefore, to recognize that, in drama, the "spectrum" fits the definition of "the image of something seen continuing when the eyes are closed or turned away." The "something seen" is the process whereby individual resources and creative potential are developed into dramatic art awareness which leads to a rich, dynamic experience of the product. The beginning, middle, and end of drama in education are here considered as three interrelated phases of activity, which incorporate the educational objectives of personal development and the artistic objectives of drama development.

PHASE 1: LAYING THE FOUNDATIONS

Since the stress in phase 1 is on personal development, while art form is deemphasized, it will be entitled *creative drama*.

It is not difficult to persuade teachers of grades K-6 that a vital function of drama in elementary education is the development of the child's resources. Educational philosophy and psychology consistently emphasize the needs of the growing child. Sometimes, because of inherent prejudice against drama, its general educational objectives have to be disguised under the pretext of fostering creativity which is considered acceptable, even desirable, in the education of the young. But when it comes to the teen-ager in the junior high grades, or the young adult in the senior high school, vision becomes blurred. Overnight the Grade 7 student has become adult enough to learn adult ways, and any type of classroom activity which implies growth or "creativity for its own sake" is suspect. As for the Grade 10 student, the appointed drama specialist usually has one thought uppermost in mind: to produce the annual school play as soon as possible. Instant theatre becomes the maxim. It matters little if the students have had drama before; it matters less if they are physically inhibited, imaginatively deprived, or incapable of communicating thoughts and ideas with freedom, confidence, and vigor. The suggestion that individual resources that have long been dormant or atrophied should be rediscovered and quickened before attempting to introduce them to the art of drama is received with amazement, scorn, and even ridicule.

Any beginning group, regardless of age or drama background, needs an initial period of exploration and orientation to provide a basis for further creative experience. Creative drama, therefore, is the beginning point for *all* drama.

PHASE 2: AWARENESS OF DRAMATIC ART FORM

This phase will be termed *improvisation*, on the grounds that improvisation embodies numerous elements of dramatic art and is a natural evolvement from creative drama.

This period of drama experience is the most misunderstood. Dramatic art and theatre are equated with *performance*; but from the preparatory stage of resource development, the student needs to go through a level of exploration into elements of drama without the pressures of public performance which preclude (or should preclude) failure. More than this, drama teachers should acknowledge the different aptitudes of children and teen-agers, and make a distinction between the drama-oriented/non-drama-oriented young adult. In elementary grades, all children can participate in creative drama; in junior and senior high schools, where drama is an option, it is illusory to assume that participating students must be capable of the type of dramatic art which incorporates public performance. It is well known that junior high and Grade 10 students often elect drama because they are counseled to do so, or because it seems the lesser of evil choices.

Many children, young people, and adults can enjoy the experience of dramatic art within the confines of the workshop environment without the need or desire to extend that experience into public performance. Improvisation, therefore, is a middle level of drama viewed as an essential transitory exploration for some, and a terminal experience for many.

PHASE 3: EXPERIENCE OF THEATRE ART

While phases 1 and 2 may be described as process, phase 3 is concerned with the experience and exploration of theatre involving performance; therefore, this phase earns the simple title of *theatre*.

Experience of theatre art involving performance is ideally limited to a minority, for while all can participate in phase 1, and many in phase 2, only a small percentage of senior students are sufficiently drama-oriented to pursue the art through to its ultimate conclusion;

such students may well continue with theatre arts as a vocation or as a leisure activity in adulthood. Nevertheless, it can be argued that there are different interpretations and degrees of performance so that, while chronologically the concept of "three phases of drama" may imply elementary, junior high, and senior high, in fact, the same three phases with appropriate modifications may easily be applied to any age group of students in the school system. Implicit in the apparent paradox is the acceptance of a style of theatre that is unconventional and therefore, for many teachers, unacceptable.

Phases 1 and 2 may certainly prepare students for traditional theatre arts programs with the emphasis on the formal (proscenium) production of a scripted play, but it must here be admitted that the stress on improvisation and flexibility of dramatic form inherent in the process tends to produce nontraditional styles of theatre art emanating from student-centered originality as distinct from director-centered imposition of an established theatre form. *The combination of flexible (often center) staging, utilization of dance and improvisation as well as script, projected images reinforcing dramatic statements or themes relevant to youth today, exemplifies experimental theatre which has certainly earned its place in the unfoldment of twentieth-century drama.* By chance (or, some may suggest, by reversion to simplistic styles indigenous to the origins of drama and dance), the demands on the young student are less technical, enabling even the least sophisticated to participate in the product.

THE THREE PHASES OF DRAMA: OBJECTIVES AND TECHNIQUES

Phase 1: Creative Drama

Objective: To lay the foundations for further creative activity through the discovery and development of personal resources.

Creative drama is an exercise or activity involving extemporaneous speech; spontaneous action and movement; imagination; simple characterization; story-making; and uses the whole self interacting with others to create a dynamic, immediate experience. It occurs in any kind of space, uses neither written script nor conscious structured theatre art form, and involves no presentation; it concerns personal experience rather than communication to an audience. Creative drama is totally non-theatre-oriented.

Creative activity has two main thrusts: originality (involving innovation) and interpretation. In theatre terms, originality is recognizable through the playwright, while innovation today seems to be mainly the province of the director who, with the designer and actor, is an interpreter of the playwright. In educational drama, the production or study of plays is interpretative creativity, with the teacher/director as the prime interpreter; into this category belongs also the dramatization of a story or poem with the teacher/leader as the main interpreter. In the argument put forward herein, *dramatization is to be found in later phases of drama when the stimulus and discipline of dramatic literature provide extended experience of material and awareness of form.*

In phase 1, emphasis is placed on original ideas emanating from individual students, or collectively from groups; imagination is an important ingredient of creativity which is considered not merely in relation to the arts but as an integral part of the vital, flexible, initiative drive indispensable to personal and societal responsibilities. Other interracting physical, emotional, and intellectual resources involve sense awareness; bodily freedom and control; oral communication; self-awareness and sensitivity towards others; cognitive, deductive, and divergent thinking; together with self-actualization or the realization of full potential in the development of abilities, with dynamic response to every experience.

The above may be termed overall objectives. In creative drama, immediate goals are centered around the development of concentration, absorption, and sincerity; confidence in all activities involving movement, speaking, imagination, and interraction with others; alertness, dynamism, and maximum effort in all circumstances and conditions; the preservation and growth of individuality, and the evolvement of self-discipline with personal responsibility for endeavor.

The characteristics of creative drama are recognizable in that extemporaneous speech and spontaneous action (movement) are utilized extensively, with all students working simultaneously most of the time, using the total space available. (It should be noted that, even during pair or small-group exercises, no section of the class is excluded or asked to become "audience.") There is often high noise emission from the creative drama classroom, particularly during speech activities. To the casual observer, there is an apparent lack of unity in that each student may be doing something quite different from the next; but the governing factor which ensures freedom rather than license is the structure of the creative drama session: the techniques involved in the early part of phase 1 are specific and highly organized by the instructor.

Any group beginning a new activity (or being introduced to a new approach) needs a clear framework within which members can operate without fear of failure or ridicule. When children or young adults feel insecure in an environment or occupation, they react in a variety of ways—none of them particularly conducive to creativity, effort, or concentration. For each exercise in creative drama there is an immediate objective, and underlying the majority is that of building confidence so that potentials may be discovered and developed.

Thus, in early sessions, students are given clear instructions on *what* to do or *who* to be and then are left with the responsibility of deciding *how* to do it (this is a challenge to some who may have grown to rely on a demonstration from teacher or parent). As soon as possible, however, the instructor begins to relinquish responsibility for ideas on what to do or who to be, providing stimuli rather than detail. An important by-product of the approach whereby all work simultaneously in a noncritical atmosphere avoiding censure or praise of individuals is a leveling of extreme personality traits: the very shy individual will begin to take a few risks, and the exhibitionist will soon realize that nobody is watching his or her antics except for the instructor, who is busy observing everyone. The accent on private and personal discovery of potential for any given exercise endorses the valued property of individuality while precluding any suggestion of conformity through uniformity. Inherent in the structured session is discipline imposed and control taken by the instructor; the simple rule of "maximum effort" plus the logic of aiming for a simple objective such as concentration demands of each participant a specific behavioral response. For example, students who chat to each other while doing an individual movement excercise are obviously not concentrating on the activity and thus cannot fully achieve the desired aim; both concentration and movement will suffer. The underlying principle asserts that maximum effort will produce development which will lead to achievement.

In the early stages of phase 1, the instructor is looking for achievement in the immediate objectives and, as these are realized, progresses to more complicated exercises; thus, having attained a certain degree of concentration and confidence while working individually, students must now discover how to apply such properties when working with others. In practice, therefore, exercises move from being person-centered to group-centered, although the total session is still firmly structured and all pairs or groups will continue to work simultaneously in activities which lack any noticeable art form.

Exercises range from discovery of space and sense awareness to movement response to stimuli: imaginative "journeys" described by the instructor and physically undertaken by the class; large crowd scenes involving speech and action; story-making from original ideas provided by the class (as an end in itself without any attempt at full dramatization, although characters and incidents arising from such stories may be used as stimuli for further activities). As the format extends to include pairs and small groups, so music may become the stimulus for simple movement situations; pair and group incidents are devised with the emphasis on action, as are situations involving mainly speech. Discussion is consistently encouraged—both as a method of obtaining ideas and planning activities, and as a means of direct communication between instructor and class. In early sessions, the topic for discussion is irrelevant, since the immediate objective is to create a climate for positive oral communication and to establish an environment where all ideas are valid even if they are not commonly acceptable or cannot always be used.

It has been stated that the non-theatre-oriented approach of creative drama is applicable, even necessary, for any beginning group, regardless of age and background. For young children in elementary grades, organic growth implies that creative drama with its accentuation on personal development can—and perhaps should—be an end in itself. The natural development of the child proceeds slowly from the "singleton" stage of early infancy into the social discovery of one friend at a time through to the "gang" or group stage; this process parallels the development of drama as outlined above. By definition, therefore, it would appear that as far as elementary grades are concerned, phase 1 can be the limit of their drama experience. On the other hand, it is unrealistic to deny experience of simple art forms to the elementary child merely because he is trapped in the unnatural division of an educational system which in June labels him a Grade 6 child, and in September a Grade 7 teen-ager. Therefore, the teacher of top elementary grades should be looking ahead, just as the teacher of Grade 7 students must, for a while, look back.

For teen-age groups, phase 1 is an essential starting point. With young children, creative drama assists in the natural development of resources; for the older student, it is a means of rediscovering personal resources and developing those which have lain dormant. Even for the drama-oriented teen-ager or adult, the exercises and activities of creative drama are necessary for the type of creative endeavor embodying originality and innovation beyond the requirements of traditional theatre techniques. By ignoring or denying this, theatre arts teachers prevent the full exploration of creative potential in their young students.

Noteworthy, however, is the increasing trend for some secondary school teachers to disregard *the need of young adults for artistic exploration*; through lack of knowledge and expertise in dramatic art, or because of a deviation in objectives, such teachers maintain a level of creative drama which produces in their students lethargic disinterest or indulgence in emotional, self-centered "freak-outs."

Artistic maturation is an important stage of development. As the young person moves toward adolescence, it is with varying degrees of anticipation, resignation, and frustration that the adult accepts the manifestation of emotional and physical maturity alongside the more manageable growth of intellectual powers. Less attention is paid to the young adult's artistic maturation, although art educators have long maintained that an interest in techniques and skills coincides with puberty.

The application of artistic maturation to drama discloses that, as the youngster approaches adolescence, he manifests an emerging interest in the elements of dramatic art form. Thus, for top elementary grades, phase 1 merges naturally into phase 2; for beginning groups in junior and senior high school, where artistic maturation is revealed and realized, phase 2 becomes an essential progression, as the discipline inherent in any art form provides at once a vital challenge to personal resources and a focus for heightened physical, emotional, and mental energies.

Phase 2: Improvisation

Objective: Introduction to dramatic art form.

Improvisation is an exercise, an activity, a scene or a play involving extemporaneous speech and spontaneous movement or action, *embodying elements of dramatic art*; it may evolve from original ideas, or from stimuli including dramatic literature; it can lead to a detailed scenario and script writing.

This definition developes from that for creative drama. The confusion among practitioners in the field of educational drama has been confounded by a failure to differentiate between a beginning activity (creative drama) which is non-theatre-oriented, and an advanced activity (improvisation) which, historically, has always had a place in the art of theatre. The instant we view improvisation in its rightful context, it is apparent that it is not synonymous with creative drama, nor is it a substitute for theatre, although it may develop into theatre art.

Phase 2 is characterized by group improvisation projects; it is important to distinguish between spontaneous "ad-libbing" which is sometimes interpreted as improvisation and the utilization of extemporaneous speech within a planned dramatic framework; also, it should be explained that phase 2 improvisation does not include the highly skilled "instant theatre" approach favored by some professional theatre groups, nor is it limited to acting exercises utilized in actor-training. Rather, movement and/or speech improvisations are devised, planned, and rehearsed from session to session, and sometimes from week to week. Major responsibility is given to the groups for ideas and organization; during such projects, pairs or small groups of students can be found scattered throughout the building (assuming that such freedom is permitted by the administration) and, if a deadline is given for the completion of a project, groups may well meet to rehearse out of class time.

Occasionally, the instructor may organize a project involving the whole class: a crowd scene (e.g., the assassination of the governor of a small country, or a band of robbers looting an empty castle); a movement drama (e.g., a *West Side Story* incident to a rhythmic record); or the dramatization of a story from original or literary sources. Written assignments are also introduced, progressing from an outline of the scene to a full scenario. Even, with older students, a simple production script.

The latter is indicative of accumulative experience in phase 2 aimed at increasing the students' awareness of elements of dramatic art. For teen-age groups, each project introduces some new component beginning with the simplest involving *structure* (objective: to work out an ending for the scene), and gradually adding: *climax* (build to a strong moment); *the event* (drama involves particular occasions or incidents); *characters* (individual differences, relationships, and how people behave in usual/unusual situations); *organization* (selection and definition; the difference between a story and a play); *dramatic statement* (what is the story line or what statement is being made?).

As awareness of dramatic art form is developed, production elements are introduced and artistic judgments stressed. With originality and innovation strongly in mind, however, little attempt is made to impose rigidity of form and techniques. Instead, groups are encouraged to experiment in *style* (realistic or abstract, fluid or fragmentary); *use of space* (shape of acting area, or utilization of whole room); *lighting* (for effect rather than illumination); and *sound* (for reinforcement, stimulus, or accompaniment). Properties and costumes are limited to extension of character instead of becoming a decorative essential so that objects and items of clothing or pieces of fabric are representational or symbolic. A special project utilizing *projected images* (overhead and slide projectors each with polarizing equipment enabling them to be used for realistic or abstract images, and opaque projectors for graphics and collages) adds a further extension which contributes to the concept of creating an environment rather than "designing a set." All the above experiences are an introduction to theatre production and design.

Personal development continues, with special emphasis on expansion of experience and on acquiring a high tolerance level when working in a group. The instructor becomes in part the initiator—providing continual opportunities for further unfoldment—and in part a resource person who solves problems and organizes time. Responsibility for creativity is shared by the instructor and the groups, and collectively within the groups. Discipline is achieved in three ways: from the instructor, from the group, and from the art form itself. The peculiar distinction of the group project is that it enforces maximum effort from each member; peer pressure demands this, but a simple rule is made that, in the event of absence (excused or unexcused) during the preparation of a group project, the defaulter must withdraw, although he or she is given the option of preparing a "solo" as a makeup opportunity.

Discussion continues to be a fundamental part of the process and is based on an evaluation of achievement in the particular objectives given for each project. Also, group projects are now presented to the rest of the class in a workshop situation: it is made clear that the presentation is for the purpose of seeing what others have been doing, and applause is disallowed to reinforce the nonperformance, noncompetitive principles. Through positive discussion, standards, criteria, and aesthetic values are absorbed and, as the work progresses, are applied by the students in practical work and in discussions.

Since phase 2 takes its place in the spectrum of drama as the natural unfoldment of artistic awareness for the young adult, achievement is now measured in artistic terms—not limited, however, to "acting" only. Drama has included movement, imagination, production concepts, organization and planning, and writing: toward the end of this phase, individual strengths and weaknesses become evident. It is possible to identify the potential writer, director, designer, or actor among those who may be particularly drama-oriented; it is also possible to recognize the enthusiastic "non-drama" person who enjoys the artistic experience but has neither special talent nor the desire to take that further step which is involvement in theatre art.

The elementary teacher, studying the excercises and projects incorporated into phase 2 of drama experience, will readily declare that many such could not only be undertaken by these grade levels, but also would be of benefit to them. This is true in the sense that, with any group, ideas can be adapted and techniques modified. Thus, a dramatized story, a "group play," or a movement drama can provide stimuli for creative writing, for arts and crafts, and can become a positive exercise in simple forms of organization; the use of media as an art extension linked with drama or literature has been successfully introduced to elementary students. If the premise of a correlation between artistic maturation and adolescence is accepted, however, then the goals of such projects differ according to the age group. The readiness factor for the extension of experience is probably the most important assessment that every teacher has to make at any given time: of all experiences, the readiness level for any kind of performance is of high significance.

Phase 3: Theatre

Much has been written on the pros and cons of performance by children and teen-agers, and these arguments need not be restated. But it is worth noting that most of the dialogue has been based on the concept of theatre performance which embodies adult techniques of acting and staging with performance to the general public. If the word "performance" with all those connotations is removed and replaced by "presentation" involving originality, dynamic natural action, and speech in an intimate environment as a workshop event for peers, friends, family, and selected guests, most of the reasons for objection are removed. An informal, "open-day" type of presentation can involve any age group, provided there is a valid reason for it, the students are at the right readiness level, the content and style of activity is within their natural capabilities, and the "audience" is private.

Unfortunately, even if such ideal conditions are observed, the decision to give a presentation transforms process into product and creates a pressure on instructor and students. One useful way of solving this problem is to call the presentation a "demonstration" or an "incomplete production." This allows the instructor to explain to invited guests what the objectives of the project have been and, in the interests of the total concept of personal and drama development, that the presentation is an example of work which has reached a particular level of attainment.

The stress on originality and flexibility of production styles encouraged during phases 1 and 2 results in an approach to theatre that is close to contemporary experimentation. More often than not, center-staging will arise, incorporating the use of levels with flexible representational or symbolic "sets." The action will include movement/dance and improvised dialogue, although script-writing will occur; and dramatic literature, scenes from plays, poetry, contemporary songs, may be interwoven to reinforce a topical theme relevant for the young student. Lighting, sound, and projected images for effective enhancement of the dramatic statement produce a theatrical event that defies classification because the intention and formation has been a "collective creation" by a group of original thinkers.

Alternatively, a play per se may be devised, embodying more conventional structure while still incorporating many of the above dramatic elements; or a story may be taken as a framework for development into an imaginative theatre event. For instance, one legend about a priest and the devil actually has only five characters: the Priest, his Cat, a Fisherman, his Wife, and the Devil. A play may be developed as follows: The characters: the Priest and his Cat; the Fisherman and the Islanders; the Mainlanders—pleasure-seeking and easily tempted by Satan and his Devils who are constantly among them and from time to time become supernatural beings or the elements of a storm that continually destroys any bridge the Islanders try to build.

The Mainlanders and Devils represent a *Vanity Fair* image through movement; the Islanders discuss their problems through improvised dialogue; the Priest and the Devil work on (and partially script) the bargain they make. The bridge is "built" in two ways: (1) through realistic mime including the climbing of ladders to represent cliffs, with lighting effects and the apparition of devils for the storms that destroy it; (2) through a symbolic dance drama as it is eventually completed. At various moments throughout the presentation, projected images depict religious pictures and artifacts, devil faces and forms, the village and the river, together with abstracts during the dance dramas. Costumes are limited to pieces of cloth and masks for the Devils. *The total production involves all members of the class in both action and technical production*: dialogue and movement are worked out by groups and/or individuals; lighting is planned, projections are created, and when students are not involved in a scene, they are working a spotlight or the tape recorder, or a projector.

One of the greatest misconceptions of this style of theatre is that anarchy prevails and artistry is absent. This can indeed happen, if the instructor abdicates liability for organization, for supervision, and for the maintenance of artistic integrity. The instructor/director in phase 3 takes responsibility for artistic decisions and aesthetic judgments, and for continuing to expand the students' awareness of the art of theatre. Student responsibility has progressed from self (phase 1) to the group (phases 1-2) to the art form (phases 2-3) and ultimately to the audience which deserves something better than "deadly theatre" inexpertly performed and produced.

By encouraging student-originated theatre exploration, the theatre arts teacher contributes to the dynamic unfoldment of theatre in the twentieth century, for some of these young adults will become the playwrights, directors, designers, and actors of the future. At the same time, this style of theatre exemplifies the demands of educators, administrators, parents, and politicians for the encouragement of initiative, flexibility, leadership, cooperation, tolerance, and various other qualities considered desirable for adults in the "person-centered society" advocated by the Worth Commission on Educational Planning.

The evolvement of theatre and drama in education throughout history has bequeathed to each generation a heritage of prejudice from without and controversy within. It should come as no surprise, therefore, to realize that many school boards and hundreds of schools deny to thousands of children and young people the right to experience drama as an integral part of their education. Only drama educators care enough to rectify and improve a situation which may well deteriorate within a decade. Surely, through progress with unity, we may avoid catastrophe and realize the consummation of our educational and artistic aspirations.

REFERENCES

Peter Brook. *The Empty Space*. Harmondsworth: Penguin Books, 1968.
Philip Coggin. *The Uses of Drama*. New York: George Braziller, 1956.
Peter Slade. *Child Drama*. London: University of London Press, 1954.
Brian Way. *Development Through Drama*. London: Longmans Green, 1967.
W. Worth. *A Choice of Futures*. Edmonton, Canada: Commission on Educational Planning, 1972.

THOUGHTS ON
THE CREATIVE PROCESS

VIRGINIA TANNER

*Virginia Tanner, director of creative dance at the University of Utah,
is as well known to leaders of creative dramatics in this country as she
is to teachers and students of dance. She has given demonstrations for the
Children's Theatre Association and has presented her young dancers at
Jacob's Pillow, the Connecticut College School of Dance, the Seattle
World's Fair, and the 1970 White House Conference for Children. Miss
Tanner's influence on dance education has been widely felt through her
guest teaching assignments, which have taken her from New England
to Hawaii. She was recently selected as "Master Teacher" by the National
Endowment for the Arts and the U.S. Office of Education, for whom she
continues to teach in its Artist in the Schools Program. In 1963 Wilson
College in Pennsylvania recognized her with an honorary doctorate.
In this essay Miss Tanner describes the creative process as she sees it. Having
her students become professional performers has never been her major
interest; helping them to become more sensitive to the world around them
and guiding them to discover their potential in movement are her goals.*

For many years it has been my privilege to be surrounded by the
beauty, the joy, the excitement, as well as the hesitancies of
childhood. What a challenge this has been!

Teaching creatively starts with imagination and ideas. Most
children are filled with both—ideas they are eager to express, and
ideas they must express if they are to live fully as children and later
as adults. To a child anything seems possible. His world is filled with
fantasy, which is frequently dimmed when parents, teachers, and
friends turn down the lights in his treasure house of imagination. A

child quickly realizes whether or not you offer sincere warmth, understanding, and interest. Only when rapport is established will he unlock the many facets of his heart and allow you to share your treasures with him and his with you. The key to guiding the child to self-fulfillment lies in sharing those moments that involve thinking, feeling, and exploring experiences. As these experiences take place the child spreads his roots in fertile soil.

When one has an honest respect for children, there is a constant search to open new channels that will increase the child's awareness of the world around him and give a deeper meaning to his daily life. In this setting most of my activities over the years have taken place.

Early in my professional studies, I realized that, in the name of dance, much damage was being done to the young. False values were being fostered in immature minds as parents were encouraged to buy "sophisticated" kiddie costumes for the local dance review. The child was being denied the real beauty of expression through dance. By approaching dance as an art form I gradually learned to recognize many basic truths; and in doing so I developed a teaching philosophy that has inspired many persons to work creatively with children. The creative approach to movement not only provides a means to enhance coordination and poise, but it also makes a marked difference in the lives of children.

During the past few years, a great deal of time, investigation, and study have been expended throughout the world to discover ways to learn more about this elusive quality called creativity. I wonder what would have been the result if, during the initial measuring of an individual's potential intelligence, equal time had been allotted to measuring his potential creative ability, and then a search had been made for ways to stimulate the growth of both these inherent qualities.

There is a great deal of truth to the statement "All God's chillun got wings," but far too often those wings have been clipped before they have known the joy of soaring. The seeds of curiosity present in man at birth can lead him to become a dedicated person with tremendous drive for his chosen work. Yet only a few, with so insistent a creative gift that it flourishes in spite of everything, realize their potential and make a unique contribution to science, art, and the teaching profession.

But what of the hundreds of thousands of children who, at the age of four, seem to possess this cherished capacity, and then, by the age of nine, no longer utilize it as a source of rich fulfillment? Could it be that unimaginative teaching methods, lack of perception, hours of unguided television, and stereotyped toys destroy the very thing that will help bring to each one his greatest moments of happiness? Are we ignoring the need for personal growth and fulfillment that allow a young person to formulate genuine friendships and to know the joy of using his leisure time with purpose and his study hours with eagerness?

The educated, creative man knows who he is, where he wants to go, and what he wants to achieve. Certain environmental agents can make this level of self-realization possible: sensitive parents, access to good libraries, stimulating teachers, religious belief and understanding, and the steady encouragement to utilize personal resources constructively in every phase of life. Wherever creative work flourishes, someone has established communication with his inner self. The creative force must not be permitted to waste itself. It must be encouraged, stimulated and given time to develop. During its growth, there must be guidance from a creative person.

This brings to mind an experiment conducted at a midwestern college. Two groups of highly sensitive students were selected for the control groups. Both units were given ideal situations as far as atmosphere and resource material were concerned. One group was left to itself and the other was guided by a highly creative teacher who could direct or encourage as the need arose. After a given time limit, the works of both groups were compared. As anticipated, the explorations of the directed group were far greater than those of the unit that had no supervision.

To be free to use one's imagination fully requires great discipline. Within each new freedom achieved lies the routine achievement of techniques and discipline—factors frequently misunderstood by people when the word "creativity" is mentioned. Readiness never comes by chance or by luck, but only when opportunity and disciplined technique, plus freedom of exploration, are joined. Working imaginatively with people does not simply mean "today we will listen to this music and follow whatever it suggests" or "take these paints and paper to draw whatever you feel" or "take this set of blocks and build whatever comes to mind." This approach represents only a minute part of creative guidance. The whole complex process should reflect the constant urging of the mind and body to reach out in new directions, to find more than one way to solve a problem so that within the structure of each new venture, the individual may gain more knowledge, understanding, and truth. These are the rudiments of working creatively with people. Nothing can take the place of persistence and discipline. Talent will not. Genius will not.

There is creative energy in all human beings. Louis Horst once said, "Each of us is born with genius, but some keep it only a few seconds." Our particular purpose is to open ways that will encourage the child to question, to investigate, to solve problems in more than one way, and to attack the problem at hand with a zest. In effect, to go beyond that which is easy. This is our responsibility, and I believe we can teach most facts creatively.

Knowledge and technique in skills cannot be overlooked or slighted. If we have no tools, our investigation reaches a blind wall. To be encouraged to search, to think deeply, takes time. And children as well as adults need time—time to try again, time to share, and time to have sensitive questions answered judiciously.

One day a little boy brought a book about rockets to class. "Teacher, may we dance about my book?" Until an idea was used from his book, this youngster could not participate wholeheartedly in any other activity. To solve the problem, we had small groups of children stand in four corners of the room which we designated as New York, Florida, Washington, and California. A rocket was launched from New York. It had to go very fast across the floor (our pretended sky) and land in Florida. Rockets were launched until each child had a turn. Finally, rockets were sent aloft simultaneously from California and New York. Each one had to travel rapidly through space, avoid collisions, and land in a different state. Before the class was over, rockets could be sent from each corner simultaneously. There were no collisions and yet each child moved quickly in space and landed in a new state. This experience allowed David to use the idea of his rocket book; and it taught the other children space patterns, to move with speed, and a valuable lesson in organization. And, needless to say, we had fun too.

When confronted with David's request, I could have said, "Oh, David, there are so many other fun things for us to do today. Let's save your idea." But I realized that his idea was so important to him that a way had to be found to use his book, not just as a pillow to rest on, something to jump over, something to hold high as he went skipping, for these ideas had no real relationship to the context of his wonderful book. He wanted to dance about rockets.

Keeping a child excited about investigating ideas is very important. One day a five-year-old greeted me with a special sparkle in her eyes. Excitedly, she burst forth: "Miss Virginia, I discovered the 'backwards going' skip, and I'll teach it to you." What a joyous moment when we went skipping backward together! Now you may think this a very ordinary thing. But pause for a moment and ponder its true worth. For this child the discovery that she had the coordination to skip backward was a new moment; nothing like it had ever happened before in her life. I was extremely happy to have had the privilege of sharing that moment with her! I might have said: "Oh, someday everybody can skip backward," and that spark, which could ignite further discovery, might have been smothered. Part of the richness of adult-child relationships is developed by the adult's ability to see through the eyes of the child. If the adult does not make room for the unexpected and can direct only his own set of plans, some of the most vital moments of teaching and learning are lost.

My son's first-grade class was given an opportunity for a delightful creative experience. Each was to select a leaf that had a particularly pleasing shape. Our little boy was curious about the many shapes he found in leaves and encouraged his family to go with him on a walk to help him find exactly the leaf he was looking for. He was delighted to find a large oak leaf that had an unusual coloring and special perfection in his eyes. He proudly took his leaf to school and entered into the project enthusiastically. The children were to use the leaf as the body of an imaginary child and add a head, two arms, and two legs. Steve took a longer time to finish his child than was allotted, and when the teacher came to investigate why he was taking so long, she discovered that he had added a cap in one hand and an umbrella in the other hand. "Just in case it rained, mom," he told me. The teacher quickly picked up his paper and with a pair of scissors, she snipped off the added cap and umbrella. It took weeks before he again dared to investigate beyond the limits of the assignment. He was embarrassed in front of his classmates, and his teacher had disapproved of his creative exploration thus killing his enthusiasm for a long time.

I shall never forget the day a seven-year-old came to class with a troubled look on her face. I didn't pry or even inquire what her problem was, but sent her off to do her special trick at the barre. Later in the class she stopped me right in the middle of something we were doing and said, "Miss Virginia, it hurts." "What hurts?" I inquired. "My tooth. It keeps pushing and pushing and pushing and it hurts all the time." The question flashed in my mind, "Could I help this child understand, through dance, this very puzzling incident?"

We gathered near the piano, our favorite talking place, to learn more about the tooth and why it hurt as it pushed its way through the gum. What an informative discussion we had. We discussed the reason why she was in pain, and then we discovered similarities in seeds as they burst through their jackets, chickens as they hatch, and a pupa as it emerges from the cocoon. Before we were through, one little girl said, "My mommy told me that my baby sister pushed her way out." With this idea of energy and growth as the focal point, we curled up as small as we could to discover many ways to push with our shoulders, our feet, our backs, our heads, until finally we broke through a make-believe barrier. Then our bodies began to stretch—opening up as fully as possible. When the class was over, each student, especially the child with the aching tooth, had a deeper understanding of this tremendous principle of growth.

Once while teaching a class of five-year-olds, I took a piece of plastic and enclosed it in my hands. "What's too big to be in my hands?" The children's answers were delightful. "My house," "the piano," "our baby," "your shoes." "Oh, yes," I said, "they are all too big. Now watch. It's something special, so special that I believe you will want to dance about it." As I opened my hands, the plastic piece slowly and beautifully unfolded. The children were enchanted and wanted to see it again. As they watched, they began unconsciously lifting their backs. The starting point in the movement pattern was similar to the previous story, but this time, the energy used was gentle because the motivation was different. The idea is the hinge upon which all art swings; and in dance as an art form, it is the idea that determines the movement patterns chosen. Fast rockets are different from erupting teeth. The *reason*, the *idea*, directs the shape—the form of all worthwhile learning, of all great art!

In my classes we share a capacity to see with what we call our "magic eye." This eye is located near the sternum, and we learn to use it to see the beauty around and above us. It helps us to "think tall." Try lifting up your back and opening the area across your shoulders. It will work for you, too. The children watched and discovered motion in the plastic piece. They knew how to use their magic eye—and they were learning to move with purpose, as they danced with their entire bodies. I had given them a piece of plastic, and each child was deep in thought as he watched the beauty of his plastic unfold.

As they began to dance, expressing what they had seen, several children tucked the plastic close in the curves of their small bodies, and when they opened up, so did their bit of magic material. Then, holding their pieces of plastic by the corner, they began dancing in a joyous, lyrical style, watching it lift, glide, swing, turn, and float as they released it or held it in their fingers. This was a delightful and meaningful experience, for the children were being encouraged to look, to feel, and to explore.

One vivid teaching experience that I recall was triggered quite by accident. My husband often calls me "Pollyanna," for I have a habit of tucking unpleasant things way in the back of my mind and then forgetting them. Because of this habit, I don't remember what made me angry one particular Thursday, only that I was. I remember that the anger seemed to fill every fiber of my body. By 4:15 P.M., near the time for my seven- to eight-year-old class, no one had come to my rescue to teach for me and I had to go to them—anger and all. It was impossible to forget my own feelings, yet to do so is one of my cardinal rules both for myself and for my teachers. The class must come first.

The children were quick to sense something wrong, so I called them over to the piano and began class by asking them, "Have you ever been really angry, so angry that you could explode?" "Oh, yes," they said. Immediately I threw out another question: "If I could see only your feet, could you show me with them how you felt?" Within seconds, fireworks were exploding. Such a variety of "feet things" in anger I'd never seen! They jumped and went down on their backs, kicked the wall, used fast and jerky patterns, and long, slow ones that seemed to build up and explode.

We then talked about other strong feelings that we had had; and for children so young, they had experienced many things that had caused them to feel deeply. One child said that she'd had something happen that very day in school, but she wasn't quite sure what her feeling was, maybe just disappointment. "Could you share it with us?" "Oh, yes," she replied, "it was during arithmetic."

They had been asked to choose a number lower than ten and then to write any two numbers that could add up to their chosen number. Her choice was eight. After doing several combinations, she suddenly thought $3 + 2 + 3 = 8$. Excitedly, she went to the teacher with her new discovery. At the moment, the teacher was not ready to accept more than the given problem and she was sent back to her seat.

Suddenly a light turned on in me and I asked the children to go from the piano to the record player and back, using three different foot patterns. Among the group, all eight patterns were used—walking, running, leaping, skipping, galloping, sliding, jumping, and hopping. We were now going to use these patterns to solve Jenna's arithmetic problem. "You are in school—doing arithmetic," I told them. "But I am your teacher. This time I will give you the answer, and you must discover how to solve it. The answer is eight. You must use any foot pattern such as skips, slides, and jumps (three things) and finish by the count of eight."

Again, fireworks! But this time, such happy ones. The children worked, they questioned, buzzing about their numbers and combinations. Over in the corner, one child was busy counting on her fingers. She did three jumps and then held down three fingers. Two fingers were left on that hand, so she did two skips. Several seconds later, she figured out (again by counting) that she needed three more things to make eight. By now she'd forgotten what she'd done with the first five fingers, so she began over, repeating the process.

Before the end of the class hour, most of the children had their answers and could do them quite efficiently. I knew that they would be working at home on this newly found way to solve an arithmetic problem and that Jenna was more than pleased, not only because she recognized my approval, but also because we had taken her idea and shared it in such a fun way with the class.

Needless to say, I, too, felt better and had begun the process of wrapping up my "Pollyanna" package of intense anger. This experience did not end here. In fact, it kept us busy for several weeks and eventually developed into a charming dance play called *Our Day*, in which we presented the events of a typical day—from getting up in the morning as sleepy heads (because of Daylight Saving Time) to solving arithmetic problems at school.

Searching for ideas to help the children has dictated and directed most of my activities over the years, even when I have been vacationing with my family, shopping, reading, or just listening. I am constantly on the alert for new ways to assist the child in exploring the realms of movement within his understanding of his marvelous instrument—his body.

Some time ago, the thought occurred to me that I had never approached movement through the use of simple lines—bent, straight, and curved. At the time, a group of nine- to ten-year-olds was exploring ideas with me and "Miss Anne" in their Art in Relation to Dance program, and we spent four months finding new ways, each week, to approach this one idea. This gave us time to look, to imagine, to search, and to share. Pooling ideas often led to exciting results, emphasizing the group's ability to select movement patterns wisely. Eventually, the more interesting patterns were integrated into compositional studies that were exciting to the students.

Since then, I have often thought how important it is when children possess the tools of knowledge and imagination to cultivate a project in which the overall result is a source of constructive pleasure. It seems to me that if we could devote a portion of time seeking that which is significantly pleasing, sensing what would promote pleasure for others, and realizing where beauty lies, then again we would be sending the roots of genuine happiness deeper into fertile soil. All too frequently young people are technically trained in a chosen art form with no opportunity to explore on their own. I believe that if improvisation on basic principles and ideas was encouraged as the technical training is pursued, we could give new freedom and inspiration to many more people.

In trying to solve the complex social problems of today we tend to ignore a special kind of hunger. If our children could have their creative selves always fed, their destructive selves would gradually starve.

I have gone to many sections of the United States to demonstrate principles that have helped me nurture creativity. At one of these times when the Children's Dance Theatre performed in the East, Walter Terry of the former New York *Herald-Tribune* wrote after seeing the performance:

From the first there was beauty. But more important than the loveliness of the setting was the vital innocence of the dancers themselves. They looked like children and not miniature adults. They danced themes of their own choosing and of their own creation. It is difficult to describe the most potent intangibles. But the best I can do is to say that the children danced as if they had faith in themselves, had love for those who were seeing them, actively believed in their God, and rejoiced in all these.

The *Christian Science Monitor* added: "This work is the result of an idea, a search for beauty and truth that never ceased unfolding." Children involved in such work are not likely to become "school dropouts" or juvenile delinquents.

As I recall our first visit to the East, an incident at Jacob's Pillow comes vividly to mind. While a mass "bravo" echoed throughout the theatre, one of the starry-eyed children whispered, "Miss Ginny, why are they calling for Provo?" which, as you may know, is a city in Utah.

Within this philosophy of teaching, we try to help the child have enough of a professional attitude about dance so that it can extend into his other endeavors. We guide them to discover their own potential in movement by helping them to go beyond that which is easy; by enhancing their awareness and knowledge of the tremendous power of rhythm, both breath and metric; by letting them discover the joy of clean line in movement; but always encouraging them to move with ease and agility, balance and control. They are encouraged to contribute patterns to the many dances that have been composed and then to compose their own dances. These have been our goals through which the children can find beauty—a beauty that comes from belief in self.

How do you achieve these goals? Where do ideas come from? How do you know what to teach each age level? How long do you work with each child before you give up? What do you do for the student who depends upon and is satisfied only to follow other children, to use other children's ideas rather than his own? Can you teach the child rhythmic movement without a pianist? These are all thought-provoking questions to which I have found answers through a deep respect for the child and trust in my "intuition" based on experience.

One little boy was hesitant to join in the class. In fact, he did not venture away from his mother until the third week. Finally, he became so excited by the crepe paper streamers being used as a teaching prop that he decided to share in the fun and become a real member of the class. This situation raised one question: How long do you work with a child before you give up? Briefly, the answer is that primarily we do not stop until the mother gives up. As long as the parent cooperates and does not become discouraged, a wholesome atmosphere is maintained within which we can work.

Another question arose from the hesitancy of some children to use their own initiative in searching for ideas. What do you do for the pupil who depends upon and uses other children's ideas rather than explore for himself? Teaching a child to use his own ideas is a very important part of all teaching.

In the beginning, some children must copy others to get ideas, but during each class, they are encouraged to think for themselves. Simple movement ideas that can spark teaching will come about by asking lead questions that are within their understanding; in doing so, the child is encouraged to find his own patterns. For example, How far can you stretch? Can you reach as high as the ceiling? Can you reach down to the floor without bending your knees? Could you make a tunnel and have both feet and only one hand touch the floor? These simple ideas motivate a child to do the movement for himself.

Let one group touch something prickly and sharp, such as a starfish or cockleshell. Have another group touch something smooth and round, such as a small ball or a hard-boiled egg in the shell. Ask the children to show you a pattern with their arms that reminds them of what they touched. See if each group can find words to describe what they think the object was like. "Prickly," "bumpy," "hard," "sharp," "rough," "pointed" may be words to describe the shells; while "smooth," "round," "hard," "curved" may be used for the ball or egg. With this vocabulary you can help them find contrasting movement patterns.

In one course on creative movement, a teacher who had applied these ideas to her first-grade class related that, as a result, their trip to the bakery had a great deal more meaning. The children wanted to dance about their experience. They had seen large paddles mixing the dough, the slow rising of the dough, the way the dough was cut, and the loaves of bread moving in rows. This visual experience served her class as impetus for creative movement.

Another teacher found that "moving" need not be set aside as a special project. It can be put to immediate use for many ideas that arise during the day. She related that early one day the children had been making tunnels with their bodies, and later in the afternoon they were learning to recognize the small letter *m*. It was then that a little boy said, "Teacher, an *m* is like two tunnels hooked together." Her students had no difficulty in remembering *m* from that day on.

Students must be given ample time to think about the things they are being asked to do. Equally important, the teacher must thoroughly understand the movement problem being presented to the children. Again, ask leading questions: Do you really know what you are going to do? How are you going to start? Will you stay in place or move about? These questions stimulate answers and ideas that will help the shy child transfer the general movement idea into patterns of his own.

Many simple objects can be used to inspire movement—a feather as it gently floats and falls to earth, a ball as it bounces and then gradually stops and rolls. Any one idea of motion can serve as the impetus for creative exploration. Take a swing, for example. What is there that has a swinging movement? Of course, most children have experienced being in a swing and realize that the path of movement is one that goes forward and back as well as up and down. But other objects move in a swinging motion. The pendulum of a clock, windshield wipers, clothes on a clothesline, a golf club as it strikes the ball, a girl's skirt as she walks are just a few additional ideas; and each would give rise to different movement patterns. These differing patterns can be investigated by using this principle: First let the arms swing, then the legs, then the torso; now change levels, each time deciding where the base of the swing is. Choose your own amount of time and tempo—sometimes slow, sometimes fast—continuing until you feel the phrase is completed.

The potential for movement stimuli in literature is tremendous. However, there are essential qualities of excellence in children's literature that teachers must learn to recognize. In searching for poems to inspire children in creative movement, I try to watch for several elements:

First, adaptability to movement—

> Want to see 'lectricity spark in kittie's fur?
> Want to see 'lectricity make her motor purr?
> Want to see 'lectricity make her headlights shine?
> Well, meet me in the alley after dark some time.

This beautifully crystallized idea and many other delightful pieces, some of them reprinted below, are all found in Vilate Raile's book *So There*.

Second, making a fanciful statement about something real—

> What if the Spring
> Should fall?
> What if the Fall
> Should spring?
> I didn't say it could
> did I
> But it would be a funny thing.

Third, one of my favorite devices for inspiring children to explore is to trigger their sensory images—sharpen their capacity for sight, sound, touch, taste, and smell—and then to encourage their use of imaginative words—

> Ice cream has such
> a quiet taste
> So cool, so smooth, so mild
> That I don't see how
> it could help
> But make a better child.

Fourth, an emotional outlet that can arouse a feeling of empathy—

> Inside I'm purry as a cat
> When it's Spring
> I wonder why I feel like that
> When It's Spring?
> Giggles push to be set free,
> Songs sing inside of me,

Feet go tripping off in glee.
Mother says she tells by me
When it's Spring.

Most teachers, particularly those in elementary education, do not have access to accompanists, so it is only natural that the question be asked, "Can you teach the young child creative rhythmic movement without a pianist?" Yes, of course it can be done, but the teacher must first know what rhythm is and appreciate some of its mechanics.

Because of the vital part that rhythm plays in our everyday living, from birth to death, I have concentrated on finding ways in which to enhance and increase the child's awareness of rhythm and those elements of dance related to it. An extremely simple, yet delightful way to help children become more aware of rhythm is to take the syllables of a word or group of words and clap the rhythmic structure that you hear as the words are spoken. Because there is rhythm in everything, this idea opens up an endless variety of patterns. For example, find the variations in cities and states. Salt Lake City, Utah, sounds different than Seattle, Washington. After the children can clap the pattern, see if they can transfer it into their feet. The sentence "I won't do it" is a valuable one to explore, not only for its rhythm pattern, but also because it allows the child to express a negative thought which becomes a relished challenge. Note value, meter, phrasing, and quality should all be a part of the child's knowledge, understanding, and ability to utilize in many ways.

One might make tapes of various sounds that give rise to movement. The many different ticking noises made by clocks, the wailing of sirens, people talking, the train as it leaves the station, the music of a merry-go-round, the surf at the ocean—these are a few sounds that might provide the stimulus for movement, for conversation, for their own stories.

Exploring the sounds of various percussion instruments can also be exciting to a class. Movement suggested by the gong, bell, or triangle is quite different from movement suggested by the drum, the wood block, or the sand block. If the students listen to these sounds, they will find that each instrumental sound inspires a different pattern.

Another means of teaching creative rhythmic movement without a piano is to investigate interesting children's records. Many very good records are readily adaptable to teaching rhythm, and new ones are being marketed all the time. All the Bowmor records, the Silver Burdett series, *Adventures in Music*, and my own record, *Come Dance with Me*, are stimulating.

Verbalizing about teaching creatively is a very difficult process, for the minute an idea is written down, it acquires a quality of rigidity and can become stilted unless it is viewed imaginatively and used as a springboard to additional ideas rather than as just a "thing" to teach. There are so many questions a teacher should be able to answer by means of imaginative, flexible ideas. How do you take the children's ideas of the day and build a section of the class around them and still accomplish some of the needed goals of the hour? Can you relieve tense situations with your own gentleness and turn these situations into rich experiences? If you do cherish the rich imagination of children, can you guide and develop it?

The answers to these questions are some of the keys to enriching each child's potential and his power of communication both as a dancer and as a human being. In other words, do you have an all-seeing eye—one that sees everything that goes on, all at once, all the time; one that recognizes whether each child is understanding, contributing, and doing anywhere near his capabilities? This all-seeing eye should be so perceptive that by your use of it each child can be encouraged, enriched, and given a feeling of security in knowing "today I discovered something new; today I did my best."

There should be moments of stillness within each class wherein a child can think, recollect, imagine, go back over the problem at hand, or listen. These moments can be extremely valuable, not as a discipline device but as a challenge to the creative self. Discipline problems, as such, are rare where creative teaching is being done. This does not mean that there is always quiet order; much conversation goes on as children are busy solving problems. The involvement of each child with the problem at hand is what is important. True discipline never comes with threats, embarrassment, or punishment; it comes through the teacher's capacity to conduct the class with enough excitement, enough challenge, enough firmness. enough regard for each child to encourage self-awareness and thence self-discipline.

Of great importance is the teacher's willingness to change her pattern of teaching if the children are too restless. Sometimes a very quiet voice, a special piece of music, a rhythm pattern on the drum, or the sound played on a gong will attract the children who are not giving full attention and arouse their curiosity so they will want to find out what the group is doing. Of great importance is nipping a discipline problem in the bud rather than excusing the child who causes confusion with, "Oh, today he's not ready to participate." I realize there are no ironclad rules on this and that each situation is different, but the teacher who tries not to notice the confusion is only asking for more of the same.

In conclusion, I'd like to share with you responses from two teachers who were in one of many workshops that I have had the opportunity to give. These reactions express the thirst, the need, the desire on the part of most teachers to become more involved professionally with creativity.

> Creative movement has affected the way I will look at things from now on. It has reaffirmed my belief that teaching cannot be done in neat little packages to be used over and over again as each year passes. I will need to sharpen my intuition, to become more proficient in identifying the needs of my children in order that they gain the maximum. What a joy to discover that I could use my whole body and that dancing as we now understand it can be for the layman and that we can help our little people discover, through movement, so many things that will enrich their capacity for language arts, rhythm, communication, and awareness of their world. How happy I am to know that I can help my children use their creative wings this coming year. In my teaching I am sure that I have not nudged them hard enough for them to go beyond that which is easy. Next year I hope to leave imprints—ever so gentle imprints.

The second one:

> For two years I have worked with children almost totally stripped of creativity, imagination, and the power to

make use of any inner self. These deprived children have had their lives crammed full of "nothing." They have learned to hate school with its pressures, frustrations, and its constant reminder of their failures in life. . . .

But suddenly, an unseen door has been thrown wide open, and on the other side lies a wealth of fresh ideas and approaches to help these unfortunate youngsters. I have seen things I never knew existed. The ideas extending from them are inexhaustible. I can envision already great possibilities in their approaches to math, to art, to music, to everything we do. . . .

If in this next school year I can help these children in this direction so that they no longer say "School is junk," I shall think that I have found the pot of gold at the end of the rainbow. . . . I approach September with a new energy and enthusiasm. No longer will there be deadwood subject matter for me; now I look upon it as driftwood, with its freedom, its freshness, and its quiet challenge.

It is vitally important that teachers not only be aware that there is a better—a more creative—approach to routine classwork, but that they also receive encouragement and support in their creative endeavors from administrators.

A last example of the thoughtless damage done and its invisible effects: One afternoon, months after my son's experience of having the cap and umbrella cut from his leaf-child, he came to me and asked, "Mom, what can I do now?" I answered him by asking if he had done anything in school that he really enjoyed and would like to try again. He thought for a moment and then a twinkle came into his eyes as he said, "Oh, yes!" For an hour he was very busy. When he cocks his head a certain way—and his tongue goes to the corner of his mouth—I know he is completely involved in an idea. He had taken a large piece of art paper, colored pencils, and many tiny leaves from the bridal wreath bush. The picture he made was not of one child, but a whole army in action, including airplanes with pilots, parachute jumpers, men in battle, some of whom had been wounded. All his people were made of the tiny leaves; each one armed for combat. After it was finished he came to me and said, "Look at my picture, mom. And she's not here to cut it up."

Dr. E. Paul Torrance, professor of educational psychology at the University of Georgia in Athens, is an outspoken critic of educators who fail to do justice to the creative impulse. He believes that "society is downright savage in its treatment of creative people, particularly when they are young."

The price of stifling creativity is incalculable. In America the brakes are jammed on the creative velocity of children in various ways. Many authorities on the psychology of creativity, including Dr. Torrance, put part of the blame on what they term America's "quick success" orientation. In our hurry toward "success" we are not prepared or willing to cope with the frustrations and delays that are inherent aspects of true creative work.

The unprecedented need in our society today for creative talent calls for some truly revolutionary changes in educational objectives. We need to ask more than ever before what kind of people our children are becoming. If you find some answers disheartening to accept, then may I offer these solutions to the problem in the form of a plea:

Don't turn down the lights in the child's treasure house of imagination.

Please don't cut off the "caps and umbrellas."

Develop your "magic eye" as well as your "all-seeing eye."

Inspire the child to go beyond that which is easy, to explore the difficult and the new.

Listen to his questions with sensitivity and answer them judiciously.

Above all, respect the child you teach.

DRAMA AND CHILDHOOD:
A PERSONAL REACTION

GERALD TYLER

*Gerald Tyler is well known to drama educators in virtually
all parts of the world. Educated at The College, Bishop's Stortford,
The College of Saint Mark and Saint John in London, and the University
of Leeds, he has devoted his entire professional life to community theatre,
children's theatre, teaching, and organizations that further the work in
these fields. He was founder of the Leeds Children's Theatre and the
Brighouse Children's Theatre, and has initiated and organized numerous
drama and folk festivals for both adults and youth in England. He was
county drama advisor, West Riding, Yorkshire Education Authority, from
1948 until his retirement in 1974. Mr. Tyler was founder-chairman
of the British Children's Theatre Association, founder-chairman of
ASSITEJ, and founder-representative for the National Council of Theatre
for Young People. In addition, he has designed drama courses for teachers,
lectured throughout the United Kingdom and America, conducted
tours of Europe, and written for a variety of publications. Out of his wide
experience he has evolved a point of view toward children and drama
which he shares with us in this essay.*

The common factor in the approaches of teachers to creative
dramatic work and theatre for children and young people must
surely be a concern for the all-round healthy development of their
children. No two teachers will approach the subject in quite the same
way nor will the methods necessarily be identical. Every child is a
unique human being, even though some emotions, thoughts, and
physical characteristics may be generally peculiar to all. There are as

many good ways of teaching a subject as there are good teachers; I should like to be one of them.

Personally, I believe in the importance of the folk—folk stories, songs, and dances, folklore, and folk drama. Experience confirms belief that within the folk is a storehouse of wisdom accumulated and handed down over the centuries of the growth of civilized man. It is the wisdom passed on by one generation to guide the next along the road to as secure and happy an existence as circumstances will allow. Indeed, I should go so far as to say that, in spite of the heavy veneer of modern progress, the farther one departs from the folk and the more one ignores their advice, the deeper and more dangerous are the waters in which one swims. Man is making so many discoveries in education that appear to be at variance with the past that it seems to me that anyone who is busy preaching the benefits of coeducation at every level, or advocating large schools, or demanding the abolition of physical punishment in schools, or supporting a cult of youth or the breaking down of taboos would do well to stop and ask the folk what is their wisdom in these matters.

The present world is moving fast. But is it sure of its direction? And is that direction a right one? When the folk seem to demand gods or a God to worship, how far is the government of a country ever likely to succeed in demanding of its people an acceptance of state atheism? In the store of folk knowledge from unrecorded time there lies material that touches every human being in the world. There are things in folk that evoke immediate, universal, and sometimes irrational responses: things which seem to touch human beings not in the head or the heart but near the solar plexus. Why is it that the old mumming plays and folk tales never fail to capture the attention of young people and to keep their fascination with the aged, if there is not something strong and necessary within them?

In the rush of modern times many mothers have omitted teaching their children the old rhymes and stories around the evening fire. It has been left to teachers to do this job at a later stage. Some new-style intellectuals, with a passion for telling children the truth, have even failed to understand the fundamental truth of the existence of Santa Claus. In the countries of the Eastern bloc the old British children's favorite, *Punch and Judy*, is frowned upon because it is thought too violent for children to see. In Britain *Punch and Judy* comes out like a hardy perennial in spite of the regular beatings Punch gives his wife, the way he bashes the baby, and then finally hangs the hangman. There has been an epidemic of real baby bashing in England recently, but I believe it is more likely the result of a lack of opportunity to see Mr. Punch than the result of his unsocial actions. Charlotte Chorpenning made an excellent play from the story of *Little Red Riding Hood*, but the end of the play differed markedly. The story's ending, more in keeping with folk tradition, has the wolf eat the grandmother and be found later by woodmen while he is sleeping at the riverside. The woodmen cut open the wolf's belly, the grandmother pops out, and they fill up the hole with a large stone and sew him up again. The end is fantastically violent and unreal; yet the end Chorpenning gave to the play—the capture of the wolf, who wishes to live like a man but is put in a cage—is diabolical by comparison.

Cruel-hearted stepmothers are common in folk tales, but however hard this may seem on some excellent stepmothers, the stories cannot do without them. The princesses must have their good and bad fairies, and the heroes must have their dragons to slay and their princesses to rescue. The themes are evergreen and come up like spring daffodils for every newborn child. We must give all children the opportunity to hear the stories, just as we should also give them the chance to live in the open air among real daffodils.

Some children nowadays appear to have outgrown fairy stories at an early age. Does this mean that the stories are wrong, or is childhood suddenly moving too fast? Are pressures put upon children by television and modern life destroying childhood? The modern child is still surrounded by dragons and wicked ogres. It may be that a good dose of fear of the smooth-tongued witches and evil wizards of folklore is a better antidote to the sly work of drug pushers than the books to be seen in some American schools on the classification of hard and soft drugs. Are we losing out on the opportunity for children to learn through fantasy rather than meet all the dangers through the hard, immediate, and specific facts of modern life? This early period of learning and adjustment is vital and should not be made to pass too quickly. Our present attitudes may lead to more jobs for psychologists, bigger and better mental hospitals, and free contraceptives for all at the age of ten—but surely these are not compensations to be desired.

For a long time I have been somewhat dubious about many things that are said and written about child drama, creative dramatics, and theatre in education generally; and this article is my attempt to explain the whole business to myself in my own way. It owes nothing to Jung or Freud, and if Robert Ardrey and Konrad Lorenz seem to support me from time to time, then it is good fortune indeed.

It began nearly half a century ago, when in the middle of a general science lesson my teacher and friend rolled out the phrase "ontongeny recapitulates philogeny." Sonorous, catchy, and mysterious in itself, it opened up a great world of interest. We learned that the human individual grows from a single cell, soon to divide and multiply and then to follow the evolutionary journey of development. On it goes through the cell-dividing stage, the amphibian stage, on through the stage of the higher animals where the human fetus much resembles that of a dog, and on to become distinguishable as a human being, to be guarded and protected until the end of the nine-month gestation period. Then follows the next mystery, for the helpless mite arrives in a strange world with little or nothing to help it to survive; yet somehow it must adjust to the world around it and come to terms with a complicated pattern of existence. Within the short space of three or four years, the child will have accumulated as much knowledge and have become as adapted to his environment as he will do in any similar period of his future development. It is truly remarkable how all the host of sensations, impressions, and illogical human regulations of behavior are absorbed, accepted, and made his own.

It is doubtful whether the child could cope with the mass of new experiences were it not for the important contribution made by his private play. Play is his principal learning time, his rehearsal time, his preparation for the future. It is strange that his learning about his place within the environment seems best when passed between reality on the one side and rhythm, verse, ballad, and song on the other.

The role and function of drama in child education is a subject of considerable controversy. Personally I find that many people are so inclined to have and defend their own definitions that it seems best to rely on the *Oxford Dictionary* for clarity and it is by the *Oxford* definitions that I abide. Theatre is there defined as a building where plays are performed, but it can also mean the theatre arts and dramatic literature. Drama is defined as plays, literature, and situations having excitement. Education is defined as the bringing up (of the young), systematic instruction, development of character and mental powers. To educate is to provide intellectual and moral training.

From these definitions it seems to me that the purpose (i.e., role and function) of education through drama and theatre may be stated as follows:

1. To bring children into contact with dramatic literature, play making, play writing, and the presentation of plays

2. To introduce them to the pleasure of theatregoing and plays of the past and present both at home and abroad

3. To inculcate a critical approach to the theatre and to other dramatic products of the mass media

4. To encourage them to devise their own plays and to explore the possibilities offered by a variety of dramatic situations

5. To encourage study of all the related arts, particularly those involved in theatre

6. To respect moral ends in all work undertaken since, as by definition, education is directed to the moral aspect

This last point is emphasized because there is an observable tendency on the part of some young teachers to regard the taking of moral attitudes as wrong in educational theatre, with the result that children are sometimes subjected to ideas beyond their experience or critical powers and to language that society would not wish to encourage. An amoral attitude is in danger of becoming an immoral one. It would seem that our educational obligation toward the child and its parents is to eschew attitudes of personal indulgence and to remain, for the child's safety, in a conservative position.

Directly one begins to make such statements as "drama develops imagination," "drama is self-expression," or "drama has curative effects," one comes up against the fact that the same claims are made for every other art with equal justification. Drama is seen to be only one means of expressing personality or feelings or ideas and of developing imagination and creativity. This level is where drama is at one with all the arts as a force in education and, indeed, as one of its most important contributors. It is to be seen not in isolation but related to music, poetry, dance, scupture, and to any other medium through which man can express his thoughts on the world around him. Little will be communicated, however, unless the techniques of the chosen medium are acquired, nor will there be truth in what is communicated if truth is lacking in what is expressed.

Because the nuances of speech provide a multitude of shades of meaning by which man can express himself with exactness in great detail, drama has become a means whereby thoughts and feelings can be communicated with a greater immediacy than through any of the other arts, particularly so since the instruments used are the human body, the voice, and the personality. It is at this level that one can talk of expressing personality, exploring personality, or of exploring and portraying human behavior. By studying the effects of one's teaching, one may come to draw some tentative and general conclusions regarding development of confidence or personal adjustment or release of tension.

Now I am postulating a deeper level, one below the one just considered. On this deeper level one can look at life and at man and try to see what one can of the spirit of man at different times: as it is today, as it was far back in recorded history, and indeed as it was as far back as man can probe into the history of the race. At this point I wish to go back to the human child last seen arriving in this strange world, each one unique but each one showing some general characteristics. What impressions are collected and what powers are being developed during the period before birth we do not know. How the computer of the brain begins to take in impressions, relate them, produce and reject answers during early childhood is a mystery. One thing we can do is to watch children, try to see what interests them, how they react toward and learn from other children, and observe the patterns of childhood as they emerge.

Here I have set down from general observation of my own children and others around me, a number of actions that children make and things that they do, which seem to come naturally to them and give them satisfaction. They have been arranged in a rough chronological order—rough because they vary to some extent from child to child according to his readiness and to the environmental opportunities offered to him to develop. Rightly or wrongly, I have, as a matter of convenience, omitted the early stages of foot-and-hand exploration and gone straight to the time when the child is on his feet and able to move around on his own.

Some Observed Tendencies and Characteristics of Childhood

1. (up to 4 years) Need for security, the presence of mother, home and family; to be talked to and played with. The environment gradually extends and the child needs to be taken out. He needs to make noises, run about, climb, swing, to experience rhythmic motion and sound. He attaches importance to things of his own—cup, toy, etc. He develops socially—sometimes has a secret, invisible friend.

2. (4 to 5) Need for apparatus and pieces of costume for being postmen, soldiers, etc. He mimics parents and tradespeople. He plays at being cars, engines, planes, often being the car, its parts, its noises, and its driver all at the same time. He collects things. He engages in free movement and dance; he is interested in witches, fairies, and magic.

3. (5 to 6) Tendency to want to be leader, captain, king. He rushes around violently and noisily, often aimlessly. He plays games, likes mechanical toys.

4. (6 to 7) Has fears, compulsions (must tread in the squares). He plays cops and robbers, cowboys and Indians, and capturing games begin. Girls make up dances. Both boys and girls say or make up funny rhymes, take part in processions.

5. (7 to 8) Defeats the evil chance. Makes things begin and likes organized games. He creates camps and dens. Private reading can be enjoyed.

6. (8 to 9) Shows an interest in masks and likes to play drama games, bows and arrows, join in a group. He has secret ideas.

7. (9 to 10) He plays out stories in a solitary way but also plays with others, "You be X and I'll be Y." He has codes and passwords and explores farther afield. Reading is well advanced by now.

8. (10 to 11) He likes practical things, enjoys arts and crafts, has standards. Drama now quite advanced.

This whole section is set down with humility and diffidence because children vary so much. The lonely child and the imaginative child will adopt a secret friend at a very early age. The dominant child will dash around the playground and also become a leader at an early age, while a more reserved child may never develop these tendencies. It is so hard to generalize on many points of behavior. These observations and the classification may not find favor everywhere, but it must be a fact that there is a pattern and a succession of such characteristics while the how and the why and their function remain a matter of theory and research.

In *Play, Drama and Thought*, Richard Courtney's masterly examination of the intellectual background of drama, drawing as he does upon the scholarly work of educationalists, psychologists, and philosophers, the concept of the recapitulation theory is dismissed as a speculation rather than a theory. This may be so, and my article certainly has more depth of feeling than of scientific study. This is neither the time, place, nor necessity to set up an argument between Patrick White, Joseph Lee, Carl Groos, and Stanley Hall, but I must point out that considerable changes of thought and fashion have taken place in psychology and in anthropology, in particular since 1930. Perhaps on reexamination this particular speculation may now find more respect. Can it be that if the history of the individual does recapitulate the history of the race, in the mind as it does in the body, then perhaps the order of arrival of the characteristic actions and personal play of children may say something about the history of the development of the racial mind? Personal characteristics and the order of their arrival may suggest, or help us to determine, good lines for dramatic work with children. It may also tell us where to tread carefully and not to interfere.

Richard Courtney refers to the successive culture patterns in man's history echoed in children's play, which have been set by various American writers. They are given as the animal stage, the savage stage, the nomad stage, the agricultural/patriarchal/early settlement stage, and the tribal stage. Upon these pegs the various aspects of children's play are hung to make a reasonable and understandable pattern of development. All I can say in reply is that what a man learns for himself plows a furrow in the mind and that all learning must be tested as well as absorbed. Obviously I am in general agreement with these findings, which would seem to support the recapitulation theory.

It is significant that if one turns to that famous work of the last century, Sir John Frazer's account of the beliefs and practices of primitive peoples entitled *The Golden Bough*, there is a startling relationship to be seen between many of the characteristics of childhood and what is related of the practices of primitive peoples, and indeed, for that matter, to some beliefs and suspicions of the more developed. Again, this is an observation that has been made by other people, but it may be pertinent to ask how many teachers of drama have even the abridged edition of *The Golden Bough* on their shelves or use it as a source book for drama work with young people.

There are accounts in Frazer of the practice of magic; of masks and face painting; of the worship of fire, sun, moon, trees, rocks, ancestors, and animals. He deals with ceremonies attending birth, initiation into the tribe, marriage, and death. There are accounts of the festivals surrounding the seasons, hunting, and war. There are weather invocations, sacrifice, the scapegoat, virgin birth, and a host of other beliefs and customs. He covers a wealth of material that is highly dramatic, so much of it related to childhood and often finding a deep understanding in people everywhere.

Much of what is said of this link between the manifestations of childhood and the primitive practices would seem to give an authority for the use of some of it in our own dramatic teaching. Many primitive customs and ceremonies involve processions, which children enjoy, especially little girls, whose preoccupation with the wedding ceremony begins at an early age. The mammoth Prague exhibition of child art with paintings from almost every country in the world showed that the most frequent and universal subject was the wedding ceremony. The May Day processions and gala processions with their dressing up and their garlands and ceremonials never cease to attract the young. They are important, too, in the teaching of drama, for within the simple ceremony lies, apart from all the color and excitement, the never to be mentioned elements of technique and control. To keep one's place in a procession, to carry one's posey safely and one's person with dignity, is a great step on the road to self-confidence and acting. To let one's dolls talk to one another and to hold conversations with them holds the beginnings of characterization. "Come and watch me, mum," is a command that carries the early signs of wanting an audience. And when the child says to a friend, "I'll be May and you be Joanna," then drama is really moving.

Masks are always fascinating and carry a touch of mystery and repulsion. They can be frightening and give the power to frighten, an aspect that boys in particular respond to. Makeup appeals more to girls, but daubing the face is something that becomes a Brave. Here lies a subject with wide scope in both drama and general education. From painting a horrible face to devising a tribal face lies a wealth of learning. Caste masks and the married status, the painted faces of the Orient, masks of Gods and demons, animal masks, and the formalized masks of the Egyptian gods carry one's learning across the world and up and down the centuries. It is of such universal interest and human importance that it would be possible to build a whole program of dramatic activity based on disguise and the human problem of the mask and the face.

Among the many intensely satisfying lessons I have known was one developed from a simple piece of information that a friend had seen in a kangaroo dance done by Australian aborigines. In it one man pretended to be the kangaroo and in the dance was killed and borne back to the village in triumph. A class of slow learners (eleven-year-olds) made up a circle dance from which the kangaroo detatched itself, moving in and out of the ring. Then one of the spear-carrying dancers began to follow him in and out and around the circle. The circle became a line and still the stalking went on, until the kangaroo moved forward in front of the hunters who, in formalized rhythmic movement, came down and speared him in one strong symbolic action. All the dancers then mimed picking up a kangaroo and carrying it dancing back to their village for a general celebration. The absorption and concentration throughout the performance proved its satisfying nature both for the participants and for those who watched.

Man has always been preoccupied with his fragile security here on earth. He early developed a respect for the sun, which gave him warmth and ripened his harvests. If the sun failed to rise in the morning, there would be perpetual night and everything would die. The sun's blasting heat at noon also demonstrated his power for no one could look at his brightness. In the Bible we read of the people who were wailing for Tamuz, the Sun god, as he was leaving them in autumn. We can be sure that this would be followed by a spring rejoicing on his return. The celebration was often a dance and later a play enactment where the god was killed and rose to life again. This death-and-resurrection cycle is the foundation for the folk plays from ancient Greece to Hungary, from the Basque country to Britain, where the mumming plays became known as Guisers in Cornwall, Soul Cakers in Cheshire, Galations in Scotland, White Headed Boys in Ireland, and Pace Eggers in Yorkshire.

As I write this on Easter Saturday morning our Brighouse Pace Eggers have just set off on a visit to neighboring towns and villages. They went off in their white smocks decorated with rosettes, the Black Prince of Paradine being distinguished in wearing a black one. All the Pace Eggers except the doctor, dressed in a formal black suit and top hat, wore mortorboardlike hats with hoops of garlands high above them and paper streamers beneath; the streamers are the vestigial remains of the masks that at some early time covered the face. In some places today the Fool will sweep out a ring among the crowds and Saint George will slay Bold Slasher a dozen times in mortal combat, only to be revived in a comedy passage by the doctor. The words are doggerel and often without sense, and the entire play is but fifteen minutes of knockabout in the crowded streets on a cold day. The collection of money or pace eggs is the reward, but even that small compensation will go to the theatre workshop to help pay the rates! The play is like the sun; it only sinks to rise again next spring.

Nor are the myths and legends to be regarded merely as possible sources of child interest, for both these areas of recorded stories run close to the folk. Many appear to have a strong element of history. King Arthur and his knights, the wilder and more imaginative Welsh stories, and the legends that surround Robin Hood are all part of a background where fantasy, history, and folklore meet.

From where I sit at this moment I am looking across the valley to the hillside on the Kirklees estate, where Robin Hood lies buried. His history is shrouded in legend, but his name and exploits live on. He has all the necessary attributes for both play and study, and like other legendary figures he has lived on because within him are the universal characteristics of a folk hero. He was a warrior in the grand manner, one whose prowess in battle and whose quickness of wit made him admired. He took from the rich and gave to the poor; he was a man in distress of the law, who nevertheless stood for fundamental human justice. And all this is based on historical fact. As one of those men who followed his lord, the Earl of Lancaster, to defeat in a battle at Boroughbridge, Yorkshire, in the early fourteenth century, he was as a contrariant against King Edward II and was obliged to take to the woods to escape capture and death. He was an outlaw. His name has been a household word and Robin Hood plays a feature of the English May Day festivities for centuries. Many writers have embroidered on the historical facts, but it does not require much from any child's imagination to look through the trees into the valley and see Robin Hood and his band cautiously picking their way to Wakefield, where a secret welcome would be awaiting.

On quite a different approach to Robin Hood, consider the dilemma of the people of Wakefield caught up in a quarrel between their liege lord and the king! For whom should they fight? Should they join the armed men on their doorstep to whom they owe immediate loyalty of the king, a man they do not know but to whom they owe loyalty through their lord? The battle having been lost, retribution will follow; what action can the men take and what is likely to happen to those left behind? How can the men who take to the woods and become outlaws meet their wives and families? Who will be their enemies and who will be spies?

Here are a dozen problems to be discussed and solved, incidents to be played out in improvisation, stories to be made up and plays to be created. The problems are real and personal, the problems of any civil war. The great advantages, as I see it, is that the problems in this situation are similar to those in Vietnam and Northern Ireland, but they can be played out without the pressure of the politics of today. The problems of the present day are never good material for school drama because these questions are too near and too complex. No teacher is in the situation to express any more than an opinion about them nor the child to understand them. What can any child know about the rights and wrongs of South Vietnam by the North, and what can he know about the causes of the troubles in Northern Ireland? The use of modern controversial happenings and other such internal and external political struggles is an open invitation to children to be pushed politically at an early age, when the purpose of the teacher should be to develop in them a critical intelligence so that they can meet with reason the hysteria, rumor, shallow argument, newspaper reports, and manipulation by persons with ulterior motives in the years ahead.

Another confirming experience regarding the use of folk drama and primitive culture entered some forty years ago when I was reporting the Maddermarket Theatre Festival at Norwich and interviewed the director, Nugent Monk, in his fine-galleried Elizabethan music room. He said, "The Maddermarket Company began here in this room with a performance of the Norwich mystery plays." I expressed surprise that he should start with a mystery play with a company of amateurs and he said, "On the contrary, the mystery plays are right because they are easily understood; the stories are known, the dialogue is simple and straight lined, the emotions come naturally to the actors and the technique of acting has become more sophisticated as the years have gone by."

This lesson had a great effect on me, and I went away and devised a syllabus for drama with secondary school boys from eleven to fourteen years. It started with tribal dances, weather invocations, ceremonial processions, mumming and other folk plays and led on through the tropes, mystery plays, moralities, and interludes to scenes from *Ralph Roister Doister* to exciting, well-known extracts from Shakespeare. I was teaching in a tough school for boys in the hungry 1930s and the program worked.

It also told me that material from the classics, chosen with care and presented with imagination, had great appeal. Good language and universal truths are not wasted on young people. The last thing that one should do is to play down to them; just find ways of capturing their interest and do not bore them. Nobody should have Shakespeare all the time, but that is not to say that Shakespeare should be ignored at any age. Improvisations about two warring families who create such a nuisance that they are warned to keep the peace and after another brawl breaks out are stopped by the law and brought up for punishment can be played out without reference to *Romeo and Juliet*. The story can as easily be read in the newspaper.

The careful selection of material for dramatic work, whether it be original or taken from the ready-made, is most important. Drama is a form of art and the art process can be said, at its simplest, to consist of the selection of ideas, words, things, or actions put together to make a statement. On this definition much that is created daily in a drama lesson might be considered to be art, except that work must not stop at the basic process. The artistic value of the product will depend upon the quality of the selection and the quality of the statement to be made. The care in the selection and the choice of subject need our careful guidance.

Creation is never easy; to most people it comes very hard indeed, and there are no easy ways for the drama teacher to do his job. He can follow somebody's book or walk in the wake of some drama prophet. He may, by so doing, obtain some reasonable results, but in the end he must be an artist himself and work out his own salvation. To do this he must have the knowledge, the feeling, and the experience to test the materials and have the skills to produce the artistic result. All art would seem to rest on a bedrock of technique and this is true for both teacher and pupil. Both must build up their resources, their critical intelligence, and their techniques and hope for the final miracle. In teaching there is always a balance to be found in encouraging the child's creative work and in building up his resources for better work, for allowing free expression and for subjecting results to critical examination. There have to be disciplines somewhere and finally they must come from within.

Violence is one disturbing feature of drama in schools and theatres today. It reflects what is happening in the world outside. Young people have a compulsion toward scuffling and fighting; it is within them and cannot be ignored. It is no new problem. The folk would say that violence is within man and will recur time and again. The message of the Bacchae says the same thing and concludes that man must therefore learn to live with violence and control it. Discipline and control are the key words in drama teaching with youth. Children need a circle of security within which to live, explore, and experiment. As they grow older, the circles of environment and of security must extend also, but freedom of expression must always be kept within those bounds of security by which the young person does little harm to himself or to others.

The bounds of society are its taboos encased within the laws. It is one of the glories of life that youth is romantic and idealistic and it could be said that there is something wrong with the young person of eighteen or nineteen who does not know all the answers and wish to set the world to rights. Society must listen with sympathy and answer with reason, but it would be a society of idiots that let youth rule the world. Rebellion in a controlled situation is acceptable, but he who seeks to turn society into a jungle must expect a jungle answer.

Another concern in the field of drama with young people is the undercurrent in the theatre of a preoccupation with experimenting and wandering into the areas of the mind where the influence of the supernatural abounds. It may be an exploration of self or group cognition, but it does imply a journey into the uncharted twilight area of the mind. Few would deny the value of the work of Artaud, Grotowski, or Peter Brook; but they are danger signals rather than signposts in one's dealing with young people. A six weeks' course in psychodrama with young drama teachers would also seem to be a dangerous procedure, unless it is a course on what to avoid. Straightforward drama teaching of the free-form kind has problems enough, without seeking others; and while the work is based on the best of art, helpful curative effects will come as a by-product. There is a vast difference between letting art do its own work and structuring work to meet imagined needs of disturbed pupils. That is the job of the psychologist whose training is long and deep and who, even then, knows that he knows little.

Tassos Lignadis, of the Moraitis School in Athens, in writing about school drama, refers to mimicry as an attempt to escape from the limitations placed upon one by objective time scales. "To play," he says, "is to take oneself out of time and to finish the game is to submit once more to the limitation placed on one by society." In fact, he believes that growing up can be defined as learning to limit or even stifle one's imagination. The above consideration should be borne in mind in any attempt to describe the theatrical possibilities of an age group whose very existence is an absurd, raw, erotic, immediate, and dangerous drama.

If there is an underlayer to the level of unconscious knowledge seen in children's play and exemplified by what can be seen in the behavior of primitive peoples, then I speculate that it is a matrix or flux of early memories and instincts that cannot as yet be separated or defined. Yet there does seem to be an even deeper level or thread that runs vertically through them all. The question is, Where does inspiration, revelation, and ultimate truth lie? One can see man's struggling, emerging thoughts and reactions in Frazer's *Golden Bough*, but one can find more inspired thought in the Bible or in the Egyptian stories of Isis and Osiris.

Man is a thinking animal, not governed by instinct alone, and is therefore capable of the best and the worst. A friend once remarked that every vile thing that the human mind can conceive has probably been perpetrated at some time or another. It does seem, however, that within man lies a universal tendency toward law and order, and in the struggle between order and chaos, good and evil, it is order and goodness that prevail. It is in the passion play of Osiris, in the festivals of Marduk, and in the passion of Christ that these truths are revealed. Through our drama work we have the power to make them known. Above all else we must observe the child and keep him in mind, for it is surely in inspiration or revelation that Wordsworth wrote in *Intimations of Immortality from Recollections of Early Childhood*:

> Not in entire forgetfulness,
> And not in utter nakedness,
> But trailing clouds of glory do we come,
> From God, who is our home.

REFLECTIONS ON
A SPRING DAY

AGNES HAAGA

Agnes Haaga is professor of drama and chairman of children's drama at
the University of Washington. She is a fellow of the American Theatre
Association and a past president of the Children's Theatre Association. She
headed the American delegation to the first International Congress
on Theatre for Children and Youth in London, 1964, and was a member
of the ad hoc committee to draw up the resolutions for the creation
of ASSITEJ. A Northwestern University graduate, Professor Haaga
has received numerous honors and citations as a leader in the field of
children's drama. With Patricia Randles she wrote Supplementary
Material for Use in Creative Dramatics with Younger Children.

It is the first Saturday in May, the opening day of the boating
season in Seattle. And *what* a day! On such a day as this with spring
"moving in the air above and in the earth below and around him,
penetrating even his dark and lowly little house with its spirit of
divine discontent and longing," Mole cried out "'Bother!' and 'O
blow!' and also 'Hang spring-cleaning!' and bolted out of the
house."[1]

I say "Hang writing" and with Sean and Deirdre, my two
dachshunds, bolt down the hill to Lake Washington. The whole
world seems to have declared a holiday. The lake is filled with
sailboats. Those who aren't sailing are messing around the boats in
the public boat basin or bicycling or walking or playing or just *being*,
rejoicing in the day.

We stroll along our usual path near the edge of the lake. We stop.
There's something *new* in the familiar landscape—a rope is hanging

from the limb of a willow tree at the water's edge—a thick rope with a big knot at its end. As I pause to consider enjoying a swing, a fair-haired boy of eleven discovers the rope. In one long sustained flowing movement he throws himself down the bank onto the rope and out over the water. After a few swings back and forth he explores other aerial patterns. A wide circular swing takes him around the tree and back again. Then he swings out with a S-shaped movement. At the height of his flight he twists his body to the right and swings back to the bank, creating a figure 8 in the air. With a whoop of delight he re-creates the figure 8, chanting, "Around the moon and back again."

"Around the moon and back again"—shades of Aristotle—"the imitation of an action in action"—the movement of the S, spontaneously turned into an 8, an impressive physical movement—something stirs within; there's a quick shift and the movement becomes an action—a space flight. The space above the water is quickly transformed. It becomes space, outer space. The "actor" involved in an action gives himself a name . . . several names, Space Ship, and finally Space Man. His movement was that of an object, Space Ship; but in chanting "Around the moon and back again" his dialogue names him Space Man. Simple though it be, "Around the moon and back again" is dialogue—the action spoken. And as for the theme of all this, the significance of the complete action, well I could meditate the rest of this lovely day on possible levels of meaning.

How naturally *movement* evolved into *dramatic* movement and then into dramatic *action*. How simply the moving child becomes something or somebody moving; something or somebody *doing* some thing. *Imagining* is at the heart of it—imagining oneself a character in action—imagining characters in action . . . in an action, a deed done—*drama*. The sixth-grade classes at Renton Park Elementary School near Seattle call their drama hour "mind's eye." "Because," say the youngsters, "you see something in your mind's eye, and you *do* it."

And often in your mind's eye you have transformed what you have seen—given it a new name depending upon your use of it. children, like poets, seem to be engaged much of the time in "giving to any object, or thought, or event, or feeling, the name that makes its nature shine forth."[2] Pier Morgan, a university student, captured in a series of line drawings the action of a preschool boy as he—

starts out alone
discovers a *rope* lying on the sidewalk
encircles the rope like a *bridle* around a telephone pole
and gallops in place
rides free of the pole twirling the rope in the air like
a *lasso*
centers the rope at the seat of his pants like a *tail*,
still galloping
the gallop slows to a walk; the *tail* becomes a rope
once more and is trailed behind the boy as he strolls
down the street "doing nothin'"—so he says.

Too bad someone in the Federal Energy Administration did not wonder and ask, "What can you *do* with a gas-ration coupon bearing the image of George Washington as do dollar bills?" It wouldn't take an imaginative youngster long to come up with an answer. "Put it in any standard bill-changing machine in any laundromat and collect a dollar's worth of change in return." No one did ask, so 4.8 billion gas-ration coupons (printing cost: $12.5 million) will probably have to be destroyed.

My musing is interrupted. A young man on a bicycle has stopped; a baby is strapped in the seat behind him. The baby points his finger in the direction of the two dachshunds and says, "Pup-pees." "Pup-pees," repeats the father with the same rising inflection of the voice. "These 'pup-pees,'" I inform them, "are six years old." The man apologizes, saying, "'Pup-pees' is the only name we have for all four-legged creatures of the canine variety."

I think of all the names I have for these two creatures—My Joy and My Burden; Consciousness Achieving the Form of Sean and of course, Consciousness Achieving the Form of Deirdre. The latter names are newly acquired ones motivated by a recent visit to the Seattle Art Museum and gazing upon Morris Graves' soft, haunting, lovely painting *Consciousness Achieving the Form of a Crane*. Birds are a recurring subject in Graves' paintings and yet, "the objects he draws are not birds, but the bird after it nests in the mind, and his minnow is the stuff of the soul . . . he thinks with images: If the skull is a shell, the bird is the thought."[3]

A wind rises from the south end of the lake setting everything in motion. Headsails billow out in front of those boats running with the wind. Boats caught running oblique to the sudden, strong current of air bend sideways, their sails horizontal to the water. The riggings of the boats tied to the docks become wind chimes. Pennants snap. The rope hanging from the willow branch swings in unison with the branches. Frisbees, picnic napkins, human tresses, lake water, Sean's and Deirdre's ears, all respond to and are caught up in the rhythm of the wind. Then just as suddenly the wind subsides; headsails droop, horizontal masts become vertical, the music of the "wind chimes" fade; all things move gently, and Sean and Deirdre turn their ears right side out with hearty shakes of their heads.

My sister, Rita, at the age of five came in one day with two new names for a wind not unlike this one:

> The wind is God's hug,
> The breeze is His kiss.[4]

Then she ran across the room, caught her baby sister up in her arms, and gave her a big hug and a little kiss.

Naming motivates action; action motivates naming. How many names little children can find for an upward, rhythmic movement of the body. How they love to curl up tightly and unfold slowly, reaching and growing skyward. "*Who* are you growing up and up and up?" How they delight in an interruption in the rhythm at just the right moment. "*What* might stop you from growing?" Ah, here it comes—the Universal Adversary—Trouble—a Problem—the Villain—the Antagonist—or as one child called the disrupting agent—the big *No No*. How many times he must have reached upward for something, almost grasped it and then heard, "*No No!*" There was once a little boy who when asked his name always replied, "No-No-Johnny." He really thought that was his name, for he had never heard Johnny minus the No-No.

Children are quick to respond to key dramatic questions. I barely asked the question, "What stops you from growing?" when one little girl had thrown herself bodily across another child who was growing upward as a rose. She pressed the "rose" down to the "ground," then seeing my expression of puzzlement and concern informed me, "I'm the sidewalk she's growing up under." Well, that could stop a rose—but not quite. This "rose" began to grow sideways; squeezed out from under the "sidewalk" and continued her growth skyward. "Roses," said she, "just grow and grow and grow."

"They have Helpers," suggested a playmate.
"Who would help roses to grow?" I asked.
"The rain." "The sun." "People!"
What action does this begin to imitate? Ah—Joseph Campbell's single hero emerging from behind a thousand faces, archetype of all mythology, receiving a call to go beyond where he is—a call to adventure. He has his No No's, including his own refusal to answer the call—in which case there is apt to be a transformation to a lesser form of life. He has his Helpers, within and without. Saying yes to the call initiates a transformation to a new identity, a fuller life.[5]

A raucous barking breaks into my thoughts. Sean and Deirdre are chasing a pair of ducks. They always manage never to catch the ducks but delight in the chase. Some children are playing in the shallow water at the swimming beach. They are improvising rules for a game of water tag—"You can't leave the water"—"You're safe if you touch the posts." Then come shouts of "Not It!" "Not It!" "Not It!" "You're It!" There are screams as It chases the Not Its. A Not It is caught and becomes It. How intense is It's desire to get Not It. How equally strong is Not It's determination not to be caught. Such conflict in a simple game of tag.

This same intensity is present when we have played a game of tag in drama—working in pairs, each pair imposing a handicap on itself, e.g., hopping on one leg or walking stiff-legged to slow down the pace but not the intensity of feeling. All understand what they want—to get Not It or to escape It. Great fun! After this action comes *naming*; first *general* names for It and Not It—Chaser and Chased, Hunter and Hunted, Antagonist and Protagonist, Bad Guys and Good Guys, Villain and Victim. But drama is the art of the particular so we move on to more *specific* names, more concrete images as we imagine ourselves characters in an action—Cop and Robber, Cat and Mouse, the Wind and the Sea, Snoopy and Red Baron, the Early Bird and the Worm, Broom and Dust, Wolf and Red Riding Hood, the Fates and Oedipus, Fear and a Child, Machine and Man. Hunter vs. Hunted—is there any earlier plot known to man?

Up on the grassy hillside above the beach four boys are engaged in what appears to be a game of hide and seek. But not quite; it has been modified and renamed Army. The players carry toy rifles, highly representative of the real thing. Three are in hiding; a fourth, the Seeker, goes forth, rifle poised for action, to search out the foe. I am far enough away to see all the characters in action. The Seeker is edging his way around the refreshment stand. A second boy is on the opposite side of the building, his back pressed to the wall, as he inches his way along to venture a look around the corner of the stand. A gentle movement in the bushes beyond indicates that one gunman is undercover there. A fourth boy is lying on the ground. When the Seeker spies him and fills him with gunshot, he raises up and protests "I'm dead! I'm already dead!"

"O.K. O.K. O.K. You're dead."

"And so are *you*," shouts the undercover man emerging from the bushes with a "Pow Pow Pow." The Seeker drops. Now the back-to-the-wall boy dashes around the corner and after a burst of gunfire stands triumphant. But there is a surprise ending. Unseen by me and apparently forgotten by the four boys, a fifth boy has been lying prone on the roof of the low building. He lifts himself and his rifle and with a giant "POW!" brings the action to a climax and an end. The dead rise to life; there is a new initiating Seeker, and the action starts again.

As the play continues, I ponder this more complex Hunter vs. Hunted plot worked out by the players in the course of the action. The name of the game is Army. You reach for more specific names for Hunter and Hunted and you come up with but one name—soldiers—who at one and the same time are the hunter and the hunted, the killer and the killed. My immediate response to this violent action is how wonderful that there is this harmless, imaginary way to release aggressive human energy—no broken heads, no blood, nobody hurt. And the significance of this action? Ah, here I hit a snag. How simple if the name of the game were War; then the commentary is: "War = killing and being killed." But the boys have complicated the situation; the name of the game is Army and the significance of this violent action is: "Army = war = killing and being killed." True? In part, yes; but in whole? What about the situation where "Army = United Nations forces = peace keepers" or "Army = strength = national security?"

Whether this dramatic action of Army had taken place outdoors as it did or indoors (or out) in company with an artist/teacher, one would have to admire the tight mini-plot that evolved in the course of the action. There was indeed a straight dramatic line of action leading up to a surprise climax and ending; all those involved played with conviction, interacting with each other in a highly concentrated way. This was indeed an intensification of experience with an immediate replay.

Here is where the adult leader would make a difference in procedure. With an adult involved as a partner in the proceedings, there would be no immediate replay but a time of relaxation after the playing—a time for some feedback, evaluation, clarification. The focus of this clarification depends so much on the who and what and where and why of the individual group. With little children the clarification of the experience in which they have been involved might simply be individual children sharing the name they had given their upward rising movement. Sometimes involvement can be so great that it welcomes further expression in another art form and you have paint and brushes on hand so the children can now give color to what they just endowed with character and action. Living the same experience twice but in two different art forms may be a most satisfying kind of clarification.

Older and more experienced players may want to look at the experience in dramatic terms, becoming aware of the dramatic elements involved in the mini-plot. Here would be the place, it seems to me, to explore the significance of the action calmly, and with goodwill and humor recognize half-truths as in the case of the Army game. Sometimes it is broad generalizations that pop up in the playing that need exploring with much interest and curiosity by children and adult. Once in exploring the characters in Walt Whitman's poem "I Hear America Singing," one boy puzzled and distracted the others by staggering irrationally about, bumping into people, furniture, and walls. Afterward in taking a look at our efforts, we voiced our puzzlement and asked him who he was. He looked surprised as though it should be very obvious to all who he was. "I was a sailor."

"How were we to know you were a sailor?" I asked.

"Well," said he, "I was drunk."

"Oh?"

"Well, sailors drink."

"And when they drink," said I, "they drink to great excess and they stagger all over town bumping into people and—?"

The boy woke up quickly. "O.K.," he said, "I was *a* sailor, one, individual, and particular sailor who was drunk—O.K.?"

The whole group said, "O.K."

The observation of the boys using the old game of hide and seek as the spring board for their Army game and watching them work out a plot in the course of the game reminds me of a plot that was generated by a square block. In the circular playing area of the famous Penthouse Theatre on the University of Washington campus are some sturdy wooden blocks about eighteen inches square. There are also a few blocks shaped as though three of these squares had been welded together in an *L* shape. The blocks can be assembled into tables, chairs—whatever the players need. One of the boys in the sixth, seventh, and eighth grade drama group arrived early one afternoon, piled the blocks up like a pyramid, and sat himself down on the top block. To the first girl to arrive he announced, "I'm King of the Mountain."

She must have had a bad day at school for she put him down with a cold reply, "You're King of the *Squares*." He was taken aback, not by the words (he was bright enough to appreciate the play on the word) but by the tone of her voice. But he bounced back with, "If *I'm* King of the Squares, *you're* the biggest square in my kingdom."

This kind of "naming" can begin to hurt. As we are not out to hurt or to be hurt in drama, I moved in, not as leader or teacher but in a character appropriate to the dramatic situation. "*I'm* the greatest square," I boasted. "I can do the most square things in the squarest way." I began to walk square, adding robotlike music to accompany my movements. The girl laughed and joined me in a square dance—as did others arriving and tossing coats and books aside to get right into the exploration of squareness. At the suggestion of one player we embarked upon a square day—brushing our teeth, eating, etc., all in sharp horizontal and vertical movements.

Midway into the day's square chores I injected a key dramatic statement to open up possibilities for conflict, legitimate dramatic conflict. "Enter Trouble!" Before I had time to ask who or what the Trouble might be at least three players replied, "A *round* person." One of the three promptly stepped into character. "I'm King of the Rounds."

"What do you want here?" I asked.

"To be King of the Squares!" was the reply.

All looked to their Square King. "I'm going to *stay* King of the Squares!"

"On guard," cried the Round King.

A battle of swords ensued—in slow motion so no one would be hurt. All the Squares picked up the slow-motion style responding with cheers, groans, and moans as first one king and then the other seemed to be winning.

Then came a moment of stunned inaction and silence. The King of the Squares was "run through." The slow-motion camera stopped and then rolled again as slowly, oh so slowly, the Square King fell from his mountain, crag by crag—a drop and a pause, another drop and pause—until he lay at the bottom. From the top of the mountain the new King exclaimed, "Squares, bow down to your King, your new King." All bowed. Then with a twinkle in his eye (eye of the boy or eye of the King?) the King announced, "Edict Number One: All Squares must change their shapes; all Squares must become round; do you hear? *Round!*" They heard and they did become round, changing with much effort from a sharp-cornered rhythm to a circular movement as they completed the day's routine activities and retired to sleep, curled up in round balls.

We gathered in an intimate circle to exclaim over the plot created in action. We had joy in the *doing;* we have joy now in the experience of *clarifying* and *appreciating* what we have done. If we are like our Creator in our power to create, does it not follow that that likeness includes the power to appreciate our own creation; to rejoice when it is good? *And* to acknowledge when it delights us not and why? The group looked at the plot that had evolved. They were interested in the significance of the action, in the satirical style of the playing. They wanted to try another ending. What about having the "square-rounds" rebel, overthrow the King, and thus free all to be round, square, oblong, horizontal, vertical, whatever each wished to be? They exclaimed and laughed as they envisioned the climax and all the possible ways of moving as each person in the kingdom found his or her own form and rhythm and moved in that individual shape and way and yet was in harmony with all the others.

There have been times when a spontaneous experience of this nature leads into a long, continuous drama demanding research and a steady but willing commitment. "Who would dream that a simple poem like "Imaginings" wherein we are invited to create a world of our own desire behind a little red door would lead a group of teenagers into the mysteries of creation and the atom? But such was the result when one boy found behind the door a book containing the answers to all the mysteries of the world. What were those mysteries? For each his own mystery, from the awesomeness of space, the perplexity of love, the marvel of universes revolving within universes, to the moment when the Cause of all causes started things causing. The result was an exciting experience in dance and drama wherein the scientific and the biblical accounts of the Creation were found to contain no contradiction. In the process the leader as well as the youngsters had to "bone up" on atoms and elements and Genesis."[6]

The circular space of our famous theatre-in-the round on campus is by choice the locale of my university classes and children's groups in drama. I've always been fascinated by circles—

—The circular form of children's games.

—"Let's all form a circle," says the teacher.

—"I can draw you a picture of God," says the child and draws a circle. "See, no beginning and no end."

—No beginning and no end—all are equal in the circle.

—"Find your own place in space" and the child with outstretched arms turns himself about delineating in the air a circle.

—The expanding circle of communication—the child first communes with himself and then with one other and, in drama, only with those within the context of the dramatic situation. The little boy playing the Soldier in the Nativity story stands nose-to-nose with Joseph and whispers, "Go back to where you were born; you got to be counted." "I can't hear you," says an adult sitting close by. "I wasn't talking to *you*." replied the Soldier. When the players reach the age and the level of experience when they delight in communicating with those within the dramatic situation *and* with those who are looking on, there is no "don't turn your back to the audience" nonsense, for in our circular playhouse the audience is all about us. Our circle of communication has expanded naturally and painlessly to include the audience in the drama.

"Oh, I like our circular playing area," I say out loud. And as I speak I become aware of a little girl standing in front of me and the two dogs—a little girl with dark curly hair and blue eyes. Her name is Kathy and she wants to play with Sean and Deirdre. As she plays, her name, her looks, and her spirit remind me of another Kathy. At age seven she arrived for the afternoon session in creative dramatics with a book in hand and in one long unpunctuated sentence not only supplied the content but suggested the procedure for the next hour. "Here is a book of Mother Goose rhymes you pick out some *good* ones and tell them to us and then we'll choose which one we want to *do* with our partners and you ask us some *questions* and we'll make a little play all of us at the same time with our partners." In that moment I felt deeply my vital role in the creative and dramatic process these children had come to engage in for their own enjoyment and benefit. Kathy, by her action and words, was acknowledging that there is an art in guidance, in the selection of dramatic content, and in the procedure that is a partnership of the children and the adult involved.

In the sharing of the rhymes I came to "Peter, Peter Pumpkin Eater," told the rhyme and posed two questions: "Why couldn't Peter keep his wife? ("What was the problem?") *and* "Why, once inside the pumpkin shell, was she so content?" Kathy and her partner leaped up and begged for this rhyme. Their wish was granted, and they immediately went into action as had all the other twosomes. Kathy picked up a cardboard box that happened to be on the edge of the playing arena. She put it on her head and blindly thrashed about. "Peter," she cried, "there's no room in this house, no room, no room for anything—I'm leaving." And off she went, oddly enough with the "house" still on her head and mumbling, "No room, no room!" "Peter" quickly assembled some chairs in a big circle; then with a digging motion removed one chair from the circle and dug vigorously all about inside the sphere of chairs. That chore completed, he chased down his "wife"—led her into the pumpkin house; took the old "house" off her head, and stood back to see her reaction to the new one. Kathy as the wife moved about the round house, entranced and finally gave voice to her ecstasy, "Ahhhhhh space, space, space at last!"

How much space has been covered in our walk today, physical and otherwise. How much time, too; for the sun has dropped behind the hill, the boats are all nestled at their moorage, and we too will soon be on our way home. We rest for a moment on the rolling green slopes of the park across from the boat basin. The azaleas, the rhododendron bushes, a few late-blooming camellias and fruit trees fill the air with their vivid colors and their scents. All week long the gardeners have been tending them—pruning, weeding, loosening the dirt around their roots, spreading pungent sawdust over the flower beds to contain the weeds and enrich the soil.

It is the nature of these plants and trees to grow and develop. Each is programmed to grow according to an individual and unique design within. "The rose is a rose is a rose," never an azalea or a rhododendron. But there are helpers without, too—the rain, the sun, the gardeners.

Each child is blessed with an inner design of his own and endowed with innate powers to grow and to develop, to perceive, to think and to imagine, to create. In him, as "in the prophetic artist, genesis again will create the firmament and the day and night and the world of plants and animals, and into this creation he will enter and he will be its voice and its guardian

> and will give to everything its name
>   which is poetry
> and to everything its sound
>   which is music
> and to everything its color
>   which is painting
> and to everything its shape
>   which is architecture.
> and to everything its motion
>   which is dance
> and to everything its metamorphosis
>   which is sculpture."[7]

And I would add—

> and to everything its action
>   which is drama,

and

> becoming increasingly aware in the process of his own
>   unique self and his interrelationship with
>   all creatures and all creation.

This power is there, within all of us—to be recognized, appreciated, nurtured, turned to most joyous and meaningful account. But it too needs the helpers—the rain, the sun. The gardener's work and mine are much alike.

NOTES

1. Kenneth Grahame, *The Wind in the Willows* (New York: Charles Scribner's Sons, 1929), p. 3.
2. Max Eastman, *Enjoyment of Poetry* (New York: Charles Scribner's Sons, 1932), p. 29.
3. Frederick S. Wight, John I. H. Baur, Duncan Phillips, *Morris Graves* (Berkeley and Los Angeles: University of California Press, 1956), p. 1.
4. Rita Haaga, *Is the Wind Still in the Willows?* (Private Printing, 1969), frontispiece.
5. Joseph Campbell, *The Hero with a Thousand Faces* (New York: Pantheon Books, 1949).
6. Agnes Haaga, "Recommended Training for Creative Dramatics Leader," in *Children's Theatre and Creative Dramatics*, ed. Geraldine B. Siks and Hazel B. Dunnington (Seattle: University of Washington Press, 1961), p. 205.
7. Mary Caroline Richards, *Centering in Pottery, Poetry and the Person* (Middletown, Conn.: Wesleyan University Press, 1962, 1964), p. 94.

CO-RESPONDENTS:
THE CHILD AND DRAMA

ANN M. SHAW

Ann M. Shaw's professional experience began when she was appointed creative dramatics specialist in the Evanston Public School system. Subsequent teaching has included Western Michigan University, Hunter College, Teachers College of Columbia University, and Queens College, where she is presently a member of the faculty of the Department of Communication Arts and Sciences. Dr. Shaw has been a consultant in creative drama and communication development to National Follow Through Centers in Georgia, Michigan, and New York City, and has been a leading proponent of drama in the education of disadvantaged children. A contributor to many professional journals, Dr. Shaw is on the board of directors of the American Theatre Association. Her bachelor's and master's degrees were granted by Northwestern University and her doctorate by Teachers College. In this essay, Dr. Shaw discusses her view that the potential of improvisational drama in education derives from its relation to life and to drama as an art form.

What has the child to do with drama or drama to do with the child? As the framer of the question, I readily admit that the implicit assumption reflects my point of view: I believe that the child and drama are inextricably linked; and I advocate the deliberate, purposeful inclusion of improvisational drama in the education of children because I believe it can contribute to the process all of us are forever involved in, that of becoming and being human.[1]

If that sounds like a "declaration of faith by a true believer," it is. My intuitive sense that drama and the child are naturally related predates the time when, as a sophomore in college, I originated the idea of improvisational drama with children. My creation of what I supposed to be a new dramatic form was stimulated by my desire to combine my passion for theatre with my pleasure in children. It was based in the process that had developed from leading neighborhood children in "Let's pretend that . . .," a kind of play in which we made up and developed problems in spontaneous dialogue and action—our only audience the family cats and the town dogs who were sometimes drafted to be part of the drama.

My image of myself as a creative genius was shattered when my theatre professor told me Winifred Ward had been working with children in creative dramatics for twenty-five years before I "discovered" it, that she was not the only proponent of this form of drama, and that several universities offered courses or programs of study related to drama and the child. So ended my brief career as a pathfinder! Still, it was something of a relief to find that I was not alone in my interests and that there were those from whom I could learn.

Always a believer, I have become increasingly concerned with the need for the formulation of an intellectual basis for that belief. The following discussion certainly does not establish that base nor does it constitute a philosophy. It is intended to indicate my search and my current views. At best, it is only a partial answer to the opening question.

The kind of drama experience I shall be talking about is called by a variety of names: creative drama, improvisational drama, child drama, developmental drama, education drama, informal drama. I shall use the terms *creative drama* and *improvisational drama* interchangeably simply because these terms seem to be in most frequent use in the United States and are usually familiar elsewhere. Variously defined by exponents, it seems safe to say that an explication of any of these terms would include reference to a process in which a leader guides participants in exploring and expressing ideas through spontaneous enactment. Improvisational drama is appropriate to any age group: it is particularly suited to the interests, needs, and learning styles of children.

My view of creative drama and its potential in education is grounded in what I take to be its relation to life and to drama as an art form. I shall begin with a brief description of the capacities and processes which distinguish humans and are the base of the improvisational drama process and then suggest several aspects of drama which ought to be kept in mind as we advocate and practice improvisational drama with children. With this as background, I shall offer a definition of improvisational drama and discuss my views of several issues which are central to an attempt to examine the particular contribution improvisational drama might make to the growth and development of the child.

SYMBOLIC PROCESS AND DRAMA

To begin at the beginning, then, we humans are the animals who perceive and create the world symbolically. Susanne Langer contends that "symbolization is not the essential act of thought . . . but an act essential to thought, and prior to it."[2] She views the brain as not simply a great transmitter, but better likened to a great transformer:

> The fact that the human brain is constantly carrying on a process of symbolic transformation of the experiential data that comes to it causes it to be a veritable fountain of more or less spontaneous ideas. As all registered experience tends to terminate in action, it is only natural that a typically human function should require a typically human form of overt activity; and that is just what we find in the sheer expression of ideas.[3]

The symbol behavior of the young child often takes the form of overt imitation of experiences and behaving as if the child were the person, thing, or in the circumstance imagined. Thus the young child acts the mother feeding the baby, acts the jet plane streaking across the sky, acts the birthday party. Hans Furth, discussing Piaget's distinction between sensorimotor knowing and symbol behavior points out:

> When a three-year-old child plays "mother" or "going to bed," the child's gestures could not take place if the child's knowing of mother or sleeping were tied to physical actions. Sensorimotor knowing of sleeping, you will recall, is *actual* sleeping. When the child plays

sleeping we can conclude that his knowing is beyond the sensorimotor stage, that it is no longer entirely tied to the external action, and that therefore the child is capable of representing his knowing in *symbolic* sleeping.[4]

In the symbolic behaviors of children we find the earliest manifestation of the processes and form that characterize the art we call drama. Because drama was developed we have come to call this kind of play "dramatic play." It is important to remember that this form of symbolic behavior gave rise to drama and to avoid the tendency to speak of improvisational drama as if it were antecedent to life.

The child's interest in dramatic play is obvious. I once walked behind a little boy in Harlem thinking, for a few minutes, that he was either crippled or had a nervous disorder for he moved with a strange little hop and a jerking motion of his head. As I came closer to him I realized that he was intent on a pigeon that was going down the street in front of him and was imitating its walk. After a minute or so, the child turned into a horseback rider and a neighing, bucking horse which, after being brought under control by the cowboy, galloped down the street. Suddenly, the horse was pulled up short opposite two men who were tearing up the street with a jackhammer. The child's hands which held the imaginary reins grasped the handle of an imagined jackhammer, and with feet spread in imitation of the construction worker, the child impersonated the sound of the jackhammer and the actions of the man operating it.

In the first and last instances, the child was involved in imitating what he was actually seeing and hearing. As horse and rider he was involved in what Piaget would term "symbolic imitation," the figurative gestures making the remembered/imagined event present and expressing his knowing of it. Watching a child involved in dramatic play is a little like watching a one-man band. The child often acts several aspects of an event simultaneously as in horse and rider where he "Whoas!" for the cowboy, whinnies for the horse, pulls on the reins, slaps his own thigh for the flank of the horse. Still, this form of child's play is no more an exact copy of what has been or is being observed than theatre is an exact copy of life. Literal as the imitative play may seem, examination makes it clear that the child had transformed reality into selected, heightened gestures. As the child develops, these figurative gestures become increasingly selected, condensed, and sustained, as though the child somehow understood the principle of aesthetic economy expressed in the phrase "less is more." In a single well-chosen gesture as in a well-honed phrase, a host of meanings are projected.

It seems clear that conceptualizing the world outside one's skin requires the overt enactment of aspects of the "not me" world. This symbolic play is instrumental in developing the ability to discriminate self and other, breaking the bonds of intellectual egocentrism, becoming socialized. Cameron states:

> Social communication depends upon the development of an ability to take the role of other persons, to be able to reproduce their attitudes in one's own response, and so learn to react to one's own behavior as others are reacting to it.[5]

As the child's intelligence develops, the enactment process becomes internalized. However, the covert process of imagining—or imaging—self as other or in places and circumstances not physically present to one's senses continues throughout life and characterizes much of our thinking when we hypothesize our future, reconstruct the past, and plan for the present.

It may well be that the imaginative projection of self which requires overt enactment in the early years is the foundation of divergent thought and underlies all hypothetical thinking. Theodore Sarbin, a leading exponent of role theory, says:

> It is by now a truism that the learning of social roles—in fact the learning of any concept—is associated with the ability to treat an object or event *as if* it is something else. One has to adopt the *as if* set in order to group apparently diverse objects or events into a common concept.[6]

Behaving "as if" is the bedrock of symbolic behavior and fundamental to learning in any intellectual discipline. Drama is the field that is most specifically and literally derived from this human capacity. Enactment of our remembered and imagined experiences gives form to subjective feeling and celebrates our individual knowings. In this sense one might regard drama as the earliest or most fundamental manifestation of man's capacity to create aesthetic forms.

PERSPECTIVES ON DRAMA

Drama is an art. "All art," Susanne Langer states, "is the creation of perceptible forms expressive of human feeling."[7] Irwin Edman sees the function of art to be the intensification, clarification, and interpretation of experience. He says the arts "suggest the goal toward which all experience is moving; the outer world of things, the inner world of impulse mastered thoroughly by intelligence, so that whatever is done is itself delightful in the doing, delightful in the result."[8] Drama concerns itself with expressing selected perceptions of the human situation in the form of characters in conflict where the image of human action is presented in the form of human action.

One cannot be long involved in a community of persons who are concerned with drama without realizing that there are a number of views of what drama is. This has made it particularly difficult for advocates of creative drama to articulate our relation to the traditional positions and programs of departments of theatre in colleges and universities. Development of the area of improvisational drama has been further impeded by the fact that those of us who are primarily concerned with drama in relation to the child define drama differently. While agreement may not be reached, communication may be served by a brief examination of interpretations of the term.

Many employ the term drama in the sense of the first dictionary definition: "A composition in prose or verse portraying life or character by means of dialogue and action and designed for theatrical performance; a play."[9] For these people, drama is the literature of the theatre and may exist as drama solely on the printed page.

Others use drama and theatre as interchangeable terms referring to the purposeful presentation of selected aspects of human life or human skill, whether these aspects are real or illusionary. For example, people who hold this view would apply the terms drama or theatre to the circus act in which Gunter Gable-Williams actually rides a tiger who is actually riding on the back of an elephant as well as to the portrayal in dialogue and action of the murder of

Desdemona in Shakespeare's play *Othello*. The key here is the performance of actions designed to arrest attention and involve the spectator with little or no formal distinction made between those performances which constitute actual danger and those which present the illusion of danger.

Circus performers whose lives and livelihood rest on an appreciation of these differences are dismayed by the increasing tendency of audiences to respond to their skill and feats of physical daring as though the danger were pretense. Bernard Beckerman distinguishes between theatre and drama, advocating a view of theatre as an art of presentation and drama a special form of that art in which "one or more human beings isolated in time and space present themselves in imagined acts to another or others."[10] The distinguishing element in this definition being "imagined acts," that is, the presentation of illusions of reality.

In each of these preceding views of drama a staged presentation to others is implicit or explicit. A divergence of opinion is expressed by those who hold that drama need not necessarily involve either the presentation of plays to an audience nor a literary composition, that its essence lies in the purposeful selection of aspects of human experience which are heightened and expressed in dialogue and action by persons who behave as if they are the person living the experience which has been imagined. While many of us in improvisational drama do not totally reject the more traditional views, surely all of us, if we connect our work with drama at all, must agree that drama is not dependent upon a literary composition nor on the formal presentation of plays to an audience.

The broadest interpretation of drama is advanced by those who consider it to include any action which arrests attention and intensifies an experience, e.g., seeing or being involved in a car accident, and by those who insist that drama and life are synonymous as may be gathered from such statements as "Everything we do is really drama" or "Actually, all life is drama."

As you can see, interpretations of drama range from the literary work which may be considered the most objective form in that it has permanence and may be repeatedly examined, to an experience which is indistinguishable from life itself. Personally, I find the first view sterile in that it omits the dynamic of human presence; I find the last view puerile because it misses distinctions of function and form. Here are two statements on drama which reflect my thoughts on the subject and indicate the predilections I bring to the following discussion of improvisational drama. The first is a definition developed by the Attleboro Conference group.[11] It has provided us with a useful base for our discussions of issues related to drama, theatre, and the child.

> Drama is the metaphoric representation of concepts and persons in conflict in which each participant is required either to imaginatively project himself into an identity other than his own through enactment, or to empathize with others doing so. This action is structured, occurs in real time and space, and typically demands intellectual, physical, and emotional engagement and yields fresh insight into the human condition.[12]

The second is a statement by Kenneth Tynan that has been eloquently employed by Dorothy Heathcote in her discussions of drama and the child. It captures the emotive power of drama. In *Declaration*, Tynan avers: "Good drama for me is made up of the thoughts, the words and the gestures that are wrung from human beings, on their way to, or in, or emerging from, a state of desperation."[13]

IMPROVISATIONAL DRAMA: A POINT OF VIEW

The remainder of this essay is made up of personal assertions and thoughts on selected issues and topics pertaining to improvisational drama and the child. Each issue and topic deserves fuller treatment than I have been able to give it here but may be sufficient to indicate my present point of view.

Subject or Method?

The power of improvisational drama to inform the lives of children is generated by:

1. The fact that the process of improvisational drama is grounded in a form of symbolic transformation of experiential data (overt enactment of the "as if") which is essential to the

development of human intelligence and is a fundamental way by which the child makes meanings.

It is this which leads many to regard creative drama as a potent methodology rather than a subject and to advocate creative drama as a teaching approach to all aspects of the curriculum.

2. The nature and function of drama—the art which involves us in the creation and apprehension of metaphors expressive of the individual's response as he confronts life pressures, makes decisions, and deals with the consequences of chance and choice.

It is this which leads some to insist that creative drama is a subject which has legitimate claim to its own time and place in the school day.

Frankly, I consider improvisational drama to be richest in import for the child when it is defined and practiced in such a way that it includes both the process of making metaphors and the metaphor made. In conjunction with my colleagues Frank Harland and Anne Thurman, I have described creative drama as: the improvisational, non-exhibitional form of drama in which persons are led to imagine, enact, and reflect upon human experiences.

The potential of improvisational drama in the development of persons is best realized when we emphasize the process and the particular understandings with which drama is involved and is able to illuminate; when we purposefully involve children in the enactment of their individuated imaginings of the development and outcomes of those significant moments of personal and universal experience which *grip* our minds and hearts. To the extent that we do this we may fairly propose creative drama be considered the central humanistic study in the education of children. To the extent that we devote our energies and expertise to promoting improvisational drama as a panacea for personal development and the problems of educational institutions, we are profligate.

This assertion does not mean that I think improvisational drama is an ineffective methodology or ought never to be used as an approach to other curricular contents. I suspect that in the hands of a reasonably skilled leader, improvisational drama would nearly always be an effective way to capture attention and motivate interest, whatever the subject might be, because children associate it with the pleasure of play, it allows them to be actively doing something, it personalizes subject matter, and it can make abstract concepts concrete. While I question the advisability of a dramatistic approach to conceptual development in science and mathematics, except on a philosophical level, I think creative drama might well be incorporated in social studies, history, and literature. Even here, however, it is easy to founder on facts and forget the essential nature of dramatic experience. It is important to realize that while improvisational drama is developed in spontaneous dialogue and action, improvised speech and action, in itself, does not a drama make.

The point I wish to establish is this: Improvisational drama may well be an effective teaching methodology. But relegating improvisational drama to the role of "hired hand" to teach spelling, personal hygiene, how to answer the telephone or conduct yourself on a bus trip, etc., is an appalling waste of the power of drama to relate children to themselves and to others, to make vivid the actualities and potentialities of human existence.

Process and Potential Contribution

The goal of improvisational drama with children is not the development of a play for an audience, to train actors for the stage, to make required subjects palatable, nor to "keep kids off the street." As has so often been stated, the goal is the development of persons. Such a purpose places us on the side of the angels but leaves us in a similarly disembodied state unless we can be more specific about what and how creative drama might contribute to personal development. I have attempted to illustrate how the process central to improvisational drama involves the child in symbolic transformations which are instrumental to intellectual, emotional, and social development. I have argued that the understandings drama seeks to develop—that is, the meaning of personal plight and possibility, and the creation of aesthetic representations of life which making drama involves—are humanizing experiences.

To be more specific, it is necessary to look at what participation in the creative drama process requires the child to do. Throughout a creative drama session, children as individuals in a group situation are involved in: (1) recalling and using their knowledge and experience to enhance their understanding and communication of the known—and to make inferences about what is unknown and has not been experienced; (2) imagining themselves, someone else, or something else confronting problems; (3) relating to and interacting with others; (4) analyzing alternatives and making decisions; (5) exploring, developing, and expressing ideas and feelings through enactment; (6) evaluating the outcomes of their actions.

The interplay of these behaviors and the dynamics of group process may be clearer by example. Recently two of my students led a group of mentally handicapped eleven- and twelve-year-olds in improvisational drama. The children had said they wanted to make a play about "a really bad accident." Somehow a plane crash on a deserted island became the focus; the leaders and group worked for two sessions playing into being their images of danger, isolation, privation, survival, group dependency. By the third session they had managed to heal the injured, secure enough food to sustain life, agree to risk trying to reach civilization, and make a raft from parts of the plane.

The third session began with getting the raft stocked and into the water. A table replaced the previously imaginary raft, and the children and both leaders climbed aboard. "Are we ready? Is everyone here?" "Everyone's here." "Shove off!" were the replies. But Linda was not on the raft; one of the children discovered this fact and told Linda to get on the raft. She shook her head "No." They asked her to get on the raft. She refused. One leader said, "I wonder why Linda won't get on the raft?" The children posed the question to Linda. She declined to answer. One child reviewed the situation for her and reminded her of the reasons they had decided to leave the island. Linda remained silent. Persuasive appeals became highly personalized. "You can't stay here alone. You might get sick and couldn't get any food." "What if a snake bites you?" "You won't have anyone to talk to." "You won't have nobody to play with." Linda was not moved. One leader asked, "Well, what are *we* going to do?" and the children began to realize and respond to other dimensions of the dilemma—group responsibility to the majority and to Linda, individual's responsibility to the group and to Linda, one's responsibility to one's self. "I want to get back home." "So do I, but we can't go without her." "If Linda doesn't want to come with us, that's her problem." "But she'll die." "I guess we better stay." "Then we'll all die." "Everybody gotta die sometime." "Let's tie her up and make her come with us." "That's not fair." They turned back to Linda and faced her with their problem. A decision had to be reached. The tension was palpable. Reluctantly, Linda said, "I'm afraid. I might fall off and drowned!" This was a problem they could solve. "Here—you can sit right in the middle." "Man! I swim good. Don't worry!" "We'll hold onto you, Linda!" Cheers broke out as Linda climbed slowly onto the raft and, true to their word, they made space in the center of the raft and held her safe. Sighs of relief and sounds of celebration were audible as they "shoved off." The group was again united and could turn their attention to the voyage home.

Improvisational drama is no mindless or spiritless matter. Of course the profit for the child is dependent on the ways the leader employs the process and contents in relation to the particular group of children. With this reservation in mind, it is reasonable to state that improvisational drama promotes the development and integration of the child's cognitive abilities (his ability to think) with his subjective life (what he feels and intuits) with his affective growth (his internalization of attitudes and values) with his capacity to create.

On Leaders and Leading

It is generally acknowledged that the leader is indispensable to improvisational drama. Agreeing with this contention and in light of my concern that the potential of improvisational drama be realized in practice, I cannot ignore the subject of the leader. On the other hand, the subject is so important and complex as to deserve and require an essay in itself, a treatment it has received in a number of publications in the field. Here are a few of my thoughts on the subject of the leader and leading.

It is the leader's responsibility and function to take the children further in developing and expressing their ideas in dramatic form than they could have gone on their own. The principles of leading require perceiving and treating children not as objects to be acted upon but as persons who can and do think, feel, and create. One must subscribe to the view that the child's future is built on the present and that the child must be fully engaged in viewing, valuing, questioning, and questing now.

Of course the leader must know, respect, and like children. Equally important, the leader should know, respect, and like himself. One must know what makes drama and be able to use this knowledge in guiding the dramatic process. One must, also, understand the nature of the creative process; appreciating the importance of spontaneity and the consequent necessity to put ideas into action before the judge inside each of us says "It won't work. It's a worthless idea" and prevents one from exploring the potential of the unknown. Similarly, the leader must respect the function of reflection, evaluation, and revision in creative effort for refinement affirms our creative potential and is a main source of aesthetic pleasure.

In order for creative work to emerge, the leader must establish an environment, an atmosphere which fosters mutual respect and cooperative effort, where ideas are listened to and valued, where imagination is fired and fun is shared. If the dramatic process is to function fully, the leader must emphasize enactment for enactment is the method of inquiry and mode of expression which distinguishes improvisational drama. Basically, the leader helps the children to get at and develop their ideas by: selecting stimuli which focus attention, arouse imagination, and evoke a response; guiding the children in making decisions about dramatic content and in expressing their ideas in dramatic action; encouraging the group to analyze and evaluate their work.

So far as I know there is no one best way to begin work with children in creative drama. Successful beginnings seem to depend upon the leader's preferences, the abilities and needs of the children, and factors related to the situation in which one is working, such as space, time available, general atmosphere, etc. I do try to make certain that I begin with something which will grip the children's imaginations, will involve all of them simultaneously in enactment, and will result in their feeling success and pleasure.

People often ask me to evaluate the kinds of improvisational drama experiences that are recommended for children and to suggest how the experiences should be sequenced. There was a time I thought I knew what should be included and in what order, but experience has caused me to question my assumptions. Sense-awareness exercises, movement experiences, and theatre games are all valuable in developing concentration and self-confidence, stimulating creative responses, and establishing group rapport. On the other hand, beginning with story dramatization or creating dramas from a topic or problem can produce similar results. Whether these activities provide a necessary skills foundation for story dramatization or creating dramatic scenes as was once generally assumed is, I think, open to question. For the reasons presented earlier in this essay, I do think one's main emphasis should be on creating dramas rather than on exercises and theatre games.

For me, leading children in creative drama is always a demanding and fascinating experience. Sometimes it is a frustrating experience as well! As a leader one is constantly challenged to find a balance between subjective and objective involvement. Unless the leader can become honestly intrigued with what is happening, is excited by the play with possibilities, and cares about the outcome of the experience, the whole effort is dulled for the leader's concentration and vitality shape the child's response. Besides which, I am a firm believer in the leader's right to have fun too. However, unless one can simultaneously maintain one's objectivity, it is difficult to assess and deal with the needs and strengths of individual children, to guide the process sensitively and intelligently, and to resist the temptation to take over the drama. In this moment to moment process, knowing/sensing which decisions must be made by the children in order to give them ownership of the creative process and event, and which decisions the leader must make in order to involve all and deepen the experience is one of the great challenges of leading groups in improvisational drama.

In beginning this essay, I said that I regard the potential contribution improvisational drama might make to the life of the child to reside in its relation to life and to drama as an art form. I have suggested that the child's symbolic development is acquired through and manifested in processes which are the life source of drama. I contend that one of the basic ways we humans come to enlarge our knowledge of the world, to understand ourselves, to relate to others is by purposefully imagining ourselves acting and interacting in relation to circumstances which are not actually present. Improvisational drama has the great advantage of employing this discovery process, a process which is primary for the child; not alien but familiar, not painful but preferred. The instinct to play, the mimetic impulse, the necessity to symbolize, and the pleasure we derive from expressing our knowings in symbolic enactment are the life source of drama, the art form which creates dynamic metaphors of the human situation illuminated through human action. As I see it, improvisational drama should be viewed and practiced as a form of drama in which children play their images of life into being; as an experience which requires children to seriously engage in thinking, feeling, relating to others; in imaging, creating, and communicating credible representations of human actuality; in valuing life and appreciating the singularity and universality of human experience.

There is much to be studied and known before we can lay claim to the potential outcomes I have posited or fully answer my opening question, What has the child to do with drama or drama to do with the child? As I continue in my efforts to contribute to the development of a conceptual base for improvisational drama with children, I am concerned with involving children at the deepest level their intellectual and emotional capabilities allow in exploring and expressing their "knowings" of life and in envisioning and creating alternative life situations.

NOTES

1. Philip Phenix uses the phrase "being and becoming human" in his book, *Man and His Becoming* (New Brunswick, N.J.: Rutgers University Press, 1964). I have reordered the phrase to emphasize the idea of growth.
2. Susanne K. Langer, *Philosophy in a New Key* (New York: Mentor Books, 1951), p. 45.
3. Ibid., p. 47.
4. Hans G. Furth, *Piaget for Teachers* (Englewood Cliffs, N.J.: Prentice-Hall, 1970), p. 28.
5. N. Cameron, "Experimental Analysis of Schizophrenic Thinking," in *Language and Thought in Schizophrenia*, ed. J. S. Kasanin (Berkeley, Calif.: Univ. of California Press, 1954), p. 60.
6. Theodore R. Sarbin, "Role Enactment," in *Role Theory: Concepts and Processes*, ed. Bruce J. Biddle and Edwin J. Thomas (New York: John Wiley & Sons, 1966), p. 199.
7. Susanne K. Langer, *Problems of Art* (New York: Charles Scribner's Sons, 1957), p. 80.
8. Irwin Edman, *Arts and the Man* (New York: W. W. Norton, 1939) p. 34–35.

9. *Webster's New International Dictionary* (2nd ed.; Springfield, Mass.: G. & C. Merriam, 1934).

10. Bernard Beckerman, *Dynamics of Drama* (New York: Alfred A. Knopf, 1970), p. 20.

11. The Attleboro Conferences were organized by Ann Haggerty, Bart O'Connor, Barbara Sandberg, and Ann Shaw to provide specialists in creative drama and/or theatre for children a forum for an exchange of views on issues central to the field.

12. Attleboro Conference, III, 26 October 1973.

13. Dorothy Heathcote, "Improvisation," *English in Education*, 1, no. 3 (1969–70): 27.

DRAMA AS EDUCATION

DOROTHY HEATHCOTE

Considered one of England's outstanding educators, Dorothy Heathcote is currently professor of drama at the University of Newcastle upon Tyne. Her course in Drama in Education was the first of its kind to be introduced into the curriculum for British teachers. Students come from all over the world to study with her, and her teaching assignments have taken her to the United States and Canada. Mrs. Heathcote left school at the age of fourteen to work as a weaver in a wool mill. At nineteen she won a scholarship to Northern Theatre School and was tutored by Rudolph Laban, J. B. Priestly, and London stage designer Mollie McArthur. She has presented work in action over the BBC and her recent films, Three Looms Waiting *and* Dorothy Heathcote Talks to Teachers, I *and* II, *have been shown throughout the United States. Her successful use of drama with the disadvantaged has attracted much attention. In this essay Mrs. Heathcote explains her philosophy of education that accords drama a core place in the school curriculum. She sees drama as practice for living, in which the areas of feeling and social relationships are of major concern.*

It seems sensible to me that, if there is a way of making the world simpler and more understandable to children, why not use it? Dramatizing makes it possible to isolate an event or to compare one event with another, to look at events that have happened to other people in other places and times perhaps, or to look at one's own experience after the event, within the safety of knowing that just at this moment it is not really happening. We can, however, *feel* that it is happening because drama uses the same rules we find in life. People exist in their environment, living a moment at a time and taking those decisions which seem reasonable in the light of their present knowledge about the current state of affairs. The difference is that in life we have many other things to consider at the same time and often cannot revise a decision taken, except in the long term. So drama can be a kind of playing at or practice of living, tuning up those areas of feeling-capacity and expression-capacity as well as social-capacity.

Poets do this in their poetry, painters in their painting, writers in their books, and film-makers in their films. All these art forms, however, require technical understanding and often elaborate equipment; drama requires only a body, breathing, thinking, and feeling. We begin this practice of playing at an early age because we realize that identifying with others is a human act of which we are capable. It is in the nature of drama that we start exactly where we ourselves are, with our own "prejudiced" views. The diagnostic potential in drama is, for teachers, therefore, very valuable. I believe that classes have the same privilege as other artists in ordering and reordering their worlds, as they gain new information and experiences.

So for drama with our classes we must select an incident for review (not an easy thing, this isolating of key incidents), and this incident has then to be clothed with such elements as place, period, persons present at the relevant time, season of the year, or any other "fixing" device. This fixing is really the work of the class and reflects their prejudiced view. Some fixes need little assistance; others require much more elaborate preparation; but it must feel real to the players, not to some future audience. Broadly speaking, I use a very simple guide if I am in any doubt. There seem to be three ways of structuring the situation (there are probably a hundred but I have managed to isolate these three): simulation, analogy, and role.

If you choose simulation as a device, you often need to bolster reality by facts, being, and feeling. Much drama in school works on the simulation level, but it is hard for teachers to keep it believable when working with an uncommitted class. If you choose to begin with analogy, emotion can usually be the fixing device. This is the easiest approach, as it is in the true theatre tradition, which is about the spaces between people being filled with meaningful rela-tionships. All too often children never get to that kind of experience in their drama. The third way of starting is with a person who is already fixed, for example, a derelict or a policeman or a rent man, who demands (because of his own strongly fixed role) an immediate emotional response. I often work in role at first because it fixes emotional reaction. I find much prejudice against this way of working, though I maintain it is the equivalent of good paint or clay and proper tools. The proper tools of drama are emotional reaction and the state of being trapped, a state from which one can escape only by working through the situation.

Now we have a starting point. Next we need to know what this starting point is likely to teach our classes because of what it will demand of them. This is the difference between the theatre and classroom teaching. The theatre makes us think, wonder, and identify through our watching position (I know that some theatre also allows us, or pressures us, to participate more actively); the drama of classrooms allows us to employ our own views while experiencing the nature of the tensions so that, in the act of making things happen, we think, wonder, communicate, and face up to the results of our decisions and actions. The most important part seems to me to be the chance to build up the power to reflect on our actions. Without this reflection process, the full use of the work is never exploited. This process demands the building of a storehouse of images and the language with which to reflect.

Some work started in classes serves the short term as, for example, when I recently introduced a class of infant children to the Goddess Pele (the guardian of volcanos in Hawaiian literature). I wanted to make a double thrust into the area of these manifestations because I considered it more efficient to learn, on the one hand, that modern man has a scientific explanation for events, but that in ancient times man had other explanations for the eruptions. I introduced the two kinds of truth. Both kinds seem of equal importance to me, depending on which point of view stretches a class the most at the time. Both certainly deserve recognition. A much longer project, which altered radically the behavior of a class of eleven-year-olds, was the founding of a city-state in which only eleven-year-olds could live. The city-state made laws, developed a system of education (school every other year!), dealt with sickness, negotiated with adults, arranged for food, and handled finance. In the Goddess Pele experience the class stayed as it was and entertained her presence. She could come and go as required. In the city-state, however, though the children were themselves, they began to live according to other rules and to take on different burdens of responsibility.

All drama, regardless of the material, brings to the teacher an opportunity to draw on past relevant experience and put it into use; language, both verbal and nonverbal, is then needed for communication. The qualities of sympathy and feeling are demanded as well as aggression and its results. This is not always comfortable for the teacher, for the expression of the class sometimes threatens her. But if we grant that it is the artist's right to begin from where he is with his view of an idea, then we must also grant that right to our classes when they create. A second opportunity, of course, is *our* right to insist on the other side of the coin—that of reflecting on the results of our view of the event. In such arts as pottery and painting this is easy; it requires only the hands to stop and the eye to view. It is more difficult in drama because the means of expression is the same as the means of looking, namely, the person himself. Art cannot exist outside the person and take on its own life. It becomes a memory of the event.

I am much criticized for "stopping to consider," especially when "it's going nicely, thank you," but it is for this very reason that I *can* stop. I know that the event can be rediscovered. Reflection about work is one of the best ways I know to elicit trust, for I can stop work in order to show enthusiasm, to challenge, to demand more, and to show my own involvement as well as my non-interest in value judgments. The outsides of the work matter to me only when they begin to matter to the class; of course, some classes like to feel that they are doing a "proper play" from the start. I want them to feel this, too, in that case, until they find themselves more interested in the ideas than in the shape. The shape is just as interesting; but not everything can be done at once, and I prefer to leave that aspect until later. I am primarily in the teaching business, not the play-making business, even when I am involved in making plays. I am engaged first of all in helping children to think, talk, relate to one another, to communicate. I am interested primarily in helping classes widen their areas of reference and modify their ability to relate to people, though good theatre can come out of this process, too. But first I want good people to come out of it. One difficulty of drama is that often the behavior of a class threatens us because it seems inapplicable to the circumstances we are interested in exploring. Purple trees in paintings do not threaten us as much, for they stay on the paper and are obviously the personal viewpoint of the artist; drama, on the other hand, threatens the very spaces we occupy, and the attitudes of others threaten the very air we breathe.

The procedures are as follows:

1. We make the world smaller by the isolation of an area of concern.

2. We involve groups of people who, in turn, are involved in group decision taking. Groups can work in fantasy or life situations (truth). These are the same; only the rules are different. But whichever they choose, they must realize that in drama there must always be the acceptance of the "one big lie." This is an agreement to pretend that we are in the situation we have chosen. The truths are the truths of how we see the situation, our own behavior, our own language and expression, our own significant actions and the truths we find to be important to us in the situation. I have discovered that all people understand the idea of the one big lie. It is like giving well-mixed paints or good wedged clay to classes, and it eliminates the silliness that often characterizes children's work at first. One reason for self-consciousness is, of course, that the person of the child is used as the material; another, that the rules are hard to perceive. This is unlike the rules of paint and clay, where the clay falls apart and the paint runs off the paper if the mix is not right. The mix in drama is just as fundamental to the success of the work as it is for the visual arts.

3. We establish certain ground rules:

(a) First the situation must be defined. There must be a beginning that each person can recognize as true to the situation. In games the rules stand at all times when the game is played, and the players learn them once and for all. Drama rules may appear to change because the actual start must use the present capacity of the class to relate to each other. In drama the space relationship is the social health of the class, plus the nature of the game it is about on each occasion. This demands very special skills to be mastered by the teacher; books alone cannot teach them, though as we learn how to isolate factors, it will become possible to teach teachers more rapidly than we do at present.

(b) Group views must be put to use so that the drama starts where the groups are (simply because you cannot start from where you aren't). This means that the leader/instigator must find a common starting point. If the common starting point is negative, then the negative must be used—positively, of course. This is why, when I am asked what I teach, I can only give the answer, "I teach children." What else is there to teach at first, whatever the subject area? It seems to me that we all teach children until such time as the classes are committed to an interest in the particular discipline and a desire to learn the skills of that discipline. To commit classes, however, requires strategies. Far too little time is spent in training for strategies or for holding staff conferences regarding those usable strategies that successful teachers stumble upon. Indeed, there should be no need to stumble upon strategies. The study of these should be a constant in-service part of running a school.

(c) There must be some instigation to review progress. Progress can easily be seen in the visual arts, but drama often disguises progress or shows it falsely; for example, if the action moves quickly, the result can be mistaken for quality. A slower approach can suggest lack of progress. I usually take on this responsibility at first because it is difficult for a member of a group to get the ear of the class. Once the social health of a class has improved, however, it is easy for others to assume responsibility and they should be encouraged to take it.

The first leaders are often those who have language confidence, though not necessarily the most ability. Later the demand shifts from talk to action, from the repetition of facts to the understanding of feelings, by the demand for skills of different kinds (often not socially acceptable, such as picking locks or brazening out a stand against authority).

I am much criticized for instigating early review. I do it because one thing that must happen in learning is the development of a sense of commitment to work. I will not guarantee that classes work; what I will guarantee is that I will always keep the work interesting. Another advantage in early review is that it prevents rot from setting in, without its looking as if one had stopped for that reason. So review can be a "failure saver" as well as a "slower down into experience." Reviewing, to me, is a strategy.

(d) Strategies must change according to the class and the drama. Because I often work in role at first, there is an assumption that that is the way I shall continue to work. In an organically changing situation such as teaching, one is constantly seeking to make the first strategies redundant, while seeking to serve the class in other ways. I am weary of explaining to my profession that I do not do the same things every time; I start where the class can start and from then on, as we become more understanding of each other, I try to build a working relationship, in which we can take more liberties with feelings, make more demands upon each other and move more as a team.

A class with poor social health requires a more delicate strategy than one in better health, where there can be some self-help. So strategies are of two kinds: those that stimulate the class to working and those that further the action in the drama. Progression lies in the growing ability of the class to accept the discipline of the drama form and to put the work before personal interest. Concern for each member of the group, ability to take more thoughtful decisions, the courage to risk making and rejecting suggestions—all these are progressions.

There are also the art-form progressions. These are closely related to the above, of course, but there are the extra dimensions of awareness of the overview: the avoidance of anachronisms, the checking of facts, the groping with unfamiliar skills and pursuing them past weariness, the never giving up until it feels right. In other words, it is conceding that sometimes the work matters more than the individual.

There is also the confidence of making the form work for you, revealing how those rules, which seem so limiting to the inept player, help to release the brilliant player. When a class can take liberties out of knowledge rather than out of ignorance, we can rejoice. This is rarely achieved in drama because much of the time students never really understand the rules.

(e) The work must go slowly enough to give a class an

experience. This is very difficult with classes of poor social health because they do not want to go slowly. Another reason for strategy! I never object to any ideas the class wishes to work on, but I do interfere with the pace. I cannot say that this is right, but I believe pace an important aspect of work and I do much to ensure that it contributes to the best experience. This is an area that a class cannot manage for itself.

(f) Tension of some kind must be present in the drama. Teachers rarely understand how to provide it. The simple factor in making tension work is that something must be left to chance but not more than one thing at a time. So long as there is that one factor and no one in the room knows precisely when that thing will occur (though everything has been set up so that it *must* occur), we have tension.

Subtle tensions are useless in a class that will only respond to cruder ones. An example of such a tension might be waiting in the dark for an intruder to enter a room. Or a less crude one, demanding more patience while awaiting one's turn to be interrogated, knowing that one of the group will be found guilty. The pressure must come from within the situation, not from the teacher/role insisting that it be done right.

Every conceivable situation can provide the tension to suit any type of class. I remember a group of delinquent children (fourteen-year-olds) who moved very quickly through a series of such tensions, each one making the group work harder than the preceding because each one demanded more of them while allowing them satisfaction. The first was a mugging; the second a verbal threat to a lady of wealth to blackmail her son; the third a painful forging of a document that would fool the guards; the fourth a telephone call made under the nose of the police, warning a friend of a police raid. Finally, the wait outside a temple to find out whose baby—yes, baby (and they themselves were the mothers)— would be chosen to be sacrificed in a prayer for rain. They also did the ritual mourning.

One feature of using tension in teaching is the opportunity it offers for using the same situation while it apparently changes for the class. An example of this was seen with a group of retarded children working on the theme of *Macbeth* (not, of course, the text, for they could not read):

Tension 1: Aiding the King safely through a forest in which dwelt a wild, often hunted, but never captured boar of great strength and size.

Tension 2: Finding that the lair of the boar was occupied and needing to be sufficiently silent while in that area.

Tension 3: Finding that the boar was loose and might attack at any moment.

Tension 4: Finding that the old guide, who would have been able to predict the boar's reaction, had fallen sick and could not help them.

Tension 5: Realizing that darkness was falling and they were lost in the forest.

This class explored fear and responsibility each time, while apparently changing their play. Each time they carried over more of the factors involved in looking after kings. They also "grew" a vocabulary in order to discuss the subject of fear. This came about because of "teacher interference." Before the teacher can interfere, however, the class must understand or make a decision as to which factor it will reinforce and why, while apparently changing the tension. I chose the problem of having to keep the King safe because I believed it helped the class to avoid using their own instinctive aggressive behavior, which would have been to kill the boar and thus rid themselves of the situation quickly. If a solution comes too easily, there is no opportunity for a class to be stretched.

(g) Feelings and thoughts that exist inside persons have to be made explicit to the group so that it can see and respond to the expression in the group. In drama this expression takes place through what can be seen to happen, what can be heard to happen, and what can be felt to happen.

The elements of darkness and light, stillness and movement, sound and silence are held in a constantly changing expression of life. In drama these must be in use from the very start and I personally try from the beginning to introduce classes to the use of them so that they begin to be selective about the way they will make their statements, though I do not necessarily discuss them in any technical way. I might say, "How will we first know that a monster has been here while we were away?" From the answers I receive I move the class to active decisions, which can be seen to employ these elements.

It is the use in common of these elements that make classroom drama and theatre kin. In theatre they are used for their effect on other people whereas in teaching they are used to make the impact on the very persons who create the work. Drama is about filling the spaces between people with meaningful experiences. This means that emotion is at the heart of drama experience but it is tempered with thought and planning. The first is experienced through the tension and the elements; the second, through the reviewing process. Out of these we build reflective processes, which in the end are what we are trying to develop in all our teaching. Without the development of the power of reflection, what have we? It is reflection that permits the storing of knowledge, the recalling of power of feeling, and memory of past feelings.

All too often we phase out emotion in our classroom work as if it were unimportant. (Certainly emotion is harder to deal with than thinking because children do not expect to use their emotions in school.) If we take the emotion out of drama, there is only the burden left. I recently heard of a group of "Roman soldier juniors," who were expected to attack a British fort in a "noisy way but without making a noise." I do not blame the teacher, who was trying to avoid disturbing the class next door. I do not blame the children, who mouthed all the words they would have spoken, had they been permitted. They were neither fish, flesh, nor fowl as they tried to do a noisy thing quietly, while trying to be the efficient fighting machine they understood the Roman soldiers to have been. They had to do all the external things while being denied the internal experience they needed in order to find their truth. If they could have made a silent attack, out of the necessity of a silent approach, they might have managed it.

I blame only the training of the young teacher, which led him to think that what he was doing was drama.

Please note that I am not quarreling with the fact that the children could make no noise—only that they were expected to do and believe in noisy things while keeping silence. If they had decided to try to attack in silence, then their movements could have been a real experience of battle. Likewise, if they had been allowed to assume a bargaining position, which would have demanded a careful choice of words, they might have experienced the significance of the spoken language while facing an enemy who misunderstood the words and the promises.

I believe that the child and the actor have to follow the same rules. It is not possible to simplify these rules; it is only possible to simplify the demands we make. Some potters make clay work harder for themselves than others do; some painters do the same with paint; some actors say more with fewer gestures; and some musicians get more out of fewer notes. The processes are the same for the great and the mediocre, but the expressive use that is made of these processes is the varying factor. Surely we owe our classes the real material that our artists have to use. Drama is possibly more liable to criticism than other art forms because the rules exist in use, by people in action, and they never exist outside that reference except in the memory.

The elements of darkness/light, stillness/movement, and silence/sound offer an incredible range of expression. They embrace all clothing worn, all places in which persons find themselves, all words said, all groups formed, all sounds made, all gestures employed; and the teacher must master the flexibility of the elements so as to make them available at will to their classes.

The method of teaching classes is usually via the theatre exercise. But exercises have a built-in, self-destroying force, particularly when used with uncommitted classes. They have a drive toward ending themselves. True drama for discovery is not about ends; it is about journeys and not knowing how the journeys may end. Once there is real commitment to this way of learning, there is a reason for studying the factors we employ in order to isolate and practice techniques.

But let us give a few examples before we start on the means by which ideas are communicated. We have crippled our children beyond the breaking point by insisting on rewardless labor before they are given the opportunity to experience any reality. Learning about being a person comes from trying out, not by practicing for it. I am not saying there is no value in exercise skills. I am saying that we must have some motivation for doing a thing before we start imposing our theories. When drama is exercise-driven, the natural discoveries that come from emotional involvement cannot arise. Pace, pitch, tempo are discovered in the heat of the moment. Exercises exist to take emotion out, so that coolness and repetition can exist. I know you can devise exercises for emotion, but why should you with children who have the real thing so readily available just waiting to be tapped?

Recently I was working with a class of nine-year-olds who were just becoming interested in the Luddite rebellion, which took place when the first spinning frames were destroyed by the incensed weavers in 1812. The children set up a frame in "heat." That is, they knew nothing about such frames but in confrontation with an owner of a mill, who was impatient to see the frame working, they not only built it slowly from hints given in role but they also developed a sense of responsibility as skilled workers, brave men who dared build such things in troubled times. They developed at the same time a distinct feeling of the rhythm of building together. Exercises do not work so efficiently. Their value lies in the way they help to isolate a factor and let special attention be paid to it. I say that exercises are for those who have already tasted the riches of a tough and real experience. Far too many classes never get to the reality of their art because of time spent on exercises.

Drama, then, teaches in the following way. Taking a moment in time, it uses the experiences of the participants, forcing them to confront their own actions and decisions and to go forward to a believable outcome in which they can gain satisfaction. This approach brings classes into those areas that in the main are avoided in school: emotional control, understanding of the place and importance of emotion, and language with which to express emotion. We expect good fathers, husbands, honest citizens, fine sensitive friends, tolerant and understanding neighbors to emerge from the classes we teach but we have done very little to prepare them for these roles.

I should not criticize our educational system so much, if we did not profess to be doing more than making children literate. We talk of career classes, for example, and then we proceed to ignore the relevant areas of responsibility that are emotionally based, except for a little advice in the form of cool discussion. We talk about religious education in our English schools and behave with arrogance toward our children. These and many other subject areas demand a steady reaction of emotional input for thorough exploration but we often present our material in such a way that emotional material has to be treated without emotional response.

Though drama is probably discussed more today in terms of teaching and learning than it has been in the past, it is far from being fully exploited in our schools. It continues to limp along, never quite able to show its potential because the system, as it stands, preserves jealously the "one class, one teacher" syndrome, the "everybody has to be the same age in the group" syndrome, the "teacher has the secrets" syndrome, the "we can't have more than one person making decisions" syndrome, the "let's keep everything in short periods" syndrome, and above all, the "let's not have too many children surprising the teacher" syndrome. I know, of course, that pockets of superhuman experiment do exist, and I do not want to denigrate these in any way. But the basic problems remain and give rise to the apathy and the social ill health in our classes.

PROCEDURES AND PRACTICE

First, let us examine a simple table. I think that the best learning takes place when there is a balance between the two extremes, but I present them here as opposite sides of the same coin. When I am actually teaching, I am happiest in an area that lies midway between the two methods as, for example, in the Goddess Pele work mentioned earlier, where the truths of scientific explanation and myth were taught simultaneously.

Informal Approach (often referred to as left handed):
    emphasis on applying experience in the act of learning
    using the emotions to aid understanding
    being involved in the teaching

being able to challenge the teaching
taking decisions to modify the pattern of the plan

Formal Approach (often referred to as right handed):
emphasis on learning from others' information
learning through the mind
convergent learning
objective learning
strong reliance on the proven

It will be readily seen that these two methods need not be in conflict; some kind of happy medium can be found in order to give the teacher security. Indeed, it is not factual information and emotion that oppose one another; it is the approach to the class and the strategies employed. The left hand relies heavily upon mutual appreciation and mutual decision making between teacher and class. Drama is not an efficient means for straight factual teaching, but it provides a rich ground for making facts understood in action. When building a spinning frame, for example, if you are not certain of the details and are asked if all the cogs run smoothly, you either ask questions about its construction or someone tells you (there is always more information in the group than emerges at first), or you do the thing that feels right. It may elicit the question, "What about those under the shafting?"

And so it goes on until looking at a plan seems a good idea; then you may either gather around the board and draw what you think you have been building or look at a picture of a real frame. The main thing, of course, is that when you do look at a spinning frame, the illustrations must not only be of good quality but may be more complex than they might otherwise have been. The class studying the Goddess Pele worked simultaneously in the areas of correct vocabulary, technical detail, ancient beliefs, the power of Pele as seen in her person, peril to people, and the formation of new lands. In a formal approach the class would have dealt with these elements one at a time, gradually building up a factual picture. With Pele to challenge and be challenged by them, to offer her explanation in reply to theirs, the students absorbed many layers of feeling and information at once. Also, it was possible to test the understanding straight away, for many diagnostic techniques can be used during the action to test the grasp of concept and factual understanding.

The basis of all my class contacts seems to depend more and more upon a few relatively simple techniques. I plan the areas where the class will make the decisions. I also plan strategies that I shall use to get the class committed to work. This planning is always done from an inside experience approach rather than from an external tasks approach. I try to know the impact of every verbal statement I make as I make it. I select all signals with extreme care and sensitivity, even when working with my back to the wall with what I call "dragon's teeth" classes. I spend much time examining the uses of questions and the types of questions asked. I recognize a dud question and set about recovering from it immediately. One dud may take ten or more other good questions to make a recovery. I decide when and why I shall leave role and become interrogator-leader. People assume that because I use role early, I mean to go on with it. I use role in order to teach the class that emotion is the heart of drama. Talking about emotion is no substitute for feeling it. This is the advantage of being in role but, of course, it is a complicated tool and takes some patience to learn how to use it. I have not yet met a teacher who cannot use it and who does not learn more about the use of drama in her teaching as a result of its use.

I seek rather than plant information. And I never mix plans. In other words, I decide very clearly what the lesson should achieve. It may be an unplanned session when I deliberately decide to test the class in order to find out where it is; all subsequent sessions can be based on what I learn in the beginning. Or it may be a session especially designed to introduce some aspect of learning, such as the Pele work discussed earlier. It may be very specific, such as the work done to readjust opinion or to bolster confidence in order to answer questions in examination. Or it may be to help study how the text comes alive on the stage.

Drama is so very flexible because it places decisions in the hands of the classes; the teacher acts as midwife. I select all the best artifacts, literature, and reference books I can find (adult materials for the most part, as I find them superior). I do not withhold information if I can find a way to impart it. I believe far too much information is withheld from classes, or children feel that it is being withheld, which has the same effect.

I work slowly in the beginning. I do not move forward until the class is committed to the work. This does not mean that I stand still; it means that I use many strategies to keep in the same place while apparently moving forward. The social health of the class dictates this commitment, and it is my belief that all the real difficulties of drama come from social ill health. Therefore, if we want to train teachers to make use of drama, we must begin by training in strategies that develop social health as the teaching progresses. This strategy is also geared to success and approval. I work to stretch classes. I expect students to work very hard, and I show that I work hard too. I never withdraw help nor do I ever praise falsely. I give positive comment at all times, and when I want to urge further effort, I often quote my own experiences (always true but often edited to make the strongest impact and timed so as to shock the class into new awareness).

I do not expect classes to like drama automatically. I guarantee that I will do nothing to make them feel foolish, but neither will I allow them to get off the hook. I use the rules from the beginning and especially make the point that all signals, whether positive or negative, affect the work. Finally, I stress that at the present time with the emphasis upon the children's expectations, the teacher will have to initiate, guide, ask for proof of work, time the work, and be the guide and mentor throughout. With some initiative developing in the fifth and sixth forms, we are bound to find this way of working difficult and slow. Children have not been trained to trust their own ideas or their own ways of approaching work. Therefore, for the time being, we not only have to carry the burden of working against the stream but that of creating classes who will revel in taking decisions, in using emotion productively, and in exercising their skills. Finally, we must stand up against the criticism of our colleagues.

CURRICULUM DRAMATICS

ELIZABETH FLORY KELLY

Elizabeth Flory Kelly's academic degrees were granted by Smith College and Western Reserve University; additional postgraduate work was done at New York and Northwestern Universities. Her theatre experience began in childhood at the Cleveland Play House, of which her parents were among the founders. Mrs. Kelly, now a member of the board of trustees, has been an active force in furthering the relationship between this outstanding community theatre and the teachers of the Cleveland metropolitan area. Twice recipient of a Martha Holden Jennings Grant, she has pursued innovative and current practices in educational theatre both in this country and abroad. For the past twenty years she has been developing her techniques in curriculum dramatics while teaching in several independent schools in Cleveland. Her recent studies have included work with Dorothy Heathcote, from whom she has incorporated some techniques for depth learning through the medium of drama. Mrs. Kelly's present position in Cleveland includes establishment of a series of teacher-drama workshops with an enrollment of 700 teachers from 62 school districts at which these teaching techniques are emphasized.

Curriculum dramatics cannot be understood properly until we rethink the key objectives of education. Should the *basic* emphasis be placed on the learning of skills or on coping with the myriad human relationships of life? How many teacher-training courses clearly indicate the multiple, simultaneous levels of instruction, with the proper priority given to each? Could a basic problem in American education lie in the neglect of the importance of *affective* learning and an overemphasis on cognitive skills? As Harold Taylor has aptly written, thinking is an activity of the whole organism "which begins in the senses . . . and involves the emotions."[1]

A junior high school English teacher learns that her curriculum will consist of teaching "clauses, verbals, and styles of writing." When she asks if that is all, she hears, "Isn't that enough? Teaching those things *well* should certainly be sufficient." The key word is "well." What do we mean by teaching "well"? Does it include motivating students? Yet how do we motivate except by making subject skills relevant? What is the relevant area of common experience where a teacher and her "unskilled" students can communicate? Doesn't this lie in common humanness? This universal human thread integrates all skills and helps avoid the fragmentation of learning which occurs so frequently when skills are taught in isolated compartments.

We are neglecting to notice that the *point of entrance*, the *magic button*, which motivates learning lies in this human level with its interplay of people relationships. Some artists and educators are beginning to realize that, because drama is the study of human interrelationships, it can, when properly focused, be a method of teaching that not only motivates but also accelerates learning. Junius Eddy, formerly with the Ford Foundation, wrote, "The arts as processes need to be examined carefully for their application to teaching situations . . . with emphasis on affective as well as cognitive goals."[2]

Curriculum dramatics is a continually evolving, unabashedly eclectic method of teaching. Any dramatic means that motivates, accelerates, and deepens the quality of learning should be utilized. Frequently two or three learning objectives can be accomplished simultaneously through dramatic techniques; i.e., the class can experience an integrating "group dynamics" session and simultaneously "role playing" historical characters of the French Revolution. Thus the drama techniques used frequently for sociological or psychological objectives can be refocused for effective subject-oriented learning. Curriculum dramatics entails the use of drama techniques to deepen and enhance education by using affective skills of participation and empathy. It allows students the experience of testing simulated, alternative life choices. The teacher guides the students in their identification with and examination of selected pressure points of human conflict. It is with her techniques for giving the moments of reflection and insight into these human situations that Dorothy Heathcote, the great artist-teacher, has moved the techniques of dramatic improvisation into uncontestable depths of quality learning.

Curriculum dramatics avails itself of any educationally effective theatre techniques, espousing the use of both formal theatre and informal drama while using criteria for quality education. The use of these techniques, however, should be made with a knowing eye for the desired learning objectives. Although the words "theatre" and "drama" are frequently used interchangeably, the Greek word roots indicate a basic difference. Theatre comes from the Greek word "to see, to view"; drama comes from the Greek root meaning "to do or live through." When charting the variations of use of theatre techniques in education, the theatre end of the spectrum will indicate the viewing, performance, and aesthetic study of a formalized art; drama will indicate the informal doing or living through which occurs with more spontaneous, improvisational techniques at the other end of the chart. Although curriculum dramatics encompasses all oral methods of teaching subject material, the emphasis of focus is toward the informal end of the scale because of the profound educational implications inherent in "living through" drama.

The theme of the 1972 annual convention of the American Theatre Association was "Is Theatre Central to Society?" Several members of the organization who were involved in the use of theatre techniques as a *process* of education, chorused that as soon as these techniques were recognized and incorporated in teacher-training classes for their true educational potential, such a question would become unnecessary.

Too often teachers follow given curricula so slavishly that they have no time for "frill" dramatics. Of course, there is little time to memorize extraneous material or even to improvise when working in educationally meaningless areas. But education is a process of skill training in order better to cope with the myriad problems of life. Since this is so, how better can a student learn to cope than by projecting himself through the techniques of drama into simulated life interrelationships?

An inherent danger lies in the use of extraneously planned or published curriculum dramatics exercises except for rather superficial educational purposes. Classroom teachers unsophisticated in dramatic techniques may unwittingly choose such an exercise to be used as an integral contribution to their curricula only to realize later that the normal progression of learning has been arrested and no deepening insights have occurred. On the other hand, if a teacher is taught how to adapt such exercises effectively in his particular curriculum, with his specific class, and on a certain day, an exercise that might threaten to become a debilitating crutch can be recycled into an exhilarating slice of quality learning.

Let me illustrate with a specific instance: Victor Miller, of the American Shakespeare Festival Center for Theatre Techniques in Education, completed a very effective Martha Holden Jennings Foundation Teacher Drama Workshop. It revolved around the teaching of *Hamlet* in anticipation of The Cleveland Play House production to which the students were to be bused.

One of Mr. Miller's opening exercises used to illustrate the components of drama was a little gem called Airport. An obstacle course of chairs and boxes was assembled on stage to resemble a littered runway. One teacher volunteered to be the airplane. A scarf was tied over his eyes to help him simulate the conditions of a blind landing. A second teacher volunteered to act as the control tower. He immobilized himself in a strategic position just off the runway in order to guide the "plane" to a safe landing without touching any obstacles. It was an exercise filled with dramatic suspense by establishing an objective which could be attained only by surmounting a series of obstacles. It also established an unusual relationship of trust between the two actors.

A few days later, I was invited to do two half-hour curriculum dramatic sessions with a "problem" third grade. Consultation with the classroom teacher revealed a class profile consisting of three children in psychoanalysis, several emotionally disturbed remedial readers, an academically run-of-the-mill middle group, and a smattering of precocious pupils. Not unexpectedly, the gym teacher was having trouble. Learning was being impeded because of poor group socialization. My drama educational objective—learning to work together—was administratively agreed upon.

I decided *not* to begin my sessions with a primary emphasis on people because those relationships were too central to the class problem. The first half-hour session was therefore spent on preliminary, individual enactments of favorite animals coping with obstacles of nature, such as thunderstorms. The children were then asked to return to the circle and vote on their most popular animal.

(Of course, horses were agreed upon!) They were asked if they would like to enact a story about horses. After enthusiastic agreement, they were asked to count off by fives. This caused momentary consternation when they realized that the natural friendship cliques of students who had been seated together were being fragmented when those with identical numbers were asked to act together as a team. The incipient emotional upset was quickly subdued with the introduction of a preliminary story structure. The groups were to enact the purchasing of very special horses to be trained to make a trip up the Magic Mountain. The remainder of the day was spent on this selection and training.

On the second day, the Airport exercise was adapted to a specific third-grade level to be used for socializing purposes. The airport runway became the tunnel leading up the Magic Mountain. The control tower became the horse trainer who stood outside the tunnel and led his string of horses through the obstacle course. The eyes of the horses were not masked because such a request would only have been a challenge to peek! Eyes were to be closed because the tunnel was dark. Any horse that peeked was immediately disqualified by his classmates who were watching tensely just outside the crooked "tunnel" of chairs. Each team consisted of a trainer and his team of horses. Each "horse," crawling on hands and knees while clutching the ankles of the "horse" preceding him, had to move with his team as a coordinated unit at the command of his student horse trainer. The dramatic tension was superb. Better still, a heterogeneous group of third graders was learning to work together with a unified focus.

To use drama as a facilitator of quality education, the main thrust should probably not be on the development and publication of drama exercises, but on training teachers to recognize and develop the dramatic elements within their own curricula. In these days of "turned off" students, a teacher must develop material that stems from where the students are in relation to their specific curricula. Therefore, textbook exercises, unless handled with great flexibility, tend to stultify instruction by inserting what may prove to be a non sequitur at the very moment a teacher is trying to relate more closely to his class. Such exercises can sometimes stimulate the creativity of a tired teacher but should never be substituted for his creative judgment and proper adaptation.

A carefully sequenced approach for teaching dramatically un-sophisticated teachers some educationally oriented drama expertise is needed badly. Because a teacher is not working with pre-plotted stories, he must learn how to identify and to structure a dramatic situation out of a general idea and still let the students retain the satisfying feeling that they have created it themselves. This entails the spontaneous use of play-writing techniques. Here Dorothy Heathcote, with her "segmenting" technique of brainstorming a general idea to achieve a dramatic focus, has made a tremendous contribution. The teacher must know how much to organize the situation to avoid chaos, and must know where to hand over crea-tivity to the students.

It has been suggested that the test for quality reasoning is very similar to the criteria for quality curriculum dramatics. Through perception (seeing the world through one's senses) and awareness (an inner feeling or consciousness), one can draw conclusions (or find the reflective learning moment). With this order in mind, we begin using curriculum dramatics by developing a belief through the senses and then moving into the study and use of emotional drives and their inherent conflicts. The theatre's pilot work in this area was brilliantly begun by Constantin Stanislavsky.

Interesting analogies to Dorothy Heathcote's techniques for gaining the depth reflection which causes the learning insights into life were not only heralded by Stanislavsky's work in actor training, but also by the playwright Thornton Wilder in his masterpiece *Our Town*. Here, Emily, having died in childbirth, asks to relive a day on earth. She is advised against this by the other tombstone people but she insists. Whereupon she begins to relive her twelfth birthday, knowing in advance the future sorrows and separations. Very quickly the reliving of this preordained experience becomes excruciating to her. Emily bursts into tears, returning to the ceme-tery, saying that she had never realized how fast life must be lived, with no time truly to appreciate it. Dorothy Heathcote's teacher-structured learning moments that focus on a segment of life, slowing it down for reflection, are a brilliant new contribution to the use of drama in education. It thus allows the students to examine microcosms of life in order to gain this added awareness of what it is all about.

Because of the limitations of time and space, this chapter cannot include my detailed curriculum dramatics instruction for teachers. But it would begin with a careful consideration of the subject of the *art of theatre* itself with the basic principles of the actor, playwright, director, scenic and costume designers. With this understood, the consideration of a preliminary *formal-to-informal curriculum dramatics scale* with accompanying educational criteria and examples might here prove helpful.

Formal student theatre productions to be included as a part of the educational process should be assessed for their literary quality and their educational and aesthetic objectives. School time should be time sacred to quality exposure. We must ask if the time used in memorizing lines is commensurate with the quality of the lines themselves. We must remember that a line memorized at this time in life may be remembered forever. On the other hand, let us not, in our devotion to quality, neglect humor and the wittily turned phrase. *The Importance of Being Earnest* may be selected for its high style and literacy. *Raisin in the Sun* or *Skin of Our Teeth* may be chosen for equally valid educational goals. A fear of discreetly cutting to obtain enjoyable, optimum learning is regrettable.

Visits to quality professional theatre productions under the aegis of the school can serve many socializing as well as educational purposes. Frequently it is the perfect entree to understanding an otherwise difficult script. I have seen the most unlikely junior high school students memorize pages of *Romeo and Juliet* after viewing Franco Zeffirelli's movie. Understanding frequently unfolds with the emotional impact of a professional interpretation. The necessary test of quality remains as well as the teacher's decision that a specific production can extend and deepen the overall educational experience.

Professional traveling troupes that visit the schools will demand less school rescheduling or curricula upset. Productions can consist of quality plays played in their entirety. The danger arises when quality literature is unmercifully cut to fit a forty-minute assembly slot.

Theatre-in-Education troupes that visit the schools give a relatively new approach to a specific type of contribution the professional theatre can make to education. Such troupes, which have widely proliferated around the British Isles, have developed more slowly in the United States. They take a particular educational topic and develop it in either a formal or relatively informal manner. They form the bridge between formal theatre productions and the more informal, improvisational structures, often using a mixture of both. They display a great variation in quality which should probably be judged in three specific areas:

1. The professional quality of production and performance, which seems unusually high in England.

2. The willingness and ability of the professional theatre to tap sensitively into the most effective educational material. Such troupes must cultivate interested, sympathetic, and sophisticated school administrations in order to synchronize their choice of material with the latest educational expertise.

3. The troupes must have the ability to locate and develop the dramatic moments within this educational material so as to construct a theatrically effective scripted framework which will elicit true student learning participation. The Theatre-in-Education troupe enters the school with at least a partially memorized framework, often containing carefully constructed slots for student participation and creativity. The quality and freedom of the elicited student participation must be judged as well as the educational and theatric competence of the scripting. The secure, professionally sophisticated troupe is capable of handling a great variety of student participation in an effective manner. Students can quickly sense built-in, contrived reactions and answers. Quality student thinking must be required.

Formal student productions, in addition to the professionally written literary plays, contain another, relatively unexplored area: *formally written plays dramatizing curriculum material.* The educational criteria for these productions should not only be an assessment of the quality of learning that is occurring, if the lines are memorized, but also how effectively the material has been dramatically handled. A delightful example of this type of formal educational theatre was written recently by a mathematics teacher.[3]

I handed this geometry teacher a copy of *Flatland,*[4] which explores an imaginary, two-dimensional, geometric world. The teacher took the basic idea of the story and developed her own original plot: two scalene triangles, at the bottom of the geometric social ladder, which is based on the number of angles one has, find congruent bliss when married by the myriad-sided high-priest circle (who spends most of his time contemplating his center!). When the two scalene triangles unite for a kiss, they discover they have become a four-sided parallelogram. They thus have upset the whole immobilized social structure of their world! The play is enriched with lyrics bubbling with geometric terminology.

By humanizing and converting the abstract concepts into a fresh, two-dimensional world, the students have been challenged by many new learning experiences that have been illuminated with the sparkle of theatre production. The memorization of this eighteen-minute playlet has sorted out and tucked away geometric terminology and concepts into the students' memory banks.

Jelled or *structured improvisation* is one of the next steps on the scale toward informal use of theatre techniques. This type of informal theatre can be handled by the classroom teacher as a culmination of improvisational experiences in curriculum dramatics structured informally into a school performance. Because such a performance stems from curriculum material, the formalized presentation can be highly educational with built-in expansion and contraction controls to fit the size of the class. To clarify this type of drama further, let me outline a few of my own productions:

> An English class had been studying Homer's *Odyssey*. They needed an end-of-the-year play but the teacher wanted quality learning to continue. She presented the students with the idea of creating their own class odyssey. They had previously researched the word "odyssey" and discovered it meant a trip entailing a search. The students decided that their class odyssey had been a journey throughout the school year while in search of the next grade!
>
> The class had been recently introduced to symbolism through poetry. Now they were asked to study each episode of Homer's *Odyssey*, capsule the action into a short paragraph, and decide what each adventure basically represented or symbolized. For instance, the Cyclops were described as self-centered antisocial mon-

sters who could not cooperate sufficiently in order to form a community. The class decided that the one eye of the Cyclops symbolized an introverted, all-demanding focus.

The next assignment was to decide what in the students' own lives might have a similar, all-consuming focus. Their unanimous vote went to "the TV tube"! With this in mind, they began creating improvisations centered around the TV's ability to divert and draw them from the studies necessary for their graduation.

The lures of Scylla and Charybdis were symbolized by the popular local teen-age shopping center. Each episode was thus boiled down to its symbolic essence and then transposed into its modern school counterpart.

A second example of jelled improvisation occurred while studying Robert Frost's poem "Mending Wall."

The class enacted, through progressive improvisations deepened by discussion, many of the human walls we build between ourselves. A poignant improvisational scene developed in an attempt to surmount the sensory barriers of communication with a deaf mute. The students developed a kind of mirror dance reflecting their ego walls; improvisational scenes emerged around the symbolic implications of the *Berlin wall* and the *Chinese wall* as the students tried to choose explicit moments to convey these ideas. The use of Frost's poem through choral speaking and mime became the recurring theme.

Let us examine briefly the *process* by which improvisation is jelled. Several class groups may be creating around the same theme with discussion and further thinking occurring after each scene. This is where the teacher's expertise emerges. She guides and stimulates further in-depth thinking in a quality learning area. When a teacher complains that a second-grade class cannot repeat a scene, or that the children will have to perform a scene immediately or it will "fall dead," the teacher probably needs to explore one of Stanislavsky's techniques of using "the Magic If." Improvisational scenes should never be reenacted the same way twice. Such mechanical repetition is only an invitation for a scene to solidify and develop chunks of insincere "ham"! The teacher should call for a moment of positive assessment after each scene to help the group formulate the new focus for the repeat scene: "What if we now play this scene in pantomime?" "What would happen this time if all the lights went out just as the killer cocked his gun?" "What if the two old ladies still had to pool their food money in order to survive, but they basically detested one another?"

The responsibility of asking the correct question to solicit deepening learning experiences must fundamentally remain with the teacher. He cannot expect his students, no matter how creative, to be able to grasp the overall educational objectives.[5]

In this way, the basic order and structure of the jelled improvisation scenes remain fundamentally the same, while meanings and implications continue to deepen as production time nears. Not only will the sequence of action automatically be learned but also the student will feel that he retains a certain freedom of expression and exploration. By encouraging the continuation of thinking on one's feet in public, the terror of forgetting memorized lines is avoided.

Staging such jelled improvisations must remain consistent with the criteria of progressing quality learning with the least amount of technical distraction. Token costuming, lighting, and scenery will usually satisfy the students, facilitate performance, and encourage the development of creativity and belief. Heavily costumed, a child may never feel completely comfortable—simultaneously handling a shawl, a parasol, high heels, a southern accent, and a story line! Part of the learning process can consist of the student selecting the one property or portion of costume that most effectively portrays the essence of the character. Is it his monocle? Is it her long skirt?

The scenery and lighting can be handled in a similar way.

1. One or two spotlights screwed on the back of stepladders, or an inexpensive dimmer hooked into the normal classroom lights

2. Acting space designated by carpet remnants, chalk, or masking tape on the floor of a classroom or all-purpose area

3. A door or window frame with shade, a few stackable blocks or vari-sized platforms giving needed, visual variety

4. The very process of suspending disbelief by having an eraser act as a cradle telephone may add a delightful, creative touch

Young voices should not be artificially strained by being forced to project in unreasonably large auditoriums or gymnasium echo chambers. The delicate focus must remain upon the best development of the individual child and what may be shyly emerging from his inner self. An oversize audience can so easily be detrimental to the proper development of a child's personality. The teacher's educational objectives for a jelled improvisation performance should include assistance in helping the student performers learn to share effectively what they wish to convey to others. The inherent learning in proper classroom inprovisation can sometimes add this additional audience-communication experience if the scene is simply shared with another class section. But may Zeus's thunderbolts forever expunge from the classroom any teacher who exploits a child's personality for the sake of a polished performance! A teacher must never forget that naturally unfolding personalities can develop only if the medium is used basically as a process rather than a product.

A final example of jelled or structured improvisation shows a coordination of the arts with core subject matter.

> The art teacher was exposing her junior high students to the symbolic surrealist art of Miro. The English teacher wished to introduce some free-verse writing as well as the principles of dramatic interrelationships. They decided to coordinate their instruction. A specific picture was agreed upon that contained several elementary figures of stars of varying sizes, a quarter moon, and a TV antenna placed against a somber sky.
>
> The English teacher asked the class to verbalize the overall mood of the picture. The celestial loneliness was described with a series of adjectives. The students were then asked to pinpoint this mood individually with written phrases that were shared with the rest of the class.
>
> The teacher then guided the students into a study of the figures within this celestial mood. She asked them to

meditate individually on a specific figure, trying to find its inner action or drive. This was to be expressed by an action verb beginning with "I want . . ."

Teams were formed with each student representing a specific abstract figure within the painting. The students took their visual positions within the composition and tried to feel their relationships to one another. They began to act out these interrelationships in pantomime.

Meanwhile, the art teacher, keeping closely informed of the developments within the English class, had begun to introduce puppetry to the same class with the making of stick dolls representing the Miro figures. The students began to realize that the inner actions of the figures could not be realized fully by immobilized cardboard cutouts. Coils, joints, and twinkling were introduced while preserving the proper mood and inner context.

The students were then asked to introduce the dialogue between the heavenly spheres. They had been studying the writing of complete sentences and were suddenly released to write lists of connotative words, and then phrases, expressing the lonely desires of these figures. It became an exciting and freeing exercise in which all types of sound effects were written and tested orally. Although the word "poetry" was not mentioned until much later, free-verse dialogue was now emerging.

The music teacher, who happened to have a real flair for modern music became intrigued with the literary and visual efforts of his class. He helped the students compose appropriate songs and sound effects to accompany the verse dialogue. Such sounds as whisks used on metal wastebaskets, Kleenex over combs and erasers laid on piano strings, were investigated and taped!

The day of the assembly performance arrived. A puppet booth was improvised on stage by drawing the curtains to the opening required to expose the electrically controlled movie screen. Three-foot-high corrugated paper was stretched between the lower portion of the opening with gym mats spread on the floor behind. The puppeteers thus could kneel comfortably on these mats while manipulating the puppets. The program began with a slide lecture by the art teacher on the symbolist-surrealist Miro, which ended with the students' chosen picture. The movie screen was then slowly raised, revealing the puppets in identical positions to the figures in the picture. The lonely musical sounds began, and the figures moved to the haunting recitation of the verse-dialogue. An aesthetic, educational experience had been successfully completed.

As a footnote to this specialist-guided, coordinated arts performance, I hasten to add that frequently I and my students have relied on only the artistic expertise inherent within the class. I am not a musician, dancer, or artist, but I have encouraged students to experiment unabashedly with their own abilities in order to incorporate a freewheeling use of other arts with their drama improvisations.

Remembering that the inherent dramatic moments frequently lie near the solar plexus, a teacher must sense those pressure points within not only her curriculum but also within her specific class. A teacher who relates quickly to a group will enter with antennae tuned for reception rather than to broadcast immediately a curriculum that does not at the moment relate to the group. The teacher enters alertly in limbo, absorbing what Stanislavsky calls the actor's "offstage beat," before she steps into her teaching role. If a high school class has had little experience in spontaneous performance, it may feel very threatened if asked to go immediately into improvisations. Discussions, debates, and reasoning conducted from desks arranged in a circle, enabling everyone to be seen, are the easiest introductions to curriculum dramatics.

To clarify this type of informal curriculum dramatics further, several examples follow showing: (1) the educational objectives, (2) the type of curriculum dramatics used, and (3) specific material taught.

First Example

1. The study of the perpetually fascinating enigma of what makes people what they are.

2. Informal class discussion.

3. George Bernard Shaw's *Pygmalion*. Discussion stemming from what makes Higgins seemingly a crass, insensitive adult after having been reared by a wise and sensitive mother.

Second Example

1. The study of the effects of rearing a child in two different cultures.

2. An informal debate.

3. The debate stems from the reading of Conrad Richter's *Light in the Forest*.

Third Example

1. Value study of the cause and handling of cheating.

2. A student-directed discussion, alternative choice of actions tried out, and an obligatory scene enacted.

3. C. D. B. Bryan's "So Much Unfairness of Things" from *21 Great Stories*. The obligatory scene is between the headmaster and the father after his son had been caught cheating on an exam. This scene was not described in the original story, leaving improvisational freedom.

A younger class might study characterization while simultaneously studying parts of speech in a grammar class:

Character	Part of Speech	Specific Example
The name of the character	proper noun	Mr. Powers
Sex	noun	male
Name substitute	pronoun	he
His life drive or action	action verb	to grab
How character acts	adverb	ruthlessly
Character description	adjective	selfish, rude
Composite portrait joined together by	conjunction	and
Location	preposition	in, on, from, etc.
His favorite exclamation	expletive	Zounds!

Two such characters can thus be constructed with opposing drives or actions. The class has already thus settled the basic improvisational questions: who you are, where you are, what you are doing. Putting the two characters together in a scene will automatically cause conflict. (Remember the four types of conflict: man vs. man, man vs. himself, man vs. society, man vs. nature.) The ensuing *suspense* can be expressed by a question mark "?". Such combining of grammar lessons with rudimentary drama training can be enacted with different resolutions and endings.

Many *trips* lend themselves to drama when one realizes that a dramatic plot is not expressed graphically as the shortest distance between two points:

A plot can better be expressed by a rising zigzag line, illustrating an action drive from point *A* to point *B* which is interrupted by obstacles and conflicts, thus building suspense:

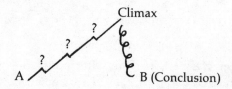

On the top riser sits the climax. The quick, downward path to the conclusion might be visualized as a spiral that wraps up all the loose threads of plot as it drops to the conclusion.

Keeping a few of these drama fundamentals in mind, a teacher can find dramatic elements in much of her skill teaching wherever she happens to be and whenever she desires to use them.

An example of using the journey plot line for improvisational and writing exercises occurred after some middle schoolers read *The Incredible Journey* by Sheila Burnford. Rather than a story about animals, the same characteristics were transposed into a group of children traveling through the dangers of a city. Even a lesson in map reading was introduced.

Curriculum dramatics has proved an invaluable tool for value teaching, where alternative choices can be tried on and results and implications can be studied. Educating to mitigate the trauma of future shock is natural material for improvisational work, which can be sparked by questions introduced by "What if . . . ?" "What if the energy crisis continues to worsen?" "What if the Atlantic Ocean is replaced by fertile land?" And an exercise in moving backward in time: "What if the French Revolution was fought with modern technology?" Change the time or place, or alter a point of view and fresh dimensions are introduced into education.

The key to curriculum dramatics is for the teacher to guide creativity into quality areas of learning rather than to be satisfied with peripheral or prescribed exercises not adapted to his particular moment in a particular class, or his individual presentation of a subject. He must not only know his subject matter, but also he must remain open to the suggestions of his students. Too often a creative teacher imposes his own creativity on a class, thus smothering the creative attempts of his students. The real trick in teaching any form of creative art is to be able to sense how much to give a class in order to guide and stimulate them. Then, exercise the discipline to withdraw from the creative activity except to help the class build, when necessary, the excitement and the tension. And finally, indicate the moments of "reflective in-depth learning" that Dorothy Heathcote mentions in her work, where conclusions and deeper meanings can be formed.

The teacher's tuning quickly into the mood and interest of the class, his ability to find the dramatic moments within his curriculum, and the structuring of those moments in order that he may indicate to his students the framework within which they can feel free to create are most important techniques. That true creativity is not dependent upon complete freedom is one of the first concepts a class must learn in any creative endeavor. All art contains inherent structure, but a neophyte frequently needs guidance in finding the correct form.

This method of humanizing learning and relating it to where the class is has been particularly effective with inner-city children. I was asked to evaluate a student teacher's creative dramatics class with a group of deprived second graders. The teacher was desperately trying to hold their attention long enough to tell the story and cast the characters of *Cinderella*. The children did not understand, nor were they interested in, kings and queens. Pandemonium had set in, heightened by several sets of hands banging on the piano. Suddenly the teacher grabbed up a spray of lily-of-the-valley she had tucked in her buttonhole that morning. "Look, children," she cried. "See what I found in my garden." Instantly she had the attention of most of the class. "What is *your* favorite flower?" she continued. She was shouted a bevy of answers. "How would you each like to be your favorite flower growing from a tiny, little seed? Let's see how tiny you can make yourselves." The focus of the class was still being shattered by an unconcentrated pair of hands pounding on the piano keys. "Softly, Sheila! Softly! Your noise is making the plants wither." Several children promptly faded to the floor! "We must have soft, growing music . . . *that's* it! See? You're making them grow." The pianist's fingers were dancing on tiptoe! "And now I shall transplant each bud to my flower bed where they can stretch their stems and grow." Tears silently coursed down my cheeks as I watched the young teacher gently enfold each little child and carry him to the "growing plot." Belief and concentration, trust and loving care had suddenly entered that room. From there the teacher could lead her class into the study of all the miracles of the beginning of life.

I cannot end this chapter without mentioning the deep indebtedness I feel to Dorothy Heathcote, the artist-teacher from England, and her work in drama in education. Her fresh techniques for adding depth to improvisation help clarify the objectives of educational dramatics. In addition, by clearly indicating the thread of human relationships that runs through almost all curricula, she has given me an answer to my twenty-year quest for a method of how to teach teachers of diverse subject areas and grade levels simultaneously. For we must all agree that it is the warmth and humanness of life that is the very heart of education.

Will the reader step back even farther, to the very beginning of my own personal quest? As an awkward little girl I suddenly became "turned on" when I discovered how to make orange-rind teeth and won a prize with my sister in a monkey-grinder act? Why was it, I began to wonder several years later, that my learning had never *really* begun, that I had never really become an integrated student, until two years after I had been graduated from college? Newer and deeper awareness only began to emerge with my study of the Stanislavsky Method of acting. That, through its focus on human emotions and motivations, furnished the central axle to the wheel of life and thus began to illuminate some of the pivotal spokes of learning.

How gratifying recently to read the following remarks by Neil Postman,[6] co-author of *Teaching as a Subversive Activity* and one of America's outstanding educators:

> What we have to do is to make the study of one's own feelings a legitimate school activity, invested with an importance at least equal to that presently given to map-reading skills or spelling. This can be done in a variety of ways ... from regularly scheduled rap sessions, to seminars in value clarification or role playing or adolescent psychology, to, best of all, the acceptance of the fact that no sensible distinction can be made between cognitive and affective learning, from which it follows that in every course, in every activity, a serious interest *must* be taken in the feeling of the students.

Anywhere human feelings and relationships need to be studied, curriculum dramatics techniques are a potentially effective method of teaching.

NOTES

1. Harold Taylor, *Art and the Intellect* (New York: Museum of Modern Art, 1960), pp. 12–13.
2. Junius Eddy, "The Upsidedown Curriculum," *Cultural Affairs* (Summer 1970): 16–17.
3. Priscilla Ford, Laurel School, Shaker Heights, Ohio.
4. A.E. Abbott, *Flatland* (New York: Dover, 1963).
5. For a fascinating lecture on this subject of teacher questioning to solicit quality student response, view the Northwestern film *Dorothy Heathcote Talks to Teachers*, Part II. (Evanston: Northwestern University Film Library, 1973).
6. Neil Postman, "The Ecology of Learning," *English Journal* (April 1974): 60.

DRAMATIZING HISTORY

JOANNA HALPERT KRAUS

*Joanna Halpert Kraus is on the faculty of State University College,
New Paltz, New York. Previously she taught at the State University of New
York, College at Purchase; New York City Community College; and
Columbia University, where she taught creative drama to Agnes Russell
School students. Her academic background includes degrees from
Sarah Lawrence, the University of California, and Teachers College,
Columbia, with further study at the University of London. She is active in
the Children's Theatre Association but she is best known for her literary
work, which includes stories, articles, and three full-length plays for
children.* The Ice Wolf, Mean to be Free, *and* Vasalisa *have all been
widely produced. In 1971 the Children's Theatre Association
awarded Joanna Kraus the Charlotte Chorpenning Cup for
Achievement in Playwriting. In this essay she discusses content
and ways of working in the classroom.*

History has often been taught as a progression of battles in
which there were victors and vanquished. Rarely is there a mention
of the anguished unknowns who paused to reflect prior to cheering
or damning any cause.

Yet, the drama inherent in decision making is the substance of
human history. The study of history should reflect more than external events, for the story of man is a progression of attitude
changes on basic issues. In the last decade alone, evolving changes
on fundamental issues can be expressed by such familiar terms as
"black is beautiful," "women's lib," "the pill," "recycling," "lunar

128

module." These brief phrases express changes that are subtly but surely altering the pattern of our daily existence.

Thus, it is in a sense inaccurate to permit only cardboard heroes and villains to parade across the textbooks of America, instilling images and ideals that often reveal sterile half-truths. Perhaps a worse sin educationally is that such a presentation is boring.

If a student is to receive any illumination from a survey of conquests and battles, he needs to conjecture on the motivation propelling the actors of certain historic scenes. He needs to comprehend the indecision, the ambivalence, the vacillating opinions that existed, for example, on the eve of the American Revolution. He needs to speculate on the internal terrors that created external events. If a student is to have any enthusiasm, empathy, or compassion for the family of man, he needs also to focus on the humanists of history, those who sought to explain or to improve the human condition. It is the humanists who have sought to make, and in part have determined, the life styles available to us.

According to Charles DeCarlo, the greatest problem facing educators today is "how to encourage in an age of large organizations, individual moral sensibilities and human responsibility."[1] Or, as I see it, can we escape from the oppressing sense that events of history simply happened to us and begin to examine the consequences as a result of human action—or the lack of it? Thus, dramatizing history can become for the participant an experience in confronting a situation and solving it with the resources on hand. For history and drama both deal with human beings at points of crises in their lives. The essence of great drama and of significant history is conflict.

In his eloquent essay "An Approach to Literature," Robert Penn Warren divided literary conflict among the following three areas: man against nature, man against others, man against himself. The classic divisions seem appropriate for the study of history and drama as well. But the creative artist's task springs from, rather than ends with, documentation. As Eugenia Collier pointed out in an article discussing the current film *Conrack*, the artist is "obligated to probe deeper than the surface reality, to answer questions (or at least raise them) about the human condition, to reveal the various dimensions of experience."[2]

Both the study of history and the study of drama should illustrate and illuminate human behavior and experience. One has the opportunity via the structure of improvised drama to not only share recorded factual data with students but also to encourage them to experience kinesthetically and emotionally the conditions under which, and the process through which, certain decisions were made that led to specific historic events.

In improvised drama the participant is the medium through which transpires the emotional range of human response. The substance of drama is conflict, people confronted and challenged by situations with which they must cope. Drama needs nothing more than a place for ideas to develop. Costumes, scenery, makeup, lighting, properties are the intricate trappings that provide the spectacle, the visual illusion. But this glamorous addition is secondary to the primary function: an illumination of human concerns.

Any teacher who does not use drama as a learning tool is deliberately eliminating one of the most native and natural tools at her disposal. The desire to play is part of the human condition from birth onward. The use of drama in education is simply taking advantage of a propensity natural to the human being.

If we as educators are agreed that education implies more than cerebral effort and that the mind and spirit can soar in the classroom, and if we as teachers working in classrooms concur with Dewey's premise that one learns by doing, then it is incumbent upon the teacher to find exercises that will provide experiences for all three aspects of human growth.

Most of those who teach creative dramatics agree with the official Children's Theatre Association's definition, arrived at after much deliberation:

> Creative dramatics, in which children with the guidance of imaginative teacher or leader create scenes or plays and perform them with improvised dialogue and action. Personal development of players is the goal, rather than the satisfaction of a child audience. Scenery and costumes are rarely used. If this informal drama is presented before an audience, it is usually in the nature of a demonstration.[3]

But, as one would anticipate, there are differences among the various practitioners. A pioneer in the area of creative dramatics, founder of the Children's Theatre Association of Baltimore, Maryland, and author of *Creative Play Acting*, Isabel B. Burger defines creative dramatics as the "expression of thought and feelings in the child's own terms, through action, the spoken word, or both."[4] Brian Way, director of the Theatre Centre in London and author of *Development Through Drama* states that "a basic defintion of drama might be simply 'to practice living'."[5] Drama is as concerned with exploring and mastering the emotional self as it is with discovering and mastering the physical self.[6] Though both Burger and Way have as their rationale the development and understanding of people, their structural approaches to this end differ. Burger's method, demonstrated in the creative dramatics classes which were the cornerstone of the Theatre's activity, moved from pantomime to mood to change-of-mood to dialogue.[7] Each step placed progressively greater demands on the creativity of the student. Way's circle of human development included concentration, the senses, imagination, physical self, speech, emotion, and intellect.[8] His exercises were designed to develop the individual areas, but he was not concerned with the point at which one commences, only that the circle ultimately be completed.

I believe that in creative dramatics a student experiences with his total being the imaginary circumstance. He exercises and trains his imagination while he disciplines his body to express what his mind and spirit dictate. If creative dramatics provides only an acceptable outlet for raging emotion, it is providing a therapeutic moment, which should have a therapist on hand to interpret. If, on the other hand, the experience develops the young person's imaginative powers, ability to conceptualize, argue, decide, and understand with his total being, then it is drama.

My rationale does not differ from Burger or Way, but I would add that in a country of conformity we need to develop creativity; in a nation where corruption is commonplace, we need to reintroduce individual integrity; in a period that is increasingly impersonal, we need to establish pride in identity; in a world where the generation gap seems sharply accentuated, we need to explore the causes of alienation; and in a terrifying time of tolerance for the intolerable, we need to develop a sense of commitment and responsibility, first to self, then to others.

The current bible of educators, Bloom's *Taxonomy of Educational Objectives*, lists a hierarchy of developmental skills in three separate areas of learning: the cognitive domain, the affective domain, and the psychomotor domain. In dramatizing historical material, one inevitably touches upon some of the skills or levels of each. However, the tendency when teaching any academic subject is to assume that the cognitive area is more important, i.e., that it is more important for the student to learn the dates and the names of little or unknown incidents than to explore the emotional reality of how individuals might have felt. I believe that this is shallow pedagogy. As George Shaftel recently stated, "History is not just a record of events. History deals with people thinking and feeling. Events are important, but so are feelings. Feelings impel action!"[9] Fannie Shaftel further commented that although there has been a push to increase cognitive content learning, it is a false notion to think that we can totally separate affective and cognitive areas. "Although some tasks are heavily intellectual or heavily emotive, behavior does not separate. . . . We move through feelings to factual material."[10]

One could not, and should not, avoid facts in dramatizing history. But facts by themselves are easily memorized and easily forgotten. Jenny Egan, founder of the Four Winds Theatre, which in its unique format explores man's past and present history, works theatrically to make the audience "feel the significance of historic facts."[11]

For too long, students have needlessly groaned their way through history. Students and tourists alike have sat and stood at historic sites, manifesting though their posture varying degrees of patient resignation, while a guide or teacher droned on. It is my conviction that creative dramatics, the participation play,[12] role-playing[13]—all of which involve physical participation as well as emotional participation—and the literate, imaginative theatrical script that combines authenticity with artistry are all viable ways of removing unnecessary dust from the tangible records of beliefs and events which, after all, shaped the present.

> History is so much more than building and an inventory of artifacts. It is a way of living that can only be transmitted to the visitor through exciting his imagination.

The dissemination of information, no matter how effective, can no longer do that. We believe that a theatrical experience, a living recreation of history can.[14]

The historian Henry S. Commager has suggested that history teachers and textbooks utilize a realistic approach to the decisions people have made in history. Many political scientists, taking their cue from the behaviorial and physical scientists, have advocated the use of simulation or symbolic models of political happenings.[15]

Despite Dewey's familiar educational motto that we learn by doing, and the subsequent supporting material by Kilpatrick, Theodore Sizer recently pointed out in *Places for Learning, Places for Joy* that almost all our education is "offered vicariously and in the abstract. Children are expected to learn how others feel by reading about them. . . . We read about the Revolutionary War, and now we know how tyrannical George III was."[16]

There are two approaches to the dramatic improvising of historic material. One serves to vivify and enhance the factual content; the other serves to demonstrate the emotional content of a conjectured, though plausible scene. In either case the participant needs to confront the problem that faces the specific individual or group and solve it within the context of time, place, and characters. As Dorothy Heathcote has pointed out, the student in any improvised scene needs to "take up attitudes and viewpoints and for the time believe in them."[17]

The Belgrade Theatre in Coventry, England, has delved into historical material in their theatre-in-education program. Stuart Bennett wrote:

With older children we used social history themes widely. Occupational mime was used to create an identity with a social role. The pupils were then, in their roles, given a common experience and put into a situation which they could only resolve through communication. The aim was common to good education and the main stream of theatre—to extend the participant's understanding of people and how they relate to one another. Secondary pupils explored the life of seventeenth cen-

tury London through improvisation and then recon-
structed the Great Fire with ourselves acting the historical roles and the pupils the people. Juniors used
similar background methods to explore the Lady Go-
diva legend and the Middle Ages. Again all the children took part all the time.[18]

The Frozen Lands, a documentary program for junior schools, related
to Shackleton's journey to the Antartic.[19]

In conjunction with the American Revolution Bicentennial Commission, graduate students enrolled in my Children's Theatre
Workshop at State University College, New Paltz, helped develop an
outdoor participation play based on the actual incident of the burn-
ing and destruction of Kingston by the British in 1777 (*Only One
House Left*).

Previously at State University of New York, College at Purchase,
my students and I developed a creative dramatics scenario on the
building of the first transcontinental railroad (*All Aboard 2-6-10 Miles
a Day*). The purpose was to stimulate interest in the characters, the
events, the conflicts, and the decisions that were part of an emerging
nation. Geography, geology, politics, immigration, prejudice, treatment of the native American, economics, ecology, private enterprise,
military involvement, modes of cross-country transportation, the
decision-making role of Congress, use of media to communicate
news—all were touched on as the children discussed, prepared, and
created their version of the history that occurred a little more than a
century ago.

There is a fascinating account by R. Verrier, Monks Public
Schools, England, in which the instructor illustrates an approach
which utilized drama, English, and history in teaching an incident
that occurred during the English Civil War involving King Charles,
John Pym, and Members of Parliament. The teaching was done with
secondary school students placed in three groups of differing
academic ability. All three groups took part in preliminary discussions, the analysis of the given situation, and refinement of the
problem; but the form of the involvement and the focus differed.

The able form of pupils showed special interest in the
legalities of the situation and the "correct" ritual of

events. This interest led them on to a study of documents from which historians themselves learn about events. They attempted to produce "original sources" such as correspondence between the King and the Speaker of the House of Commons as well as private correspondence between the King and his friends. The mixed ability form were interested in the reactions of ordinary people and the drama of the King's abortive attempt to arrest Pym. They produced a tape to "help" other pupils of "our age" to understand the situation. . . . The weaker form . . . centered around the plight of the wanted man, John Pym. They constructed group stories showing how several families living in *any street* might react to a fugitive from Royal justice.[20]

In a recent lecture by George Shaftel discussing role playing and history, he described several role-playing situations that would permit young people to focus on ethical values and group decision making. One incident occurred in the mid-nineteenth century. Two youths playing by the river chanced to see a black man struggling in the water, a white man in close pursuit. To save a drowning man might well be an act of disinterested mercy, but to assist an escaped slave in the 1850s was a criminal offense.[21] Do they see and assist? Do they see and ignore? Whatever action taken, the young people must realize the probable consequences of their behavior. Another of Shaftel's role-playing situations dealt with the members of the Interim Committee, in the midst of World War II. They had to determine whether or not to use the atomic bomb.[22] Role-playing situations grapple with moral issues and the urgent realities of the historic period, but they also demand that young people consider the ethics and values involved, which transcend any time line.

All drama should gradually move the participant from an awareness and acceptance of self to an awareness and acceptance of others.

A simple sentence from a Sioux prayer reflects the conflict in our conformist lives: "Great Spirit, grant that I may not criticize my neighbor until I have walked a mile in his moccasins."[23] In an age of conformity, some cannot even tolerate a shaggy lawn amid a block of Sunday-mown green patches. When global neighbors, less than a day's jet ride away, seem to "threaten" us with ideas, values, habits, and life styles that appear totally alien, can we possibly coexist peacefully? Incidents of history trenchantly and tragically reveal our limited tolerance. But never before in our history has it been as vital as it is today that we begin to respect the varying expressions of human behavior springing from cultural differences and respond to these differences as manifestations of the infinite variety of possibility in the species.

Dr. Shaftel believes that an individual is only tested as such when he behaves within the framework of a group.[24] We do not live in isolation. We never have. And history is as much a record of group behaviorial action as it is individual aspiration. The concept of decision making or choice, action, consequence is as crucial to the structure of drama as it is to the comprehension of human history.

In using improvisational drama to vivify and enhance the teaching of historical material, there are pitfalls. If one is dealing with specific factual data and a variety of primary and secondary sources, it is often near impossible to create the well-rounded characters or a taut drama that the playwright might wish. One is bound to some extent by statements that were made or by a progression or sequence of events that may seem somewhat implausible in the latter part of the twentieth century. Improvisational dialogue may be sincere, but flat or filled with unintentional anachronisms. On the other hand, the authentic wording of a serious statement may, on occasion, be so pompous that its forced inclusion would be self-defeating. Participants may become so intrigued with external behavior that they partially neglect internal motivation.

In emphasizing the process of involvement, the end product may not be as devoid of anachronisms or dramatic liberties as the historian might wish. For example, in our production of *Only One House Left*, there were unintentional "O.K.'s" uttered, although students knew they should avoid contemporary slang. In preparing the play we deliberately ignored the fact that the eighteenth-century Council of Safety was comprised solely of men. We encouraged both girls and boys to participate as villagers in order to involve all the children in the decision-making process. In the original letter sent by General Vaughn, the name Esopus was used when referring to Kingston. Since that would have only added confusion, we changed the reference to Kingston. Finally, when the president of the Council received the alarming news that the British fleet was at the landing, there is documented evidence that he sent a letter to Clinton. Rather than delay the improvisational exodus, we took a sentence of this letter and incorporated it into the news brought by the messenger who interrupted the Council meeting. We did this to build dramatic tension and to facilitate the immediate evacuation of the village.

The pre- and post-discussions are a vital and integral part of the dramatization process. During the preliminary discussions, the leader should elicit what knowledge the children have and supplement that with selected specific details—pictures, photographs, maps, replicas of relevant period items, in addition to evoking the possible thoughts and feelings of the characters. During the post-discussion, leaders, teachers, and parents can separate facts from opinions, theatrical devices from accurate details. The leader can help young people discover that all printed material is researched, written, and edited from a point of view, and that a profusion of sources may reveal a profusion of facts on the same subject.

One must also be careful to particularize general events. For example, when the townspeople of Kingston returned to their devastated homes and picked their way through the rubble and smoldering ashes, leaders softly suggested, "Find your home. See if there is anything left we can use." This gave purpose to the exploration and dramatically controlled what might otherwise have been vague wandering. Children quickly returned with apples, potatoes, wool, a family Bible, a silver jewel box—and burned British money!

One day after the fire a boy reported that he'd found a car. Puzzled, the president of the Council stated that he didn't know what the term meant. The boy frowned, thought for a moment, then grinned and said, "I mean a horse and cart!" Children often confuse historic time lines. They are apt to lump great lives together under that amorphous term, the *past*.

But dramatization of specific incidents can help intensify one's interest or stimulate one's enthusiasm in acquiring more knowledge of a place, event, or historic period. (The careful detail in describing class distinction, cultural attitudes, daily life displayed on the B.B.C.'s TV program "Upstairs, Downstairs" stimulated the interest of the American public in Edwardian England to the extent that a new series on the same subject will be aired in the fall.) When children become intellectually, kinesthetically, and emotionally absorbed in solving a problem, whether the event is in the past or present, they are capable of passionate intensity.

From the historian's viewpoint, improvisational dramatizing of history serves as a motivating session or as a stimulus. But it is these very excursions into the thoughts and feelings of other people in the past, confronted with an urgent problem to solve, that develop the basic skills we hold so high in our current educational thinking: the ability to concentrate, to move purposefully, to develop ideas, to function effectively as an individual within a group. I have referred to the last skill as the ability to preserve the "I" within the "we,"for I believe that is the ultimate test of a truly democratic society.

In an age where our children may well be ambassadors in space, should we not give some attention to that quality that puts us higher than the beasts, albeit lower than the angels—the capacity for empathy?

NOTES

1. Charles DeCarlo, "Molding Integrity Seen as Key Teaching Task," *New York Times*, 16 January 1974, sec. C, p. 79.
2. Eugenia Collier, "Once Again the White Liberal to the Rescue," *New York Times*, 21 April 1974, sec. 2, p. D11.
3. Ann Viola, "Drama With and For Children: An Interpretation of Terms, *Educational Theatre Journal* 8 (May 1956): 139.
4. Isabel B. Burger, *Creative Play Acting* (New York: Ronald Press, 1950), p. 2.
5. Brian Way, *Development Through Drama* (London: Longmans, Green, 1967), p. 6.
6. Ibid., p. 219.
7. Burger, *Creative Play Acting*, p. xiii.
8. Way, *Development Through Drama*, p. 13.
9. Fannie and George Shaftel, "Working with Feelings Through Role Playing" (Lecture-demonstration at the Association for Childhood Education International Study Conference, Washington, D.C., 17 April 1974).
10. Ibid.
11. Jenny Egan, introductory remarks at *The Raree Show*, New York, N.Y., 21 February 1974.

12. A participation play is an extension of creative dramatics in which the audience becomes part of the action and determines portions of the play.

13. Role playing is a process in which a problem is presented, generally related to value structure and human relations. Various solutions are explored, enacted, and discussed by the participants.

14. Vernon D. Dame, superintendent, Manhattan Group National Park Service. Program from *The Raree Show*, The Four Winds Theatre, February 1974.

15. Fannie and George Shaftel, *Role-Playing for Social Values* (Englewood Cliffs, N. J.: Prentice-Hall, 1967), pp. 9–13.

16. Theodore R. Sizer, *Places for Learning, Places for Joy* (Cambridge, Mass.: Harvard University Press, 1973) p. 75.

17. Dorothy Heathcote, "Drama and Education: Subject or System," In *Drama and Theatre in Education*, ed. Nigel Dodd and Winifred Hickson (London: Heinemann Educational Books, 1971), p. 57.

18. Stuart Bennett, "The Belgrade's Bones: Fifth Year of Theatre in Education" (Bulletin, Belgrade Theatre, Coventry, England, 1971), pp. 4–5.

19. Rosemary Birbeck, "Theatre in Education" (Bulletin, Belgrade Theatre, Coventry, England, 1969), p. 2.

20. R. Verrier, Appendix IV, in Dodd and Hickson, *Drama and Theatre in Education*, pp. 173–74.

21. Fannie and George Shaftel, "Working with Feelings."

22. Ibid.

23. Saint Francis Indian Mission, Saint Francis, South Dakota.

24. Fannie Shaftel, Discussion, Association for Childhood Education International Study Conference, Washington, D.C., 18 April 1974.

"ACTING" AND CHILDREN

GRACE STANISTREET

Grace Stanistreet, founder of the Children's Centre for the Creative Arts at Adelphi University in Garden City, Long Island, is a pioneer in the field of the creative arts as learning. Whereas the majority of programs offer children's theatre, creative dramatics, or movement classes, the Adelphi program includes all performing and visual arts in its curriculum. This multidisciplinary approach, with its emphasis on individual development, has attracted many visitors since its inception in 1937. Grace Stanistreet has published two books, Teaching Is a Dialogue *and* Learning Is a Happening, *and has been in constant demand as a workshop leader and teacher of teachers. In 1972, Adelphi University conferred an honorary doctorate in recognition of her long record of distinguished work in the field. In this essay she explains the point of view that has guided the work of the Children's Centre from the beginning.*

ATTITUDE

Theatre activity can help youth to face and adjust to reality when. it is understood by the teacher that to create the illusion of reality, the actor must be able to recognize the drama of the real. Too often, teachers of dramatic activity for children believe that fantasy, not reality, is the way to stimulate the child. They resort to magic and gimmicks as lures. They "play" at theatre. They dramatize many stories, but "acting out" is not enough; story playing does offer children opportunity for emotional release, but we have overemphasized this aspect. Growth and learning are made possible by a serious approach to the study of acting as it relates to living. Techniques for acting are techniques for living, but they need to be related and applied. Children like to work seriously and to be challenged by an activity for which they have the equipment.

Theatre stripped to its essence—the presentation of life problems —is a natural means of expression and of learning for the child. An eight-year-old expressed his understanding of acting: "Acting is all about knowing who you are, what you are doing and why." Another said, "You can't do anything very well if your heart isn't in it. I think acting is all about heart and feelings." Such expressions indicate a child's response to a serious approach. Yet many teachers fortunate enough to work in this area continue to take the playful approach, which is unworthy of both adult and child. It is true that when this is the only approach a child knows, he will play along with the adult. In so indulging the adult, he may demonstrate a greater maturity than that of the teacher. The teacher who leads the child step by step to a recognition of acting as a demonstration of life and to an awareness of his equipment, and who provides the opportunity for its use, is rewarded by enthusiastic response and proof of competence.

Do I mean by the above statement that fantasy is ruled out? No. Fantasy has a place in children's acting class because it requires knowledge and deliberate capers of the imagination. But imagination, soaring without a base from which to depart and return, is like a plane that has lost contact with the control tower. Fantastic tricks of imagination, magic, and props to stimulate result in theatrical pretence unworthy of either adult or child.

PERFORMANCE

Some confusion exists about the terms "creative dramatics" and "children's theatre." Some view creative dramatics as a spontaneous activity and children's theatre as a planned, memorized, directed play. They see the activity as creative, and children's public performance as not creative. In my opinion, the activity is a long-term preparation for eventual performance. Activity concerned with any form of communication requires a receiving station, and reception by an audience can be a vital contribution to a child's development. But the audience itself must be prepared and educated to play its part. How this is done is not our concern here. And the children coming from the classroom activity to a performance must be prepared by an attitude toward performance, which views it as an enlarged classroom. The material of the performance itself should be an outgrowth of the classroom activity, not a new experience achieved through an artificial process. As we hope to extend all learning in the classroom into life, so performance can be a bridge between the classroom and the world.

A successful performance enjoyed both by actors and audience can make the activity more meaningful and delightful. But a performance by children should not be repeated. Repetition of a performance requires a special skill to achieve the freshness and newness of the first time. This requires work and study for performance sake. In children, we develop skills for the sake of their contribution to growth; for example, courage and confidence to think, feel, and act harmoniously for an immediate purpose.

In further justification of the statement recommending one performance at a time, it is my belief that the emphasis must be placed on the process by which performance is achieved. Repeated performances place the emphasis on the product rather than the process. Further, the repetition, even though dialogue may be improvised and not memorized, tends to lose the original vitality, and therefore lessen the satisfactions derived.

Children and teacher must see performance as sharing rather than showing. It is an opportunity for children to learn the responsibilities of both initiator and receiver. They should see performance as a cooperative endeavor, not an exhibition of "me."

TEACHER QUALIFICATIONS

The teacher of acting for children must approach his work with respect and a sound knowledge of theatre as a medium of communication. He must have an understanding of the creative possibilities in conducting the formal (the play) or the informal dramatic program in the classroom. Many assume that the classroom work is creative and the play is not. Either will be as creative or uncreative as the director, or teacher, is creative or uncreative. The creative teacher-director is concerned with what happens in the course of the preparation of the play. This justifies the play as an activity for youth and determines the quality of the result.

A specialist who teaches acting to children should be able to teach acting to students of any age. The reverse need not be true. The teacher of adult actors is not necessarily a good teacher of children. But principles and concepts are shared by both. The teacher of children needs, in addition to his knowledge of theatre, to know how to apply this knowledge to serve children's needs which means he must like children and know how children learn and grow. The teacher of children knows he teaches more effectively by indirection than by direction. That is, he must present in himself all the qualities he is dedicated to developing in children. There is in his attitude an understanding of and respect for the natural capacities of children, and an attitude of humility that admits that he can learn from his students. There is no trace of patronage, sentimentality, or superiority in his approach.

Good acting is the result of a creative process. The process may be initiated by the director or the teacher, but it takes place within the individual. This inner activity results in overt action. This is self-direction. Arriving at his ends by a creative process makes it possible for the actor to achieve the totality of being, or wholeness, that we desire for children. This goal supports those who would have all schools include acting experience for every child. But the experience can be effective only under the guidance of a creative teacher, and there are too few teachers of such understanding. Perhaps this is because not enough situations demand this quality and kind of teaching. This will continue to be true until the public recognizes the difference between a superficial and a real approach to youth through the avenue of theatre. The public must be led to understand that the superficial approach results in imitation and exhibition. The real approach produces creative thinking, feeling, and acting individuals.

One problem is overcoming the concept that acting is for the stage and only for "talented" people. Presenting the study of acting as a means of successful living and learning is not enough to change these concepts or to overcome the fear that acting lessons will make a child exhibitionistic. Indeed, it can do this if the child is studying acting for professional purposes. On the other hand, if the teacher presents acting to children in its simplest form—acting is doing—they accept and understand it. And if they are *to do* (to act), they must *be* and *think*.

RATIONALE

This kind of activity may be new to children, but they respond to it. It is an opportunity to use what they have and to succeed because they are not in competition. It is harder for adults to accept and understand, for they are often suspicious that acting is solely recreational, a fun thing. The following dialogue was written to help parents understand.

PARENT: Why do you refer to your classes as acting classes rather than dramatic classes? You say they are classes for children and laymen, for educational and developmental reasons. I thought acting referred to classes designed to train the professional performer. Acting makes me think immediately of the so-called talented child, who is being trained for the professional stage.

TEACHER: Lessons that an actor ought to learn are lessons for living life. What are the stage, drama, theatre but selected, re-created life situations and problems? Therefore, the actor needs to know first how to live his life role, how to be himself, how to be an authority on himself. This is a prerequisite to understanding and being authoritative about the roles he may assume.

PARENT: But doesn't dramatics do this?

TEACHER: In the dramatics club or class the lessons generally begin with an assigned role. This is what the student expects and wants. The layman, whether child or adult, loves the chance to get out of himself. It is generally thought of as a desirable "release." The truth is that the assumed role may make the student more conscious of himself, because he looks for his effect upon others. He is concerned not with *what* he is doing, but *how* he is doing. He may have changed himself externally, but internally he is unable to encompass or identify with the character. The character cannot absorb him because he is self-absorbed. He is thinking (while going through actions of his character) his own thoughts, feeling his own feelings. He is a house divided. This kind of acting for effect may seem to succeed but contributes nothing of lasting value.

Dramatics class implies dramatic performance at some time. Often the class exists for the preparation of a performance. An acting class is concerned only with the growth of the individual.

PARENT: What are some of your reasons for teaching acting to the child or to the layman?

TEACHER: What are the qualities you desire to have, to make life more satisfying, to fulfill yourself? Would one of them be greater self-confidence or trust? The actor must know and trust himself. Whether or not he is aware of it, when he acts a role, he reveals himself. There is an idea that acting is good for the layman because it's a kind of defense or disguise that permits him freedom to do what he could not do in his own role—the "release" I mentioned earlier. Encouraging a child "to put on an act" does not develop his personal strength. It makes his need to hide greater. The first lessons, then, must be directed toward helping the individual trust himself, helping him not to be afraid of showing what he is—to perform rather than to put on a performance.

PARENT: I do not go along with you all the way on the idea that play-acting is bad. That is what you are saying, isn't it?

TEACHER: No! Play-acting has a place in the acting class but I am trying to make clear that the first concern of the serious teacher is to help the child accept himself. There is much play-acting that goes on in an acting class for learning purposes. What I am doing here in our discussion is stripping to fundamentals.

The teacher can then go on to explain her other reasons for teaching acting. A second reason may be that acting—honest, sincere acting—requires the harmonizing of all parts of the individual—the thinking, feeling, doing parts. Education is concerned with developing wholeness for health and for learning. Experience with acting is one way this can be done. What happens when you see something that offends you? Your whole being is focused in protest; you say, "Oh, no!" And when you speak there is no mistaking your meaning. You have expressed thought and feeling in words and action. This is you functioning sincerely. Good, sincere acting requires response of the whole being.

A third reason is that in our society we are judged by our public speech and behavior. I do not mean standing up to make a speech. Public speech and action is that expressive behavior called for in group situations of any kind—classroom, parties, meetings, games—wherever interaction is called for.

In the intimate familiar situation all people are capable of being individuals, expressing feeling freely without inhibitions. Very young children generally have no inhibitions. They act themselves, often to the embarrassment of adults. But they lose this freedom in time. They catch the pervading disease, "What will people think?" They become self-conscious and, to be sure, they are not different from others. They follow the crowd. They learn to hide what they think or they stop thinking. Voice and action in public becomes tentative. It is apparent that the individual's concern is with the effect of the utterance and not with the truth. Acting must be concerned with truth. Youth needs confidence to be itself in public as well as in private. I do not mean an undisciplined self and offensive behavior, for this is as unnatural as putting on an act. I mean the ability to function as freely in a group as in the intimate situation, to speak out, to move the body with ease. Notice the narrow vocal range, the limited, tentative gestures of many people in the public situation. They are dull, lifeless, and ineffective.

A fourth reason for teaching acting is that it is natural to play-act. Children learn by re-creating life situations, by being mommy, teacher, nurse, etc. And all of us enjoy in varying degrees a little limelight. Limelight is as necessary to growth as sunlight. Because it is natural, there is enjoyment in acting and thus possibility for learning also.

A fifth reason is related to wholeness. The actor's instrument is himself—his whole self. Many teachers become preoccupied with the physical instrument, forgetting there must be something behind the front, and herein lies a danger. The visible agent must be expressive of the inner agent, which is where the responsibility lies. The inner agent must be a storehouse of riches to be selected and expressed visibly and understandably. In working with children in an acting class, the teacher's concern is less with the outer means than with the inner. He feels responsibility for developing and building these inner resources. He does it by cultivating the avenues of the senses, opening them wide. He helps the child to recognize and become aware of sights, sounds, textures, temperatures, smells, tastes in the world around him. He provides opportunities to put these sensations to use so that they will remain forever in the storehouse of memory. And in widening these avenues in and out, there is the possibility of developing an ability to see that which is invisible.

A sixth reason—and though I state it last, it is by no means the least important—acting is communicating. It is strange that in a world so communications conscious, there is so little person-to-person communication. Communication is interaction. Interaction indicates that something is happening here and now. The actor must achieve not only person-to-person contact but person-to-group. He learns to assume responsibility for both initiating and responding alternately. He learns that the initiator is responsible for the response he receives. He learns that alert and active listening is essential to achieve vitality and interest. He learns the difference between talking at and talking with, the difference between recited dialogue and spontaneous dialogue. He learns to speak out and not to be afraid of the sound of his public voice.

At this point the dialogue might proceed something like this:

PARENT: I see. I like "building the resources." This means developing a resourceful person. You have made a good case for acting. But how do you teach it?

TEACHER: That is the most difficult question to answer, for there is no prescription. A teacher with the ideas I have given you will find his own ways to achieve these ends.

I indicated that the first lesson in acting should establish self-trust. The teacher might begin with a simple exercise, such as asking the student just to stand quietly and look at the group. Or he might ask him to look at an object, while he himself is the object of group attention. He might do any number of things to help the student achieve the ability to focus. In focusing upon a person, thing, or idea, wonderful discoveries can be made. The first and most important is that the attention is transferred from self to object. When this is achieved, personal freedom is achieved. A second thing that occurs is awareness of the relationship between self and objective. With relationship we discover identity. This illustrates the biblical phrase, "he who loses himself will find himself."

These goals are not achieved one at a time or in any special order, but every exercise contributes to the progress we seek.

PARENT: But doesn't the student become restless in an acting class when he is not always acting? Is he satisfied with the simple exercise you suggest?

TEACHER: A good question. If the teacher is a "good actor," the members of the group are challenged constantly. Each can have a chance as soon as he is ready. Because the class is designed to have the student discover and learn for himself, there are continual surprises and delights. At no time does the teacher sit and hand out information or criticism. There is constant movement. The challenges provide opportunity for each to do what he can; and there is the expectation that what each does today will be refined and improved tomorrow. The class is a continuing investigation of capacities and means. It is not that in such classes the students never act. But they are asked to act the experience that is theirs at the level of their growth. The result is beautiful acting because it is truth, a visible expression of inner conviction.

PARENT: How does this study benefit the student in his life role?

TEACHER: It will benefit him according to his needs. The child who doesn't know "what to play" will discover that he can make up his play. The child who never reads will begin to take an interest in words because words are important tools for the actor. The child fearful of "wrong answers" will develop spontaneity of expression because he is unafraid. The child who insists on dominating every situation will no longer need to dominate because he's had recognition. The child failing in school because he couldn't concentrate will do better. The child who never has anybody to play with will begin to attract playmates.

Of course, this doesn't happen in ten lessons. This must be a continuing activity—art of the child's life. "Trying" an acting class, a dance class, an art class, etc., is part of the difficulty in our society. These activities must be sustained and ongoing to have real growth value. One of the many fine things about a class in the arts, whether it be dance, music, acting, or visual art, is that as the individual grows, the work is made more challenging. The child need not be held back by a classmate who is less able. And even in the heterogeneous class, the teacher can meet individual needs because he is not bound by a syllabus nor expected to produce a group, whose members know the same things at the same time regardless of individual native equipment.

PARENT: You have given me some insight, but I'm afraid I cannot visualize such a class.

TEACHER: Is it important? How can I describe a class that takes its direction from needs, interests, and abilities? A class whose source of supply is the individuals within it? A class that has no text, no syllabus? It is the parents' role to investigate the philosophy, the point of view, the purpose, the principles, and the attitudes of a teacher. Then, if the investigation is satisfactory, to have faith in the teacher. Refrain from asking a child, "What did you do today?" If it is difficult for a teacher to describe such a class, how much more difficult for a child. What happens is dependent upon the conditions of the moment. What is right today may not be right tomorrow. This is true of all creative classes, whether in the arts or academic subjects.

Returning to your immediate concern about the value of the acting class, however, let me say: acting is an art form. It is the art most closely related to life. The study of acting should mean natural transference of its values to the art of living.

Parent and reader may remain unconvinced. You may say, you speak of the lessons the actor must learn that are lessons for living. If the actor has learned these lessons, why is he not a happier, healthier person? Some actors are. Those who are not may have learned the lessons well but no one ever told them that these apply to life and living. They think they need props, stage, play, costumes in order to use the learned lessons. Techniques are turned on with the lights and turned off at the end of the play. The actor needs help to see that these lessons should be integrated with his own being and should be his to use to make life richer and more satisfying.

What are these lessons? Concentration (focus on the here and now); productive use of imagination (making it work); observation (awareness of environment, persons, self); self-projection, sensitizing the senses so they remain open; discrimination (making choices); discipline of body, voice, mind, communication (verbal and nonverbal); and elimination of inhibitions and fears. These are all lessons that can help an individual achieve the most from life. Few of them are stated goals of a public or private school curriculum; but for the teacher of acting, these are the fundamentals of his work with students.

The following dialogue suggests the concepts and some techniques needed by a teacher who is using acting for developmental purposes:

PARENT: You speak of lessons in concentration. What would you do? How could you make such a lesson interesting?

TEACHER: Maybe I'd put a plain card on the floor, then ask the children to focus—giving it all their attention for as long as possible, to see what would happen.

PARENT: Have you any idea about what might happen? I'm sure I haven't.

TEACHER: I've done it myself. One thing that happens is that everything disappears but the card. Children say, "Everything went black but the card," or "It seemed to move."

PARENT: Do you think children would do this? It seems silly to me.

TEACHER: It doesn't to them. They enjoy the challenge. To see how long they can stay with the card. It is a challenge to do what the teacher knows they can do, if they try.

PARENT: I'm still not clear. How would you go about a lesson in imagination?

TEACHER: I'd let them "Scamper."

PARENT: What is "scampering?" I've never heard of it.

TEACHER: It's a technique. A procedure where we take imagination on a guided tour.

PARENT: I don't follow.

TEACHER: Do you know the edge radio has on TV for educational purposes?

PARENT: You tell me.

TEACHER: Radio makes the listener work. He has to visualize in order to follow the action. TV does all the work. All the viewer does is look. Do you see?

PARENT: Yes. Radio makes it necessary for the listener to use his imagination, his experience, his knowledge.

TEACHER: "Scampering" is a technique devoted solely to one end —exercising and guiding imagination. It is like radio in that it supplies cues to the imagination. For example, the music bridge comes in slowly in a minor key. You are prepared for a change, a somber change. The sound man prepares a sound. You interpret it as a door closing and you are right because someone says at once, "Janie, are you home?" "Scamper" gives the listener, who is sitting in the dark (because his eyes are closed), specific cues. The teacher says to the listener, "Go to your favorite place in your house. Are you there? Don't answer, just nod your head." In "Scampering" no verbal response can be given, only an inner response. The teacher says to the listener, "Will you perform some action that is usual for you in this place? . . . Someone is calling you. . . . You answer—not out loud. . . . Open your eyes. Were you able to do all you were told to do? Who would like to tell us about it? What happened? What did you say?"

PARENT: I guess I really do see.

TEACHER: We all understand that visualization is important for many reasons. And all of us in the arts have done something with it in relation to a variety of lessons. But to isolate it, to make it a technique, and to name it makes it available. It becomes another specific tool and a procedure. It adds another dimension. Perhaps it satisfies productively the need that daydreaming, which is unproductive, satisfies.

PARENT: I'd like to go back to your lesson with the card. That interested me, but somehow I'm not satisfied. Can you defend it beyond the obvious?

TEACHER: Yes, briefly. What we focus on or pay attention to we relate to. Do you realize the importance of this? I used this lesson once with a group of teen-agers. A week later one of them said to me, "Thank you for the lesson with the card. I learned why I didn't like science." Curious, I asked her why. Her answer, "Because I never paid enough attention to it."

PARENT: She was very perceptive. That was unusual, wasn't it?

TEACHER: Yes. Ruth learned and was able to articulate the learning. Others may learn but at the moment are not able to state it. But if I work with students long enough, they will articulate because this is one of the acting teacher's goals. It is not enough to "know what you mean"; you must find the words to express it.

PARENT: I am beginning to understand. You have identified for me some of the trees in what seemed an impenetrable forest. By the forest, I mean the abstract materials that seemed mysterious and vague. You have identified some of the practical learnings possible and also named some of the tools you use. You said "Scamper" is a tool?

TEACHER: That's right. Brainstorming, doodling, and games are all tools used by teachers who work in the arts for purposes of growth and learning.

PARENT: I expect your biggest challenge lies in the education of adults like me, who know only how to evaluate learning by the sum of knowledge put into a child's head.

TEACHER: True. "What have you learned? What grade did you get?" Such questions are the only way the average parents evaluate their children's school and teachers. The concern is with input. They have difficulty understanding that "output" is the only way input becomes meaningful to the child. When we can express what we know in our own way, to use for our own purposes, the knowledge is then truly ours. Strange that with all the emphasis on communication these days, few recognize it as a two-way street. It is not enough to understand. We must make others understand us. We want children to read and write because ability with language is essential to communication skill, but we do not see it as more than the decoding of words.

For years we have accepted the arts as therapy. All that is needed is to involve the patient in the doing. Involvement is the key to therapy. It takes a teacher with knowledge of the patient, of what he can and cannot be expected to do, of how to engage his interest and keep it going. In the use of the arts in education, we need teachers who "know" their students and who are working to develop many skills—not "how to" skills, but skills for living and learning. They need to know how to create new attitudes on the part of adults toward art *as* education. They need to know and name the specific goals and to identify the learnings possible. These lessons are not yet in the books. We who use the arts for learning have been guilty of vagueness. If we want to overcome this, we must dispel the mystique through clarity and precision. It is not enough that we know what we are trying to accomplish; it is our further obligation to communicate it to others.

REFERENCES

Scamper is available from the D.O.K. Publishing Co., Buffalo, N.Y., 14215.
Teaching Is a Dialogue by Grace Stanistreet is available from Adelphi University, Garden City, N.Y.

THE THEATRE:
A SIDE VIEW

MOSES GOLDBERG

Moses Goldberg is associate professor of theatre at Florida State University. He was granted a B.S. degree in psychology from Tulane University, a master's degree in child psychology from Stanford, and a second master's degree in drama from the University of Washington; he received his Ph.D. in the theatre arts from the University of Minnesota. Professor Goldberg, one of the youngest leaders in the field, has contributed numerous articles to professional journals and other publications. His most recent work is a college textbook entitled Children's Theatre: A Philosophy and a Method. *He is an exponent of involvement drama and is known for his innovative theatre productions.*

It is traditional to study the theatre from what I would call a "top" view. One looks at the particular forms of theatre that currently exist or that have existed in the past. Whether one is dealing with historical style, such as Elizabethan drama or the Peking Opera, or with a modern institution—Broadway, Happenings, Grotowski, Absurdism, etc.—the investigator in a top-view study is interested primarily in description and analysis. What was Shakespeare's stage like? What do his plays mean? How does Grotowski direct? What kinds of plays have made how much money on Broadway? What is the significance of sound imagery in Chekhov? All these questions view the theater and the drama as developed to a specific point. Since the theatre exists in such and such a form, they postulate, we can examine its form and the meaning behind the form. In studying form, we are studying the *surface manifestations* of the theatre—hence my phrase, "the top view."

The top view concentrates its attention on the artist's theatre. Most studies try to discover the intention or method of the theatrical practitioner. Those few top-view studies that do concern themselves with the audience are interested primarily in a discrete reaction by a specific audience to a single stage event, such as measuring the galvanic skin response of an audience member to a moment of tension, or analyzing the variables that produce a laugh at a specific line. Again, these are investigating a surface manifestation—a top view.

What I should like to propose—and this is certainly not intended to replace top-view studies, but rather to supplement them—is that we also study the theatre from the side view. In addition to looking at surface manifestations of the theatre, we need to find out more about its developmental processes. I should like to see a major area of theatre research opened up under the general heading of Developmental Theatre. In this subfield we will take a side view of theatre. We will ask two major questions:

1. Why and how did the art of theatre emerge?
2. How does the theatre become increasingly relevant to the life of the growing individual?

Because this approach is built upon the fundamental assumption that both the medium of theatre and the audience's aesthetic sense are in a state of change, side-view researchers find it less meaningful to look only at a single manifestation of art or a single audience response. We must look at growth—at sequence; and this can best be diagrammed as a view from the side. *Developmental theatre is defined as the study of change in theatre form or audience experience.* (Those few side-view studies that are being done today generally deal with the change in an artist's method; such as the development of Shakespeare's language through the various periods of his life.)

Since the side-view approach is comparative, i.e., it assumes two or more levels of related events, it suggests a need for relating levels of theatrical event to levels of growth in other areas—human development, economic development, spiritual development, etc. And this, in turn, suggests a need for an interdisciplinary study of theatre, particularly in dealing with the first question above. A study of the emergence of the theatre as an art medium may properly focus on an analysis of primitive man's changing psychological and sociological patterns. The significance of the interaction of magic, religion, theatre, and other now distinct but originally synonymous expressions of man's inner psyche may be investigated most appropriately by a team of researchers: a theologian, a sociologist, a historian, a psychologist, an anthropologist, and an aesthetician—all working together. Or, since there is much truth in the saying that "Ontogeny recapitulates phylogeny," it may be reasonable to investigate the development of the theatre art by looking at dramatic play in modern children in order to discover why and how they evolve, for themselves, the elements of the theatre. Perhaps this is the true function of that activity that many have called "creative drama." Perhaps what creative drama is supposed to be is a process of guiding the child to create—for the first time and out of a basic human need—an art form, which can be conveniently called "theatre," since that is what all the other people who have created it—also for the first time—have agreed to call it.

By taking the creative drama approach to the study of the development of the theatre art, we are learning why theatre appeared, as well as studying the child as an emerging artist. It is also possible to study the second area of developmental theatre—the increasing relevance of theatre to the audience—by studying the child as an emerging audience member. It is not a coincidence that the field of developmental psychology (the study of changes in behavior) focuses most of its energies on the child. If we are to study change, we must go to where change is most noticeable; and that usually means to young people.

We can, I hope, hypothesize that the individual develops as an audience member; i.e., he at one stage is an "immature" audience member, and at another stage—which is chronologically subsequent to the immature stage—is a "mature" audience member. I shall speak of this later stage as "aesthetic maturity." Aesthetic maturity may or may not be related to physical maturity, social maturity, intellectual maturity, emotional maturity, or spiritual maturity. These are all areas in which the development of the individual is recognized; and educators are aware that a person may be mature in one area and very immature in another. Maturity is hard to demonstrate, but immaturity is relatively easy to locate—in a young child. Therefore, the field of developmental theatre is committed to a study of children, both as emerging artists—perhaps in creative dramatics —and as emerging audiences—again reminding us of an existing label: children's theatre.

Developmental theatre, then, can include both creative drama and children's theatre. But it goes beyond both. It is by no means confined to children. It is concerned with all theatre as it develops and evolves, and all individuals as they mature in aesthetic sophistication. Perhaps, as a concept, developmental theatre brings creative drama and children's theatre squarely into focus as part of the "real" field of theatre. Perhaps, in the long run, we would benefit if we forgot the terms "children's theatre" and "creative drama" and talked only about the development of artist and audience. How does the art of theatre emerge from man's basic inner needs? How does aesthetic maturity evolve in the audience member? These are the two questions, slightly refined, which developmental theatre asks.

At this point in my own research, I am particularly interested in the second question—the one that deals with theatre from the point of view of the developing audience. I want to discover how we can help the individuals in the audience reach aesthetic maturity. I want to discover the sequence that each individual goes through in proceeding from immature to mature. I want to find or create the techniques and methods by which we as researchers could learn more about these concepts. And this means using the resources and methodology of the artist and the behavioral scientist to probe developmental theatre.

It means, primarily, creating a research laboratory that is essentially a theatre devoted to developing aesthetic maturity and that is equipped to experiment with various means of accomplishing this goal, and various methods of measuring its successes and failures. This laboratory must, of course, be a theatre that is fully artistic and entertaining. Otherwise, it will bore its audience instead of developing it. But it must also be a laboratory in which experimental failure is accepted as a necessary possibility, and in which artistic temperament and public recognition are subordinated to sound research methodology and audience development. Such a laboratory could study audience age levels as one major component of development, and would probably carry out much of its investigation with young audiences; but it would not be a "children's theatre." It would be a developmental theatre.

The creation of such a theatre laboratory would be a project worthy of a national funding agency with a public charge to develop aesthetic maturity—such as the Kennedy Center or the National Endowment for the Arts. However, it is most likely to result from a complex union of an educational research laboratory, such as the Central Midwestern Regional Educational Laboratory, Inc. (CEMREL); a regional theatre with a commitment to artistic standards and audience development; a major university, which can justify an experimental function for an arts unit; and, hopefully, the financial backing of the private and public foundations.

One of the key strengths of this new laboratory would be the ability of the researchers to manipulate variables, much as the behavioral scientist does, and to measure, in a systematic way, the changes that result. One example of the simplest kind of project that might be done would be an investigation of how the age of the protagonist affects any change in audience attitudes or feelings. Many have hypothesized that certain ages of audience will identify best with certain ages of hero, but never has this theory been tested reliably. Changes in audience attitude could reflect changes in audience identification, and attitudes can be measured statistically.

One method for approaching this problem might be to choose a play—such as Harris's *Androcles and the Lion*—in which the age of the protagonist is not a terribly significant artistic factor; and then to cast the part with several actors of different apparent ages. In order to control for quality differences, the researcher might choose to use several different actors at each of three or four different age levels. Perhaps as many as twenty different actors would be rehearsed in the role of Androcles; but, in every case, the rest of the production and cast would remain as exactly uniform as possible.

The next step would be to develop a quickly administered measuring instrument—perhaps a questionnaire or adjective check list—that would find out the extent to which seeing the play had effected changes in the attitudes expressed by the audience, which in turn would suggest the extent of identification with the various heroes. Similar instruments exist in the literature of psychology and education, and would be usable here with some adaptation. Then, the theatre would present the play twenty times—or forty or sixty times to help remove extraneous variables such as a "down" performance—and measure the results.

Discovering the factors that influence identification would make it possible to go deeper and deeper into those variables which make the theatre experience a developmental one for the audience, and each new discovery makes finer and finer control of variables practical. Obviously, it will be a very slow process to uncover all the relevant variables. But, over time, significant information could be amassed with some confidence. Each study points out directions for further profitable research, or closes the door on an unprofitable line of inquiry.

One could not, of course, begin to predict what the long-range results of such a theatre laboratory might be in terms of building a popular audience for the theatre in this country, or in terms of enriching the lives of individual theatregoers; but it is hoped that such a project would have very tangible benefits as well as important scholarly ones. One goal of such a theatre would be to pinpoint the sequence of experiences most appropriate to the readiness level of the individual audience member.

For example, all other things being equal, it may be aesthetically unwise to do Molière for a particular audience before it has had a chance to see an example of commedia dell'arte. Perhaps the commedia experience provides, in some as yet unknown way, the "vocabulary" the individual needs in order to take the most from the Molière experience. And perhaps Molière, in turn, prepares the individual for Sheridan or Shaw? I have sometimes asked my graduate students to rank-order all the plays of Shakespeare in terms of the ideal sequence in which they would show them to an audience. Without my telling them why or how to make such judgments, they were still able to do it in a remarkably consistent way. Various students in various classes consistently rank *Midsummer Night's Dream* and *Macbeth* before *King Lear* or *Troilus and Cressida*. *Romeo and Juliet* is invariably seen as being more appropriate to a younger audience than is *Love's Labours Lost*. There must, therefore, be an intuitive understanding in these students' minds of sequential aesthetic experiences.

The Developmental Theatre student might begin by analyzing these intuitions, reducing them to possible categories, or criteria for judging one play more mature than another; and then proceed to test these criteria experimentally in the theatre laboratory. The result of such a study might have practical application to season selection, or curriculum planning in a high school, and might even reliably inform the Broadway producer that he is making a financial mistake to do a certain play the season after another play has covered the same aesthetic ground.

The development of specific aesthetic concepts is another area for research, and may lead to specific applications for the playwright, director, or producer. The audience member learns and changes by going to the theatre, and he also learns how to learn from his future theatre experiences. If we can find out how to maximize these kinds of learning, we are guaranteeing that the theatre will become more *useful* to the individual (without, of course, implying any loss of entertainment values).

For a ready example, let us look at the concept of "death"—surely one of the most personally relevant and yet difficult concepts in human existence, and, paradoxically, one of the concepts least prepared for in the traditional education and socialization of the child. In the theatre, the equivalent concept is "character death." "Character death" does not precisely equal real death, for a character has no life to begin with; but he has an aesthetic life, and can therefore suffer an aesthetic death. Perhaps the theatre should begin with this concept by merely teaching that there is such a thing as "character death." Perhaps this is done on the simplest level—as in a play for five- through eight-year-olds—by the witch screaming out, "I'm dead!" and then taking off her costume, revealing an actor whose role is finished. Of course, this is all hypothesis. There is no evidence yet to show that this, indeed, should be the first stage of introduction to this concept; and certainly no reason to attach this stage to the particular ages mentioned.

But, to continue with speculation, perhaps the next stage should introduce the individual, and perhaps ages eight through eleven represent this stage, to all of the various ways to conventionalize character death. In a realistic play, we conventionalize death with indications of pain and weakness leading to collapse and a lack of movement. In an heroic play, death may be indicated by rhymed couplets, or a spectacular fall from the balcony into the moat. In some Oriental drama, a red cloth placed over the face means death of the character. All these are equivalent concepts and all enable the individual who views them to learn the vocabulary of the theatre. In this second phase, the major emphasis is on learning how to learn from the theatre by learning how to translate its conventions into meaningful concepts.

Perhaps, in early adolescence, the individual next learns to cope with the significance of character death in terms of its relationship with the real concept of death. He begins to *use* his translation skills at this stage as he learns to compare the death of a major character with the potential (or actual) death of one of his own acquaintances or relatives. Perhaps, in a fourth, late adolescence, stage, he learns how to deal with his own death by manipulating the character death of an identification model in his thoughts. A mature attitude toward death may simply require that he judge character death in terms of its necessity or appropriateness. Perhaps the aesthetically mature individual is the one who can say, "That was a good death, that a bad one, that a needful one, that a wasteful one." If the character deaths he has experienced through a series of plays can lead him to equanimity about the real ones he must experience, then the theatre has been useful to him. Obviously, it can be most useful if the particular concept is manipulated in the most effective developmental sequence; and my continual use of "perhaps" above indicates that we do not yet know what that sequence is. But we can discover it—in the developmental theatre laboratory.

The concept of manipulating growth, by the way, is a bit frightening, particularly when the manipulation is being done by people with whom we do not agree. But even more frightening, to me, is the concept of leaving a powerful developmental tool like the theatre unexplored—an unknown weapon in the hands of whatever naive practitioner might chance to put on a play. As the theatre becomes recognized as an educational force, public interest in its wise use will certainly replace the peripheral regard it now holds. Hopefully, the goal toward which the individual will be manipulated will not be political expediency, but rather aesthetic maturity.

The implication, of course, is that aesthetic maturity is a good thing; that fostering its development would benefit both the theatre and the audience. I see maturity—which can be defined somewhat inadequately as the ability to make the appropriate response—as desirable. Maturity in every area of human growth is important, and that should include aesthetic maturity. The arts are a powerful means of finding out about and manipulating concepts of the universe. I have spoken about "vocabulary" and "translation." The arts are a language system, a way of organizing knowledge and a way of expressing knowledge. Maturity is simply fluency in all available languages—verbal and nonverbal. The developmental theatre researcher and practitioner study ways in which the language of theatre may have come into being; how its referrents evolved; how its syntax was developed; and especially, how each individual learns the language.

In conclusion, developmental theatre is seen as engulfing and replacing children's theatre and creative drama as subject areas. It is, after all, not theatre for *children* that motivates us, but theatre for *people*. We seek a way to make the art relevant to the human being, and we devote so much of our energy to young human beings because they are more educable and less isolated by psychological inhibitions, social contexts, or intellectual interests. We want to develop a nation of aesthetically mature human beings who will continue to use theatre in their lives as adults. In addition to bringing pleasure to the immature, our purpose is to bring them to maturity (through entertainment, always through entertainment). The developmental theatre seeks to open up channels of knowledge and communication to the individual. It seeks to teach him a new language with which he can reach out to the universe. It does not view him from the top—a "finished" product. It views him from the side—growing, stretching upward towards his fullest potential as a human being. In the last analysis, reaching that potential is the only goal worth having.

SMOKING CHIMNEYS

LOWELL SWORTZELL

Lowell Swortzell was introduced to child drama at the Children's Museum of Washington, D.C., where as a child he participated in creative dramatics classes and attended touring productions of Clare Tree Major. While still a teen-ager he began writing plays, an area to which he has since made a notable contribution. His one-act plays and play reviews have appeared in a variety of periodicals and his anthology, All the World's a Stage: Modern Plays for Young People, *was hailed by the* New York Times *as an "outstanding book of the year." Professor Swortzell has taught at Yale, Tufts, Hofstra, the University of Wisconsin, and New York University, where he is currently director of the program in Educational Theatre. He and his wife, Dr. Nancy Swortzell, initiated this program, which includes substantial and innovative work in the area of child drama.*

In a review of *Children and Dramatics* that appeared in the *New York Times* in 1966, I wrote that Richard Crosscup's autobiographical account might rank among the most important statements on educational theatre since the pioneer work of Winifred Ward in the 1930s. While in retrospect my esteem for this volume in no way has lessened, I am troubled by the phrase "pioneer work," and wonder if I had any right to use it then or now in application to child drama.

Advances, to be certain, have been made since Miss Ward arrived on the scene to lead two generations of teachers through her courses, books, workshops, and lecture tours, and to spearhead the particular practice of educational theatre that came to be known in the United States as creative dramatics. Her students in turn, joined by others who emerged independently, spread their knowledge and experience from coast to coast. So the geographical frontiers have been won, settled, even absorbed into much of the educational landscape, if not so far deeply into the cultural life of America.

But because "pioneering" means more than mere homesteading, we may wonder how far we have come in first discovering and then developing this thing variously labeled child drama, educational theatre, developmental drama, youth theatre, participatory theatre, children's theatre, drama-in-education, or whatever *you* may term it.

Historians speaking of the pioneer spirit in America like to recall a characteristic adage often attributed to the father of Abraham Lincoln, "When you can see the smoke from your neighbor's chimney, it's time to move on." When visible in our field, the smoke mostly emerges in puffs too small and too infrequent to suggest it derives from work securely sustained. Some of it seems more the result of fires of confusion than of certainty, some of it reflects eagerness to serve children unsupported by preparation to do so, and some of it appears to be screens sent up to conceal a lack of anything else to reveal. Certain reasons for this widespread obscuration are explored here, along with some of the currently popular forms it takes (instant theatre, audience participation, Story Theatre, Reader's Theatre, and commedia dell'arte troupes). Yet genuine fires do burn, and vigorously in places, albeit their intermittent significance is too rarely noticed (and appreciated) and up to now seldom if ever causes neighbors either to move or to improve their own efforts. In time these fires, also discussed herein (some genuine experimentation here and in England), may come to be regarded as "pre-pioneering" efforts but for now they constitute signs of life that breed thought, generate productivity, and perhaps spawn creativity. Moreover, they invite criticism, which cannot exist unless significant artistic activity first exists to demand its presence; criticism is proof of both neighbors and their smoking chimneys.

A PLACE TO BEGIN

No matter what aspects of educational theatre (and it is an enormous field) claim the services of teachers or the attention of students, nor whether together they strive for fully finished productions or for fulfillment of an exercise or class, everyone requires a philosophic concept or aesthetic principle to govern his operation. Creative teachers, like other artists, hope to develop their own theoretical positions through practice rather than accept ready-to-wear credos lifted from pages of books, even good books by established authorities. The best do, of course, and the rest must be encouraged to keep trying until they satisfy their own requirements for hypothetical foundations and structural systems.

Likewise, everyone, be he director, actor, teacher, student, participant, or observer, needs to locate a starting point from which to take up the experience of educational theatre. Can there be one place that appropriately applies to areas as diverse and complex as the playhouse, the schoolhouse, the playground, the community center, the street, and city park? Can there be a single position that launches young people towards an understanding of dramatic literature and theatrical performance? Indeed, can they commence collectively and simultaneously? For me, such a spot has been identified by Richard Crosscup in his observation that the validity of an activity resides in its meaning.[1] He is speaking of dramatic activities in the classroom while I am speaking of drama in general, in the classroom and everywhere else. Simply by substituting my word "action" (Aristotle's, actually) for his word "activity" we arrive at the essence of drama: the transformation of an audience, be it pupils or playgoers, when it recognizes the meaning of an action. Crosscup states the aesthetic process we experience when we lead children in dramatic play of even the most informal kind and it is the same process we undergo when we see a play: we establish the "relationship between *doing* and *meaning*, and between *meaning* and *being*."[2] The relationship of action and idea and idea and existence, our own and that of others, is the one we hope to establish when we write, direct, or act plays, just as it is the connection we attempt to make when we teach courses and conduct workshops in the creative arts. It is the *creative* connection, the one by which we can transform others as well as ourselves.

And it is one that frequently remains unmade or not fully completed both in education and theatre. Pressures to move from one activity to another in the classroom, as well as from one act to another in a play, or from one point to another in an improvisation, can impede, prohibit, or altogether destroy possible connections. This failure results from the harried teacher, unclear writer, insensitive leader of creative dramatics, careless play director, or the well-meaning but inept actor who has not carried the process through each of its essential phases to its comprehensive conclusion. Somewhere during a performance or dramatic activity an action is not communicated, experienced, or transformed into personal significance and the child remains unreached, uninvolved, unchanged. It is when the creative connection is made with regularity in the theatre and classroom that we best achieve artistic as well as academic goals. And the public now often confused about our activity, once convinced this modus operandi is central to children and dramatics, will no longer look upon us as surrogate baby sitters filling idle hours with idle amusements, for they will witness actual creative growth in children; and if they also participate, in themselves as well.

ANCESTORS TO GUIDE US

If we wish to trace the aesthetic evolution of this basic creative procedure from its beginnings to the time of Ward, Crosscup, Hughes Mearns, and of their more recent British counterparts, we sooner or later find ourselves contemplating Plato and Aristotle. We discover, for example, that such a twentieth-century sounding phrase as "memory is in the muscles," used today to describe the interdependence of intellect and action, goes back to the hills, of Athens if not beyond. Aristotle, noting that action is motion and motion is always explicit, observes, "He who performs any action, not knowing what the action is, nor to what end it will lead, nor about whom action is conversant, acts from ignorance essentially, and therefore acts involuntarily." And when speaking of memory he argues, "No memory is a habit but rather an action," adding elsewhere that "those who are very young and very old labor under a defect of memory on account of motion." To Aristotle, man's ultimate happiness is found in an activity which he practices to his perfection and self-sufficiency.

Philip Coggin in skillfully outlining the origins of drama in education notes the particular influence of Jean-Jacques Rousseau upon modern creative drama.[3] The eighteenth-century philosopher distinguishes sharply between professional theatre, not to be tolerated because it encloses people in dark caves, and participatory theatre, to be encouraged because it sets people free to express themselves in market squares where they dance, march, and sport their physical dexterities. "Turn the spectators into a spectacle," he says as progenitor of the creative connection, "make them actors themselves: make each one see himself and love himself in others so that all may be the better united." To accomplish this, one certainly must turn action into meaning and meaning into being. This advice is echoed in other words throughout the nineteenth and twentieth centuries. Goethe speaks of improvised drama: "I think this practice very useful among actors, and even in the company of friends and acquaintances. It is the best mode of drawing men out of themselves, and leading them, by a circuitous path, back into themselves again." The poet Shelley speaks of drama as the teacher of self-knowledge and self-respect: "Neither the eye nor the mind can see itself, unless reflected upon that which it resembles. The drama . . . is as a prismatic and many-sided mirror which collects the brightest rays of human nature and divides and reproduces them." Wagner speaks of dramatic action: "Without it, or without any reference to it, art representation is arbitrary, unnecessary, chancy, incomprehensible," but with it comes "the urge to bring the unconscious and the involuntary in life to itself as necessary to understanding and to recognition."

Martha Graham in introducing her 1974 company of dancers to New York City told her opening-night audience that to her "theatre was a verb before it was a noun; it was an act before it was a building," which of course is to say that civilization all along has made the connection advocated here in its development of the performing arts. First came the act, which required the verb to describe it, then the meaning which necessitated the noun to name it, then the theatre in which to perform it and through which to interpret and communicate it to others. Certainly, had such acts not significantly affected his being, man would not have constructed theatres in which to re-create them and in which to glorify their meaning, century upon century.

THE PROCESS IN ACTION

The creative process suggested here may be seen at work to some extent in every youngster. But for purposes of illustration let's examine an individual childhood that reveals its steady progression and undeniable power. Paul Zindel, the Pulitzer Prize dramatist of

The Effect of Gamma Rays on Man-in-the-Moon Marigolds and author of several novels of marked appeal to adolescents, has delineated his own creative emergence and artistic self-discovery in a short essay significantly entitled "The Theatre Is Born Within Us."⁴ Not until in his twenties did he attend his first professional play and by then he already had written two of his own, a fact that leads him to believe that the seeds of theatre were inside him all the time, growing constantly from birth.

As a young child he became aware of his surroundings by exploring new neighborhoods to which he and his mother moved on Staten Island, each echoing a separate culture of distant lands as he roamed among heritages of Sicily, Ireland, the Near East, and Africa, observing their customs, hearing their languages, testing their foods, and sensing their varied values of life. By the age of ten, he says, he had gone nowhere but had seen the world. Long before this he had discovered marionettes, and had constructed box scenes, those miniature depictions of cycloramic life constructed in a cardboard box that elementary classroom teachers fostered in the 1930s and '40s. He had gazed fascinated for long hours into aquariums, insectariums, and terrariums. He had discovered the local movie house which claimed most of his Saturday mornings. "What a great love," he remembers, "I had of microcosms, of peering at other worlds framed and separate from me." During this time he discovered patterns of life as he watched thousands daily rush to and from the ferry and noticed the happy-go-lucky few who flew small airplanes on weekends. Then at the age of eleven he stopped what he calls "eavesdropping on the world" and entered into it.

His first acts as a participant in life were to play a small role in church entertainment, to sing at school, and to be swung around by a roller-skating champion. Garnering no distinction or particular sense of accomplishment from any of these endeavors, he began writing for school assembly programs where his ideas were all borrowed and mostly bad from the start. Then tuberculosis removed him for a year and a half at age fifteen from the real world and he went back to observing, this time from the sidelines of a sanatorium. When he returned to school he wrote a play about cancer and for it won a Parker pen. In college he finished another; no Parker pen. And he saw that belated first play on Broadway, *Toys in the Attic*, which permitted one of its stars, Maureen Stapleton, to move him deeply enough to think that the theatre could become "my religion, my cathedral."

But one incident more than any other in this list of rather commonplace events transformed him. Late one evening in a Greenwich Village alleyway he saw as many as twenty people leaning out of apartment windows shouting and throwing money down to an old woman who was bent over several cans, eating garbage with her hands and ignoring the coins and bills that began to surround her. That graphic moment lodged itself permanently in his memory: he kept wondering why she did not take the money and buy food. When he later described the scene and how much it disturbed him to his friend Edward Albee, this playwright explained the act in the simple words, "She was doing penance." The essential connection was made. Zindel had found the missing meaning of the action and, in his terms, it "exploded" his consciousness, so that he never again would be the same person, or the same playwright.

Paul Zindel came to be a creative individual not by a unique path but by a universal one. With perhaps the exception of this last event, nothing extraordinary takes place in his chronology. Others may not grow up on an island of such diversity as Staten, but most towns and cities offer a mix of races and cultures to study and absorb. Today's children no longer are urged to express themselves through cardboard-box scenes but they are stimulated in far more creative activities. Some may not win early recognition for their artistic attempts but many, many do, and often in more encouraging forms than Parker pens. Few may find today's professional theatre a suitable vehicle for passions sufficiently strong to be termed religious but perhaps some still may be attracted and moved even by its momentarily waning glamour and talent, or, more likely, by the energetic and burgeoning imagination of the mass media. Not every youngster, like Eugene O'Neill and Paul Zindel, gets whisked off to a sanatorium at a critical point in his creative and intellectual growth, but most, if only for brief periods at a time, withdraw through sickness or by choice from the social to solitary life. They too observe the world before they enter and participate in it. They may not become playwrights or even members of a theatre audience, but this destination is not the essential aim of the creative process in action (although newcomers always are welcome to both ranks, of course).

In using drama our primary purpose is to bring each sphere through which a child passes in his development into its sharpest focus. By fully experiencing these microcosms in performance in the theatre and in direct participation in the classroom he can become a knowing person, able to recognize the meaning of his own and other actions and to be changed by their significance. Of course, if along the way he also becomes able to create experiences which foster this process in others, as Zindel did, so much the better for all of us.

Why, if the seeds of theatre are born within us as Zindel believes, and if the creative process is part of every child's development as stated here, are we only now pioneering the field of child drama? Why do we have too few Paul Zindels and too many others unable either to recognize the meaning of their actions or to be transformed by them? What halts the process and stifles creativity? Part of the answer to these complex questions obviously lies within our own ability as teachers and artists to complete the creative connection, to bring those spheres into focus, to provide the experience of the microcosms, and fully and truly to perform in the classroom and theatre. Once more we must acknowledge only fractional and occasional success. Even those most dedicated to creativity in education can be at fault if their class work merely outlines the process but does not embody it or if their productions only suggest but do not actually implement it. Yet we all know drama cannot describe an action but must do it, theatre cannot indicate an experience but must create it, and these same tenets are equally true of the creative process in child drama.

An examination follows of several popular practices and forms of performance that in my opinion often fail to communicate and connect a child's knowledge and being, and a look at several others that I believe are beginning to succeed with encouraging regularity.

INSTANT THEATRE

Get-rich-quick schemes, forever a part of daily life, now pop up in child drama with the con-artistry promises of on-the-spot rewards. The seller claims that when the purchaser employs methods developed over long years of practice, he (along with mass consumers everywhere) is guaranteed instant creative success. The buyer of such hocus-pocus utopian systems should beware, remembering that inasmuch as there can be no such thing as infallible prepackaged creative drama or factory-made children's theatre, there should be no reason to get either wholesale. Nor in shopping for valid sources of information should we succumb to promotional labels and ballyhooing with which courses, workshops, and conferences sometimes are merchandized. Whatever a jacket may pledge, no book of "how to" rules or shortcuts delivers fully effective means to stimulate significant expression. All you have ever wanted to know about educational theatre is not between the covers of such a text or printed on cards in a kit awaiting purchase at a campus bookdealer. Cookbook methods of creativity can lead only to the nadir of self-expression and should bear titles similar to their culinary counterparts, such as "Child Drama for Those Who Hate Child Drama," perhaps made more accurate if corrected to read "Child Drama for Those Who Hate Children." Those who deny the genuine creative process to young people by using secondhand and shopworn techniques must also hate themselves for they withhold from everyone the joy of original and spontaneous collaboration.

AUDIENCE PARTICIPATION

I have long possessed a desire deeply macabre (or perhaps worse, perverse) to just once have the enormous pleasure of attending a performance of *Peter Pan* at which when the big moment arrives to save Tinkerbell by applauding not one person can be heard to clap. "Say you believe in fairies," my ideal Peter pleads, and hundreds of voices in unison reply "No" or "Never, Never, Never," or better still, "Not on your life." How delicious to see the actress faced with this ultimatum forced to improvise to save her own life as well as to get offstage. As for Tinkerbell, she too, poor dear, would have to come up with some new way to recharge her batteries without troubling the paying patrons.

All this sacrilege arises not from Barrie's misuse of the device but from those who ineptly have imitated him decade after decade and coerced innocent spectators to perform to little or no dramatic purpose or theatrical effect. Audience participation often is required, like so much else in children's theatre, because the author or director thinks youngsters enjoy such moments, a conclusion arrived at no doubt from their own childhood memories of excitement in helping

Peter to restore her/his friend to glowing health. So, time after time, Barrie gets the blame for having created a tradition that now has become an artistic albatross able to destroy the reality and beauty of an otherwise thoughtful production.

I almost had my wish come true in London at a Christmas performance not of *Peter Pan* but of one of its more feeble descendants. Printed inside the programs was a large solid red circle to which no reference was made until late in the second act. At this point we were told by the hero that the only way to stop the villain from taking over the entire city was to confront him (the villain was a fey witch in a sequined *Folies-Bergère* costume, played by a man) with red spots, the one thing in the world able to render his magic powerless. What red spots the audience wanted to know, having long since forgotten their programs. They had to be told where to find the spots, but this didn't bring the moment off either because by now they could no longer locate their programs. A mad (and decidedly maddening) scramble ensued during which children went through pockets, crawled under seats, looked in mommy's purse, snitched programs from one another, or like myself said, "The hell with it!" The actors, mind you, unable to continue without red spots, became equally annoyed, saying in polite British desperation, "Oh, do hurry up!" Finally, enough battered programs were unfolded, pieced together, and assembled to destroy the evil spell, and the play limped forward, but no one felt he had participated in a victory, and there was no sense of triumph. Only a hundred or so mussy programs.

The entire sequence was arbitrary, presented for its own sake, to be endured simply because the author/director felt it was necessary to the occasion but nevertheless failed to make it so. Why hadn't red spots been mentioned earlier and the moment properly prepared for? (Barrie skillfully set up both his scene and his audience when he did it!) And more important to ask, why does a director think he is entertaining a child when in reality he is only giving him the opportunity to move about, make noise, or in this case perform janitorial services for the management by tidying up the floors? None of these activities are what theatre is all about, in fact each is better experienced at home or anywhere else other than in a playhouse. Unless, of course, they can be made to relate to character or plot in ways that are clear, enjoyable, *and* essential.

But even then might not the time have arrived for a moratorium to be declared on audience participation in general? Each new attempt seems weaker than the last. Invention it appears has dried up; the bottom of the barrel, as the above instance illustrates, reflects faces of bored youngsters. Until some fresh and disciplined examination is made to revivify and justify this tired tradition, we look in vain for creative smoke here: the house and all that was in it burned down long ago.

Alas, the problem cannot be erased so readily, even if every director and playwright agreed it should be, for in the public mind (and this includes students taking college courses in child drama) loud and robust audience participation *equals* children's theatre. They think if we but cause audiences to shout advice to the hero, to come on stage and kick heels, or to play mass party games, and if we but bring this activity to a pitch of perspiration and exhilaration that demands upon arrival at home a shower and a nap, we have a good show, probably a great show, at any event a popular success. A critic writing in the *New York Times* claimed, "This is what children's theatre is all about." On the other hand, if we but leave young people in their seats to watch a performance at which they are expected to respond spontaneously as civilized playgoers, we may have a dull show, a flop, a decided disappointment to a large percentage of the audience. So determined are some directors to turn theatres into playgrounds that dramatists often turn scripts into handbooks for conducting physical and vocal sallies. All too few write real plays for children to see and hear, plays in which they may recognize meaning in the lives of the characters and apply it to themselves. Theatre can offer no better form of participation than taking part in the creative process of a genuine play genuinely performed. Yet at present child audiences often are denied this opportunity as they are kept occupied in revels appropriate only to celebrating New Year's Eve.

STORY THEATRE AND READER'S THEATRE

Story Theatre, an entertainment devised by Paul Sills working with a group of highly skilled actors, first at Yale University, then on Broadway, and finally in a short-lived television series, has encouraged a host of imitators from coast to coast. How many, I wonder, really know what they are imitating? How many have been attracted to this theatrical form because it seems to be a simplified method of production? And this it may be except for the actors who in their vocal and physical command must be multitalented and constantly personable paragons and for the director who in his stage cleverness must be both magician and genius.

Even the imaginative Mr. Sills did not always attain these distinctions, as his eager nonprofessional disciples might remember before following too closely in his nimble footsteps. While warmly received by critics and audiences, his first edition of *Story Theatre*, the one drawing largely upon Aesop, the Brothers Grimm, and contemporary folk music, was summed up rather accurately by Walter Kerr as a pleasant evening but scarcely a breakthrough in either theatrical technique or dramatic format. The second edition, based on Ovid's *Metamorphoses*, attracted less enthusiasm from critics and audiences alike and disappeared all too swiftly (indeed, it contained some lovely moments, most of which, again, resulted from the loveliness of the people performing them). The third go-round, utilizing documents and materials depicting events in the American Revolution, closed abruptly out-of-town after being declared an artistic shambles.

The published version of the first *Story Theatre* provides only the lines spoken in performance which are and always have been royalty free to readers of Aesop and Grimm; the style of performance is not free but neither is it described nor prescribed in the text. So, actors and director must begin exactly where Sills began, with the words. But the theatrical shape they are to be given can be constructed only in the disciplined collaboration that exists among actors trained in inprovisation and long experienced in working together. If Sills and company couldn't shape and construct them with consistency, how many of the rest of us are apt to succeed? Yet largely because it appears to be a cheap means of mounting a show and, above all, because it looks easy to achieve, how many of us will try?

For many the real lure to Sills' work, as it is to Reader's Theatre, another worthwhile style of performance when carefully prepared by experts as able as Emlyn Williams, John Gielgud, or Michael Redgrave and the Royal Shakespeare Company, is the false assumption that productions can be undertaken in much less time than that given to regular offerings. Perhaps by the Royal Shakespeare Company they can, but when given by the second-year acting class of the local high school or college, they require more rehearsals precisely because the actor is *all* and without theatrical embellishment he must emerge better than he normally manages to appear. This means prolonged preparation periods that foster his technical growth and allow him greater mastery of vocal delivery and physical expression. And this means hard work, and lots of it for everyone concerned, which when accomplished and repeated on a long-term basis well might produce an artistic breakthrough, at least at the local level, and perhaps beyond. Both adult and children's theatres need more Paul Sills and more concepts like Story Theatre and Reader's Theatre at their best but for reasons of authentic ensemble experimentation and innovation, not for purposes of saving expenses of budget, creative effort, or time.

COMMEDIA DELL'ARTE TROUPES

Familiar today in college and community theatres is the actor interested in improvisational techniques who decides to band his friends together to troupe to schools, hospitals, homes for the aged, prisons, streets, and parks and there in a reckless and sometimes self-centered manner to perform their impromptu wares in what is one more instance of instant theatre. A nomadic schedule and a lack of scripts delude such groups into thinking they share characteristics in common with the Renaissance-and-later companies who created a great popular theatre in the Italian commedia dell'arte. So popular, in fact, they could be seen in their heyday as far away from home as England, Scandinavia, and Russia, and enjoyed by everyone even when no one understood a word spoken by the immensely agile and communicative comedians.

In the last two decades Italian companies carrying forward this illustrious tradition have visited New York City to prove that good commedia staging and acting still knows no language barriers. The bona fide mastery of this art form obviously comes from long years of perfecting timing and physical dexterity to make performances look spontaneous, effortless, and inspired when in reality they are plain hard work. (We must face the fact there is no escaping the term "hard work" however far back in history we may go in search of extemporaneous theatre or however much freedom of expression we may gain today.) But this very lack of work, tradition, and training results in some of our current troupes who if they entertain

at all amuse mostly themselves rather than the young, old, hospi-
talized, or jailed audiences before whom they play the fool, or to be
more accurate, before whom they often simply appear to be foolish.
Hamlet knew what he was talking about when he forbade his clowns
to enjoy themselves by laughing or setting others to laugh by
departing from their declared purpose: "That's villainous and shows
a most pitiful ambition in the fool that uses it." Yet many villainous
and pitifully ambitious young actors presently use precisely this
philosophy of "anything for a laugh" in the name of commedia and
children's theatre.

Any actor who assumes to take up Harlequin's motley first should
prove his right to wear that long honored and most respected of
comic uniforms through rigorous training and enforced nonpublic
apprenticeship lest we produce a generation of spectators who mis-
takenly equate history's disciplined commedia players on tour with
today's fun-loving commune playmates on ego trips. True
commedia can enrich our being while carefree imitations may lead
us merely to wonder what our ancestors found to be hilarious for
three centuries. A serious loss of laughter in our lives will result if
slapstick is permanently replaced by slapdash.

GENUINE EXPERIMENTATION

If the smoke spreading from improper improvisation and infirmed
instant-theatre techniques is cause for critical pause in an assessment of the growth of our field, we must not lose sight of spontaneous and participatory activity that constitutes genuine theatrical
experiences for playgoers and performers. In both children's theatre
and creative dramatics the best new works and practices regularly
result from experimentation and unremitting testing in studio,
classroom, rehearsal hall, and the creator's head.

Anyone who has seen The Paper Bag Players knows to what
original heights improvisation can be taken, although the Bags, as
they call themselves, do not actually improvise in performance but
rather in the long developmental stages of their individual programs.
A child senses that the Bags' is a world wherein anything can happen
not because it can (or does) but because theirs is a stage wherein
simplicity forbids clutter and prompts freedom to move and to
make-believe. Their selectivity of an action or an idea appears to be

right and exact probably because it results from trying and discarding a multitude of other possibilities. Theirs is a style in which discipline imparts a security and confidence that in performance becomes the essence of spontaneity. To these considerable attributes the Bags display a grasp of teamwork and interplay exemplified in the title of one of their shows, *Group Soup*, a smooth and well-balanced blend of showmanship. They emerge in performance as a bunch of kids involved in playing imaginative games with one another and with spectators of various ages and cultural backgrounds but always with command of everyone's attention and interest. Now well into their second decade as the major professional company for children in New York City, they continue to develop new themes and techniques at a self-determined rate of artistic progress in a creative process that distills concerned experimentation into carefully prepared entertainment.

The long-running revue *The Proposition Circus* improvises routines from suggestions made by the audience, resulting in a cabaret style of production of appeal to both children and adolescents. Here informal techniques are the means and end of the entertainment and the instant creative process becomes the finished product. Even when performed by experts, as is here the case, the results are certain to be uneven but more often than not amusing to watch and sometimes exciting to be present at as unexpected or inspired events take place.

Our best directors have encouraged experimentation both in scripts and production procedures. John Clark Donahue of the Children's Theatre Company of the Minneapolis Society of Fine Arts created a highly personal style of writing and staging dramatic fantasy in his *Hang on to Your Head* and *Good Morning, Mr. Tilly*. Tony Stelblay of the Hopkins Eisenhower High School in Hopkins, Minnesota, often has collaborated with students and production staff in the total creation of an original production, such as the spirited *The Capture of Sarah Quincy*. Others have mixed conventional-script elements with freer nonstructured components in the hope of achieving a dynamic form of production. At New York's City Center, for example, a group of professional players have begun a play or revue in a more or less traditional manner, then stopped the performance at a point of high interest to divide the audience into several groups, each headed by an actor who supervised the improvisation of a unit of action required to complete the story. After a short rehearsal period, the play proceeded with the children becoming the players for the remainder of the program. At the University of Massachusetts, the performance, at least on one occasion, halted several times to invite an exchange between actors and spectators on the choices open to the characters and to determine thoughts and responses to the actions performed. In this way, director Carol Korty moved her audience inside the play and its people to become part of its machinery and to contribute to its heartbeat, leading one observer to write, "What was stunning and exalting about this piece . . . was its directness in handling powerful and sensitive emotional material and finding an absolutely true tone throughout." Obviously, the creative connection can be made through improvisation and participation when experimentation takes place at this level of artistic achievement, which, the same critic noted, met not the needs just of children "but of everyone who wants to be his or her own person."

Of course, the risks and costs of experimentation are high and producing groups must be prepared to take and pay them. When the Program in Educational Theatre at New York University presented the American premieres of *The Tingalary Bird* and *Winterthing*, money was lost as both plays failed to attract large audiences. Yet these problematic but original works deserved to be seen in this country just as serious students of child drama needed the experience of producing them. Moreover, both plays merited full productions if to be properly tested, with special attention given by designers to their technical demands, and with utmost consideration given by directors to their fascinating pitfalls. If no great activity took place at the box office, every other area of the theatre bristled with the excited industry of creating new plays for children that in their exploration of unusual themes, moods, and images really were new. More of us working in child drama willingly must take this kind of risk and be thankful for the criticism, even negative, that results. However expensive a gamble, genuine experimentation is essential to progress.

THE YOUNG VIC

In 1974 the Young Vic made its first appearance in New York City bringing with it three plays and a reputation as one of England's keenest repertory companies with a particular knack for attracting thousands of young people to its starkly plain cement-block auditorium to fill singularly hard and unreserved benches which sell for one low price of admission. Since 1969 this company has won critical and popular praise at home and abroad for producing lively mountings with little, sometimes no scenery and only economy costuming. In this country the Young Vic played in two handsome theatres with prices increased five times above what young people pay in London. Public response was limited at first; even with a rave review from Clive Barnes, *The Taming of the Shrew* drew only a handful of spectators to its Saturday matinee. Fortunately, as enthusiasm spread, larger and larger audiences found their way to Brooklyn to see the spirited *Shrew, Scapino,* and a revival of Terrence Ratigan's nostalgic comic romance, *French Without Tears.* Soon some of the excitement that surrounds the company in London began to emanate in New York, especially for its contemporary staging of Shakespeare and Molière. *Scapino* (adapted from Molière's commedia dell'arte play *Les Fourberies de Scapin,* written in 1671) several months later was brought to Broadway to become a commercial hit at still higher box office prices.

The creative smoke rising from the Young Vic, both in London and New York, signals zippy direction, often by Frank Dunlop who also administers the company, and stylish acting by a group able to move and to speak at rates of speed frequently Olympian in their record-breaking dash and dexterity. Jim Dale, one of the most facile of the actor/athletes, flourishes an original manner that wins audiences of all ages who at the end of a performance may find themselves willingly playing imaginary musical instruments in an improvised orchestra he conducts with audacious cheer. (Audience participation, kept to the curtain call of *Scapino,* could not interrupt the speed of this theatrical track meet, which although it appears to be improvised actually is precisely mechanized. Nothing, says Dale, can be added or changed in performance, not a word, not a beat.)

Hopefully, the success of this visit will spur our own directors and actors into forming American counterparts of the Young Vic. But because we have no Frank Dunlop to make productions young and no Jim Dale to make performances ageless, they may think it can't happen here. This is nonsense. Both men are major talents in the British theatre who maintain professional careers outside their duties at the Young Vic. And when they are away others take their place with equal success. Their gifted presence, though treasured, is not indispensable to the artistic life of the company. What is? Good plays, for one thing. The repertory of the Young Vic is filled with major works by Pinter, Beckett, Stoppard, Genet, O'Casey, Osborne, as well as by Sophocles, Shakespeare, and Molière. Dunlop and Dale, and all the others who are part of this bright company, give themselves the best material in world drama upon which to perform their popular miracles. In his rave review entitled "Molière Never Looked Younger," Walter Kerr wrote: "*Scapin* can take any kind of updating; he lacked calendar and wrist watch to begin with." Knowing how to select and then to make so-called classics and modern masterpieces appeal to a wide spectrum of young people is the great success of the Young Vic, for on almost any night in London you may see youngsters in the company of older brothers and sisters and take satisfaction that *together* they enjoy the play.

Here the play *is* the thing, and this directors and actors make known to audiences by giving it their full energy and inspired but not sacred respect. Jim Dale in interviews that accompanied his elevation to Broadway stardom reminded reporters who think his Scapino is mostly his own invention that every word he speaks was written by Molière. If he brings the character to life in contemporary terms, it so happens those also are Molière's. Dale has connected the meaning of Scapino's action to modern being, much to the delighted surprise of thousands of playgoers, young and otherwise.

The Young Vic, of course, is not perfect, however worthwhile has been much of its work. As yet it has not evolved a satisfactory style of play production for young children aged five through twelve, although its experiments in this field are noteworthy from time to time. The unhappy incidence of audience participation mentioned earlier took place as part of one embarrassingly unsuccessful attempt to win and reward these children as the company has their dedicated adolescent audiences. Along with the rest of us, they must continue to investigate this need, and one hopes with that same rapture and determination they presently give to Shakespeare and Molière.

It would be ironic and tragic indeed if the field that wishes to pioneer sensory and social awareness in creative development should isolate itself by its own self-absorption and blindness to the work of others. This danger is very real today as we, for the most part, continue to grow inward rather than outward. In the theatre, despite exceptions noted here, we still retread familiar fairy-tale plays instead of testing new works. In the classroom, despite major changes in student interests and values, we still invoke proved activities of the past instead of attempting untried experiences. How many teachers put students through Viola Spolin's exercises year after year as if they and not she had written *Improvisation for the Theatre*? How many students talk about Jerzy Grotowski without reading *Towards a Poor Theater* and relating its meaning to their own artistic development and lives? And perhaps more important to ask, how many of us pursue careers as teachers and artists without connecting child drama to every other field concerned with young people? Who draws upon the findings of specialists in child psychology, child development, child behavior, educational psychology, educational sociology and anthropology, linguistics, language development, creativity, and so on, to enrich our work and ourselves? Who has studied the forms of games children have played throughout history and world civilizations to see how they might illuminate child drama and children's theatre?

If we don't make these connections, or teach our students to do so, we may come to be characterized in the manner of that ancient prophecy: "The fish will be the last to discover water." Like fish, we guide children scurrying through a universe at once timeless and everchanging; but unlike fish, we must lead them to recognize both their surroundings and themselves. Theatre and drama most effectively provide this opportunity and challenge, which when completely met will end our pioneering with smoke in the chimney that can camouflage nothing because it results from a creative process that contains its own reality and validity.

NOTES

1. Richard Crosscup, *Children and Dramatics* (New York: Charles Scribner's Sons, 1966), p. 7.
2. Ibid.
3. Philip A. Coggin, *The Uses of Drama* (New York: George Braziller, 1956), pp. 222-25.
4. Paul Zindel, "The Theater Is Born Within Us," *New York Times*, 26 July 1970, Arts and Leisure Section, p. 1.

"PLEES MAKE MORE"

AURAND HARRIS

Aurand Harris, with twenty-one published plays for children, is one of America's most-produced children's theatre playwrights. His plays have appeared in twelve foreign countries. He is the winner of a dozen play-writing contests and was the first recipient of the Chorpenning Cup, the annual award given by the Children's Theatre Association to an outstanding children's playwright. Born in Missouri, Mr. Harris received his bachelor's degree from the University of Kansas City and his master's degree from Northwestern. He has taught creative dramatics and directed productions in the public schools of Gary (Indiana), William Woods College, Teachers College of Columbia University, and Grace Church School of New York City. He holds strong convictions regarding the function of drama in education, both formal and informal, but in this essay he addresses himself only to the question of writing a play for a young audience.

I was lucky. I was in the Chicago area when three great women were making children's theatre history in America. I was on the campus of Northwestern University when Winifred Ward was teaching her concept of creative dramatics and was starting the Children's Theatre of Evanston. To me she was an inspiration, and continues to be a critic and a friend.

Charlotte Chorpenning was writing and directing formal children's plays at the Goodman Memorial Theatre, showing her audiences and students what good children's theatre could and should be. I saw her plays, analyzed and learned from her technique, and along with hundreds of children enjoyed her Saturday productions.

In Gary, Indiana, Mildred Harter Wirt was pioneering Auditorium in the public schools, using the elements of theatre as a

181

pivotal subject in the school curriculum. My first experience in children's drama was under her encouraging supervision, teaching twelve classes a day in creative and formal drama. Winifred Ward, Charlotte Chorpenning, Mildred Harter Wirt—I started my children's theatre career at the right time in the right place.

Since then children's theatre in America has grown in quantity—more than 1,500 producing groups—and grown in quality—our productions at the recent international ASSITEJ meeting were first-rate. It is exciting to be a children's playwright in these expanding years.

I am often asked, "Why do you write for children?" A simple answer is that I like children and I like what children like in the theatre. When I write, however, I do not think, "I am writing a *children's* play." I write the best play I can, using the best characterizations, the best dialogue, and the best theatre techniques I can muster. I do not write "down" to a child. I write to please myself, an adult. I do use a child's theme for a plot. And there are certain adjustments—such as shorter playing time and quicker motivations, less dialogue and more action in developing the plot—but I do not find these limitations a handicap. Rather, they are a dramatic challenge and a good discipline. A children's play is lean and vigorous; it moves with an unyielding beat to a satisfying conclusion. If, as I write, all goes well, the finished play is one I like—and so do children.

I have continued to be lucky. Year after year I have enjoyed daily contact with children—teaching, observing, and learning. This consistent rapport, I feel, is essential in writing for children. Some writers, skilled craftsmen, do not succeed either in fiction or drama because they do not know, respect, or try to understand the world of the young. They have never shared or laughed or cried with a child.

The empathy a playwright has for a child's world is reflected in the first step of writing a children's play, the selection of material. Good plays have the same qualities that are found in all good children's literature—plots simple enough to involve the child, complex enough to challenge him, and emotional enough to satisfy him—all of which contribute to the revelation of a universal truth.

Many children's playwrights write only original scripts. One successful Englishman always devises his own plots because, as he confided to me, he finds doing research dull and adaptation hard work. It can be. But I find a good children's story can trigger my imagination and start me writing a play at once. While if I wait for a blinding flash of inspiration for an original plot, I may wait and wait and wait. Personally I enjoy doing research related to a situation that I find dramatic. From such searching I have learned a great deal about human behavior, social customs, and history in a profitable and painless way. It can also add interest to my conversation when I casually mention that Thomas Jefferson was the first President to wear long trousers, a historical fact that I found in my research for *Yankee Doodle*.

The time spent and the techniques used in adapting a story, I find, help me to organize my thinking, clarify the theme, and crystallize a dramatic concept. There are several ways in which one can treat a story in preparing it for the stage.

I have *dramatized* some stories, keeping faithfully to the text. In *Steal Away Home* I changed only that which was necessary to transfer the printed page to the stage. The characters were fully developed by Jane Kristof in her book. She also had written an exciting, straightforward plot. I had only to *adapt* it, to give the characters realistic dialogue, to make the scenes visual in action, and to give the play a mood and tempo which heightened the suspense of two boys, runaway slaves, escaping on the Underground Railroad.

I have written plays *suggested by* stories. Here it is the idea, the theme of the story, that is used and that the playwright treats in any manner he feels he can make theatrical and effective. Along with most children's playwrights I wanted to write a Pinocchio play. But the little puppet was already the hero of several scripts. I needed a new approach. In my research I discovered a second Pinocchio book, *Pinocchio in Africa* by Cherubini, which describes further adventures of Pinocchio. I wrote a play *suggested by* the book. I changed the locale from Africa to America where the same adventures happened to Pinocchio with the natives of America as did with the natives of Africa. He swam the Atlantic Ocean instead of the Red Sea but escaped from the same strange fish. I called the play *Pinocchio and the Indians*.

This was an early play written before I learned that many children's theatre people tend to be purists. (I include myself among them now.) Pinocchio is a familiar and popular hero. Children expect a play about him to follow the traditional plot. They want to see the scenes they have read and reread and loved. My departure from the cherished and expected was, I am afraid, too removed. Cinderella should always go to a fairy-tale ball, not fly to Mars. If you must write such a new treatment—and I am in favor of any original writing—don't call her Cinderella, but instead, perhaps Cindy. I did this, in fact. I used the Cinderella theme in a modern teen-age play, *The Moon Makes Three.* The youngest sister, waiting to become glamorous, goes with the aid of her grandmother to a Halloween masquerade party. There she dances with a masked stranger, and at midnight she is left with one of his shoes, the only means with which to find him by the final curtain.

Most children's plays based on stories are adaptations. Most of my plays are. This is a happy combination of using much of the story but fashioning it in an individual, dramatic and theatrical form. I *adapted* Phyliss McGinley's *The Plain Princess.* Her comments, accompanying her final approval, were to this effect: She liked the unity of the play—I had condensed it. She liked the individualizing of the characters—I had given each daughter a definite personality. She liked the theatrical stage effects—I had heightened each change in the Princess's attitude by a visual stage picture. She liked the spirit of fun and fantasy—I had only underlined the feeling of *her* book.

The most popular play I have written is *Androcles and the Lion.* It has had over 5,000 performances, been translated into four languages, been given in such distant places as Nigeria, Czechoslovakia, and Midway, South Pacific. *Androcles and the Lion* is based on an Aesop fable, but I wrote it in a definite theatrical style. It is played as it might have been performed by a group of commedia dell'arte actors in Italy in the sixteenth century. So far is the content of the play from the simple fable that the publisher wisely describes it as "adapted very freely."

Whether it be an adaptation or a dramatization, I have found using a good story as the basis for a plot the best way for me to start writing a play. And I must admit I find it easier. The plot and the characters are there, even the title. If it is a good story the theme is usually universal and has a wide appeal. The title is known, which gives it immediate interest to children and parents. I feel more secure with a proven property. Instead of spending time and energy, or feeling doubt about an original plot, I prefer to start thinking in theatre terms immediately, outlining and *writing* the play. It may be a part of the director in me, but this is what I like and enjoy—taking a scene and making it come alive with actors for an audience. I feel if I can write a good play, one I like and one which children like; it doesn't matter if the plot is original or not. The important thing is that the finished play should be good theatre and entertaining to children. I might add it is also a comfort to know that Shakespeare usually used someone else's plot, and Shakespeare did very well.

The important thing is to start the writing. Original plays are often sparked by an idea, a character, or a dramatic situation. Stories and poems can be used as source material. There are two folk songs that I think have dramatic potential, but as yet I have not found a style, a concept that fits them and which I feel is right for me. Some scripts are written upon request. I began working on *Buffalo Bill* at the invitation of an American company that was to tour Europe. My problem in writing it was to make a hero out of a man whose claim to fame was killing off our native animals. The tour never materialized, but I *wrote* the play. Another play I might not have undertaken without outside stimulus was *The Flying Prince*. I was commissioned to write it by the Indian Embassy and the Washington Children's Theatre. It was given a gala and exciting premiere in the nation's capital during an International Theatre Month.

The most difficult part of writing for me is doing the outline and beginning the first draft. The joy of writing to me is rewriting and more rewriting. This can prove to be a rejuvenating experience if I feel I am making the script better each time.

I do not intend this to be an essay on how to write a play. Writing is a personal and unique craft. If I were a clock maker, after constructing twenty workable clocks I would have a certain confidence that the next clock I made would run. After more than twenty plays, I have no assurance that the next play I write will work. Each play is a new uncharted exploration that develops an inevitability of its own. When all goes well, the finished play can be a work of joy. But because it is shaped by fallible human hands and heart the result can be, and often is, disappointing for both the author and audience. There are certain general and elementary principles that are helpful to a playwright—building entrances and exits, developing rhythm in dialogue, showing all the important scenes *on* the stage—but each writer has his own and best and eccentric ways of creating a play. I outline. I write with a pencil on a clipboard. I chew the pencil. I mark out, insert, draw arrows on the pages until I must type my scribbles to be able to read them. When there in a typed form, the play suddenly takes on a professional look which spurs me on to the next scene. No matter how or when or where—even in the bathtub where I have had some of my best ideas—it is only after I am so filled with the characters and the scenes that I feel forced to give them life, that I can start to write a play. Then I spend a long enjoyable time acting on my imaginary stage. And I fall in love with the characters.

In children's theatre there is a cry for more plays. Literature looks to the past and to many languages for its masterpieces. Children's drama in America is young and does not have a full library of native or foreign classics. America is young. In its first century it fought for survival and built a nation. There was little time for the arts. Also, it is only in this century that theatre has become respectable, that America has started to overcome its early Puritan prejudice. In the early years, no lady or her children attended the theatre and certainly they never performed in it. A theatre for children was inconceivable. This lack of cultural heritage is one reason there are so few plays.

However, children's theatre slowly has been building a library. A few American playwrights have been contributing consistently; a few forward-looking publishing houses have been printing more children's plays; and recently there has been an international interest in, and exchange of, plays with other countries. But as times have changed, so have theatrical styles and conventions. Children have changed, even the auditorium structures have changed. Older plays have begun to show their age. So more plays, new plays, which suit our changing attitudes, styles, and children are needed. An extending theatre must not only continue to make use of its past but also keep its doors open wide to the new works.

There is also a cry in children's theatre for "better" plays. This is the continuing cry on Broadway, in the movies, and on television. It is a cry I am sure was heard by Shakespeare and Sophocles. When I began to write for children, the cry loud in my ears, I vowed to myself I would try to write a "better" play. Of course I did not know quite what it was or how to do it. Several plays later, I discovered what others before me must have discovered: There is no perfect play for everyone for every occasion. There is a need in America not for a "better" play, but for many kinds of good children's plays to satisfy the many different tastes, standards, and demands.

The demand for, and the receptiveness of children's theatre to, all types of plays is another reason I find writing for the young stimulating. I have experimented with traditional fairy tales, a modern barnyard comedy, a musical melodrama, a historical epic, a circus script with audience participation, a lyrical tale of the East, a dark comedy, an old fashioned farce, and a patriotic musical review. I have no illusions that any of these plays is a "better" play. I wrote each because I felt that particular story and style would produce good theatre and good entertainment for children. There has been a wide variance in the popularity of these plays which, I think, reflects in part the wide scope of needs and tastes in children's theatre.

A playwright does not write for himself alone, no matter what romances he may have at his typewriter. He writes plays hoping that they will be performed and be enjoyed by audiences. A production of a play is of necessity a cooperative effort, and the playwright as an honored parent slowly diminishes in importance. In the beginning he is almost a deity, having imagined a new world. He grows less important during rehearsals, and at the final performances he is looked upon as an outsider. This is as it should be. The actors have taken over the characters. The action and the dialogue belong to them. Author? Who is he? The typewriter ribbon, the umbilical cord, has been cut.

The cooperative venture of presenting a play involves many people. Those who first read it and select it. Later those who interpret and mount it. These people may hold a variety of opinions. They may differ widely in their tastes, demands, and standards. America is not a small, homogeneous country. It is big. Accordingly children's theatre covers a wide spectrum reflecting different mores of different regions. Art is always controversial. It is healthy that in a democracy we can voice our approval and disapproval of theatre tastes. It also can make for confusion and disagreement in theatre practices and standards. Even as small and provincial as Broadway is, the critics often do not agree on the merits of a play. The playwright should be aware that there are certain questions in American children's theatre upon which people, respected in their professional fields and who will produce his plays, often disagree.

Should a play be acted by *children* or by *adults*? The answer to the question may dictate the playwright's approach. Because Shakespeare knew his female parts would be played by boys, he no doubt wrote fewer parts for women, fewer scenes, and often had females disguise themselves as men. If children's plays are performed by child actors, then it would seem characters should be written that lie within the acting scope of most children. I have directed plays both with an all children's cast (which is often a necessity in educational drama, ages seven to seventeen) and with a mixed cast of children and adults. It is my personal feeling that, ideally, any play is best cast with actors whose types and ages are closest to the characters they are playing.

Should or should not a children's play have audience participation? This directly affects the playwright. In plays for younger children, audience participation at times can be used effectively. But for older children watching a formal play, overt participation can often be a distraction, a breaking of the necessary dramatic contact. When the aesthetic distance is destroyed and the audience loses its belief in the world of make-believe, then it becomes a part of an informal happening. There are times when audience participation can be dramatic—the one time Barrie used it in *Peter Pan*—and it can give variety if it is used legitimately and sparingly. I have used it. It is one kind of children's drama. But I feel it can never be the "blood and bones" of children's theatre. From observing some children's plays, I feel that audience participation was not used legitimately to heighten an effect, but to cover up inadequacies in the script and production. It appears that audience participation is at times the only way some producers know to gain and hold attention. To me, in the theatre a party is not a play.

Which type of stage is best suited to children's drama? Theatre-in-the-round? The thrust stage? Or the proscenium arch? The physical stage on which his play is to be performed affects the playwright. Shakespeare wrote for the Globe Theatre. He knew the upper stage could be used for a balcony, the inner stage could be used for "discovering" scenes. He knew there was no scenery, so he could quickly change locales; but he also knew he must write descriptive passages to inform the audience.

The children's theatre playwright does not know upon what type of stage his play will be performed. Some plays, both adult's and children's, can be staged successfully in several ways. Some cannot. Since most children's plays are fantasies and a fantasy lends itself to imaginative and unusual staging, different kinds of physical stages can often be used. But to me, fantasy fades with proximity. The theatre by its nature is illusion, and to me, illusion is strongest when there is an aesthetic distance. Perhaps because I was trained in the proscenium-arch theatre, I usually write with a picture-frame stage in mind, carefully visualizing each scene with stage right, stage left, and footlights. Children are visually minded, and what they see is of utmost importance. As I write and as I direct, I try to visualize what the child will see as a stage picture, changing minute to minute, in scene to scene, and it is easier for me to see that the grouping, movement, emphasis, relationships, etc. are clearly and visibly pointed if the play is framed in a proscenium arch.

The in-the-round, or to a lesser degree, a thrust stage, makes for a closer physical intimacy between the actors and the audience. A rapport and an intimacy are important in a children's play. Certainly the upper balconies and the back rows of a large auditorium are bad and should never be used for children's audiences. But for me theatre-in-the-round has often been *too* intimate. I do not like to see the perspiration of the Brave Little Tailor as he strikes seven at a blow, the obvious makeup of the Cat Who Walked By Himself, or the sprays of saliva from King Oberon. A proper aesthetic distance can create the illusion that Pocahontas has built a glowing fire, although in reality it is only a light bulb covered with orange paper. Another problem is that the audience on the other side of the magic circle can become more entertaining—or distracting—than the play. Also, every movement in any play, especially a children's play, should have a definite and meaningful motivation. But too often the movement on the in-the-round stage seems to be motivated only to help the audience see most of the actors most of the time.

The stage with a limited thrust can be a happy medium between the arena and the proscenium-arch stage. Here scenes can be played closer to the audience, yet there are side entrances and a solid backing for scenery and lighting effects. For several summers I have directed on a modified thrust stage at the Harwich Junior Theatre, and I have found with some changing most plays can be effectively staged. In the thrust, as well as the picture-frame stage, Peck's Bad Boy can confide his thoughts to the audience with intimate asides, yet all the audience can see his pranks at the same time and laugh together.

Should children's plays have intermissions or not? Certainly this is a concern of the playwright. Intermissions are a theatrical convention which changes with the years. The adult theatre in America has in its short history gone from five acts to four, three, two and to an occasional long one-act. The popular children's plays of Charlotte Chorpenning were usually divided into three acts, which corresponded to the popular form in the adult theatre in her time. There is a tidy unity in three acts: Act I, exposition, introduction of characters, beginning of conflict; Act II, complications, with a high point at the second act curtain; Act III, short and with a satisfying resolution of the conflict. Intermissions can be used for various reasons. The dramatist may use an intermission to show a passage of time; the actor may use it to catch his breath; the audience may use it for physical release after a period of emotional concentration, or for a trip to the bathroom; and not least, the producer may use it to supplement the box-office by selling candy and refreshments.

Most children's theatre producers do not think of an intermission in terms of the structure of the play but think of intermission in terms of its effect on the audience. Can or will an audience of children sit still without a stretch? Can an audience of children be controlled if there is an intermission?

I have written three-act, two-act, and one-act—with prologues and epilogues, depending on the nature of the material. The average child who is old enough physically and emotionally to enjoy children's theatre is capable of sustaining attention for an hour and a half, and will if the production is good. However, I feel any audience needs "relaxers" during the performance. This can be accomplished by scenes devised for that purpose. I try to do this. And it can also be done by stopping the play—intermission. I also do this. In my opinion it is the play itself, as an artistic form, which dictates and determines when, where, and how many breaks there should be. These should be observed. But each producer has the choice of observing them with intermissions of several minutes or by simply closing and reopening the curtains and letting the play continue. The play then can retain its intrinsic form, and each producer can be true to his theory of intermissions. Those who want full intermissions can let the children wave and call to their friends or search for a lost glove. While those who want no intermission can get the audience out before the assembly bell rings, and have no worry of house-program airplanes flying from the balcony.

There are many more questions that affect the playwright. What length should a play for children be? One hour or longer? Should the cast be small for touring or large for a community project? For what age span, if any, should a play be written? Should there be less fantasy and more realism in style? Should children's plays deal with current issues and problems—segregation, divorce, women's lib? (Children's books have grown to include best sellers with such themes as abortion, drugs, death, sex, and the Vietnam war.)

The answer to these questions as far as the playwright is concerned should be determined not by outside opinions or pressures, but by the material *he* selects and the approach *he* feels is right. The running time of a play should be as long, and only as long, as it takes to tell the story effectively. There is no place in a children's play for extraneous padding. When I wrote *Circus in the Wind* I constantly resisted the temptation to insert theatrical circus acts which, though entertaining, would have interrupted the action.

The cast should include only those characters necessary to the plot. Too many characters confuse a child. There are, however, legitimate situations which can utilize "mob" scenes. This helps to make a more flexible-size cast. When I wrote a children's version of Molière's *A Doctor in Spite of Himself* I included in the household (a rich one) several additional maids who, when they appeared together, caused one critic to mention them as a clever Greek chorus.

The story itself and its treatment will determine the best age of the audience for the play. Many good plays appeal on different levels to all ages. One reason I suspect for the enormous popularity of *Androcles and the Lion* is that the fun of the commedia dell'arte style appeals equally to the youngest and to the oldest.

The playwright will choose his subject—contemporary and realistic, historic or fantasy—intuitively. He will choose a theme to which he feels attuned. I have started and later had to stop writing on a theme to which I found I could not relate, while most of my best scenes have been the easiest to write because I knew them, I understood them, I felt them. Although writers should be aware that producers have different opinions, standards, and needs, and the writer may try to meet them as far as artistic integrity will allow, the playwrights who are giving the American children's theatre its vitality, its inovations, and its stature are the playwrights who are writing what they believe, who are following Shakespeare's good advice: "to thine own self be true."

A play is as good as its production. The first plays to be given for children in America were produced mostly by dedicated individuals whose sincerity and effort overshadowed their lack of training and professional standards. Slowly this has changed.

There have always been a few professional companies presenting, sometimes touring, plays for children. But until recently there have been but few and those not of long duration. Bravely they have done, and continue to do, their best with the ever-pressing problem of inadequate financial support. Children's theatre, like most performing arts, can rarely pay its way. The professional children's theatre companies need the best talent to produce first-rate productions, but without sufficient money this is still a problem. Like the opera, children's theatre in America is a luxury. When it is recognized as a cultural force, as is the opera, and supported, as is the opera, children's theatre may also become grand.

The important growth in children's theatre, however, in both quality and quantity has been in the many regional groups. The best of these are usually located in university or civic areas where a pool of trained and interested people provide a reservoir of talent. It is their productions that have broken a vicious circle in which children's theatre was caught. Previously, because most children's plays were produced by well-intentioned amateurs, children's theatre did not mature in professional quality. And without artistic excellence, children's theatre continued to be considered an amateur stepchild. That has changed. A new circle is beginning. Because many children's plays now are being produced by trained people, children's theatre is maturing in quality. And as it proves itself in artistic excellence, it is attracting more talented artists, and hopefully the momentum will grow until the best directors, actors, technicians, and writers will become a vital part of children's theatre. And hopefully the circle will extend and include the best artists of Broadway, television, music, and the dance. Theatre complexes will be built for children's performing arts; and a large, regular audience will emerge throughout the nation.

Since in America there is no Little Broadway to give children's theatre a focal point, a place of national prestige, or to set high standards, the future, I believe, of children's theatre lies in the universities, the civic, and the regional theatres. They have trained theatre people, physical facilities, and a budget. I have been a playwright-in-residence at several of these types of theatres. Their enthusiasm, talent, and high artistic standards have stimulated me. If these and other regional centers continue to train, encourage, discover potential talent, increase the number of productions, and undertake tours of good children's plays, I feel that we can achieve a national theatre for the young that will rank high in the international world of children's theatre.

Born in the slums to do social work, growing rapidly enough in seventy years to be an invited guest as an educational and cultural force at the White House Conference on Children and Youth, children's drama in America is a twentieth-century phenomenon.

I am optimistic, although a bit impatient. I, along with others, will continue to write the best plays I can because I believe that good children's theatre is a child's rightful heritage. And I like my fan mail:

> *I injoyd your play   I laft   It is real*
> *—like my dog   plees make more*

If I am a bit impatient, it is because I would still like to be around when children's drama reaches a national standard of excellence in writing and production, when it is accepted and supported as an established twenty-first-century cultural tradition. I would like to be around when children's plays are regarded as dramatic literature, placed on library shelves, chosen for inclusion in the Ten Best Plays, even considered for the Pulitzer Prize. Then the time might come that I am waiting for, when a child, asked what he'd like to be when he grows up, answers proudly, "A children's playwright."

Date Due